Comparatively few memoirs of the Napoleonic period from the French side have been published in English. These memoirs of an officer in Napoleon's army provide a fascinating picture of that army in action in victory and defeat—at Eylau and Jena, at Wagram, in the Peninsula and at Leipzig; of the army's organization and morale; and of the life and views of the class from which the writer came, the bourgeoisie.

Charles Parquin enlisted in 1803 at the age of sixteen into the 20th Regiment of Chasseurs. His memoirs cover the twelve years after his enlistment during which he rose from the ranks of the light cavalry to become, after being commissioned in the field, a captain in the élite Guard. After campaigns in Prussia, Poland, Austria, Spain, Saxony and France—and the many amorous adventures which enliven his account of them—he was at Fontainebleau to record the melancholy scene of the Emperor's farewell to his Guard.

As a writer Parquin is entertaining and spontaneous. His descriptions of military events are concise and exciting. Above all, his devotion to the Emperor stands out, a devotion which eventually led him to a prison sentence for supporting Louis-Napoleon's abortive landing at Boulogne, serving which he died in 1845.

at the Royal Military Academy, Sandhurst.

MILITARY MEMOIRS

Edited by
Brigadier Peter Young

D.S.O., M.C., M.A., F.S.A., F.R.HIST.S.

Charles Parquin

MILITARY MEMOIRS

Charles Parquin

Napoleon's Army

Translated and Edited by

B. T. JONES

ARCHON BOOKS
1969

ARCHON BOOKS
1969

First Published 1969

This edition first published in the United States of America by Archon Books, 1969, Hamden, Connecticut

Printed in Great Britain by W. & J. Mackay & Co Ltd, Chatham, Kent

SBN: 208 00763 6

Contents

Note on the Series

by PETER YOUNG

In planning a series of this sort, there is a bewildering variety of factors to be considered. Of these perhaps the chief is the fundamental question: 'Why do people read Military History?' Is it because truth is more attractive than fiction? Baron de Marbot, although his tales had unquestionably improved in the telling, has an interest which Brigadier Gerard, despite the narrative skill of Conan Doyle, cannot rival. Marbot's memory could play him false in matters of detail, but not as to the sense of period. He brings to life the atmosphere of the Grand Army in which he served. Marbot, regrettably, is too well known, both in French and English, to parade with the veterans of this series. We have endeavoured to present memoirists who for one reason or another are relatively unknown to the English-speaking public.

In modern times, memoir-writing seems to have become the prerogative of generals. One is not, however, without hopes of finding a voice or two from the ranks to conjure up the fields of Flanders or the deserts of North Africa. Of course, we have not rejected generals altogether. But on the whole we have tried to rescue 'old swordsmen' from oblivion. The fighting soldier is more attractive than an officer with a distinguished series of staff appointments to his credit; the tented field has an appeal which the dull round of garrison life cannot rival. We have also avoided those veterans who, their Napier at their elbow, submerge their personal recollections in a mass of ill-digested secondhand campaign history. These are the most maddening of all. What details they could have given us had they chosen to!

The trouble is that memoirists take so much for granted. They assume that we know all about the military organization and tactics of their day. And so we must just be thankful for small mercies. You will not get a fight on every page, but gradually a picture is built up. One comes to visualize the manners of a bygone age, to see how people then could endure the privations of a campaign, the rough surgery of the battlefield, or the administrative neglect of their commanders. In the end we come almost to speak their language, and to hear them speak.

Introduction

'The French I have observed to be a people fond of glory and sentiment, and a story of *la Gloire et l'Amour* will always excite their admiration.'

EDWARD COSTELLO: *Adventures of a Soldier*

Denis-Charles Parquin died on 19 December 1845 at Doullens where he was serving a sentence of twenty years' imprisonment for his part in the abortive attempt by Louis-Napoleon to seize power following the landing near Boulogne in 1840. It was during this detention that Parquin wrote his memoirs. They were to be in two parts, the first dealing with his life up to 1814 and the second with the events which had led him to the ignominious situation in which he found himself. The original edition of the first part, which forms the basis of these present memoirs, appeared in 1842; the second part was never published. Yet the role played by Parquin in the politics of France after the Restoration of 1815, although a minor one, was sufficiently public, and publicized, for the sad contrast between the fullness of his early life and the futility of his later quest to emerge clearly. No doubt the irony of his position was abundantly apparent to Parquin as he recreated the picture of a past carefree life which had started in 1803 with the 20th Regiment of Chasseurs at Abbeville, such a short distance from Doullens.

Parquin's memoirs cover the twelve years following his enlistment, a period during which he rose from the ranks to become a captain in the Guard. But after being an active participant in the great events of the Empire, he could not find under the Bourbons the same sense of purpose he had previously known. Although not directly involved in an army conspiracy of 1820, he refused to denounce others and he was put on the retired list. Life became so unpleasant for him that he moved to Switzerland and it was here that in 1822 he married Mademoiselle Cochelet, Queen Hortense's reader. When Parquin and his wife settled near Arenenburg, the Bonapartes' place of exile, he discovered in the person of Napoleon's nephew the cause he had been seeking. Parquin became one of the first members of the Bonapartist movement and, as chronicler of the glorious days of the Empire, he fed the growing ambition of Louis-Napoleon.

The political results of the 1830 Revolution were not welcomed by Parquin, but at least the change in France allowed him to resume his military career and he returned to serve as a squadron commander in the gendarmerie. In 1835 he was given the rank of lieutenant-colonel in the *Garde municipale de Paris*, the presentday *Garde républicaine*. In 1836, however, came the opportunity for action in the cause to which he was devoted. On 28 October of that year Louis-Napoleon attempted to win over the garrison at Strasbourg in an effort to supplant the Orleanist regime. Parquin, transformed for the occasion into a brigadier-general, was one of his prime supporters, but the attempt failed in an atmosphere of farcical incompetence. To play down the affair the authorities had the chief conspirators tried at Strasbourg, but thanks to the pleading of his brother Jean, a distinguished lawyer from Paris, Parquin was acquitted. His military career was of course at an end; he was dismissed the service in December 1836 and the payment due to him as a member of the *Légion d'honneur* was stopped.

Now he could give himself over entirely to the service of Louis-Napoleon and he toured Europe in order to win supporters for the Bonapartist cause. When, however, the Orleanists seemed to be stealing the thunder of this cause by themselves bringing back to France the body of Napoleon from St Helena, Louis-Napoleon rushed into a venture which was doomed from the outset. Chartering a steamer and accompanied by only a few faithfuls like Parquin, he sailed from London and on 6 August 1840 landed near Boulogne, hoping to win over the garrison and ultimately the French nation. Within a short while the attempted coup d'état had pathetically petered out and all the members of the landing party were prisoners. This time the government took things too seriously for there to be any escape for Parquin and at the trial in the September of that year before the Peers of France he was one of the supporters of Louis-Napoleon to receive twenty years.

One may be tempted to wonder at the misplaced optimism and naïve rashness which provoked Parquin's downfall, yet these characteristics were present in the man from the start. In his memoirs, Parquin is describing a period when rashness and optimism were harnessed to the service of an ideal. He would probably have been disillusioned with Louis-Napoleon in the role of emperor, but the hope that the nephew might emulate the uncle was an inspiration to the man who, when questioned before his trial about the part he had played in Louis-Napoleon's attempted coup, answered: *J'étais son aide de camp, je l'ai suivi partout sans demander pourquoi.*

This same unquestioning loyalty emerges from his memoirs, but now the background is one of brilliant and honourable action. Not surprisingly, they were seized upon at the end of the century by a public which sought heroes of whom it could be proud. One notable presentation of the purely military side of Parquin's story was in the lavish series of *Récits de Guerre* in 1892, the year after republication of Marbot's memoirs. Set against the mood of the turn of the century, this interest in the glories of the Napoleonic age is understandable, but such works are valuable not merely for chauvinistic purposes. Parquin writes as an eye-witness of a momentous, turbulent period and he produces a human and personal document. His entry into the army at the age of sixteen in 1803 coincided with the beginning of Napoleon's absolute ascendancy and after campaigns in Prussia, Poland, Austria, Spain, Saxony and France, he was to be at Fontainebleau to record the melancholy pageant of the Emperor's farewell to his Guard.

Parquin's was a commendable career, less brilliant than those of some of his contemporaries, but one in which he was entirely immersed. It would be impossible to see him in any other role, yet he had embarked upon this career in spite of the objections of his parents. Parquin on several occasions expresses bitterness at his family's seeming lack of approval and encouragement. This was not an uncommon reaction in a minor bourgeois family. The Revolution had given the bourgeois class new power and prestige; they had gained most from the upheaval and in many areas such as politics, commerce, law and education they had risen to the top. Their rise had been favoured by Napoleon's organization of society where talent led to advancement and where protective measures supported French industry and importers. When, however, Napoleon's policies brought conflict with England, the resulting commercial pressures were to harm industry and commerce most. Parquin's father, as an importer, would have had little reason to enthuse about the army, the basis of Napoleon's authority. Parquin sadly comments that when he was at home in Paris in 1814, although he was a captain in the Guard and although he had been decorated, never once did his parents express their pride in his achievements.

Napoleon demanded not only the physical support of the army, but also its spiritual involvement in his grand design. That this was given is revealed by the utter devotion to the Emperor which stands out from the pages of Parquin. To serve him was a glorious undertaking, but it also drew young men away from the influence of parents and their outmoded political notions. Napoleon encouraged men to present him with petitions and the brave and the loyal were promoted and richly rewarded. Since all were liable to be called for military service—and Parquin mentions the case of the well-to-do young man who received a peremptory call to the colours the day after he showered the Emperor with dust—the young men of France were moulded in the service of an Emperor who lived among them and called them *mes enfants*.

The 20th Chasseurs which Parquin joined so eagerly was a regiment strongly imbued with this family feeling and he gives numerous examples of the spirit of comradeship which existed within it and which contributed to its fighting efficiency. He also frequently mentions the coveted honour of transfer to the Guard, which often happened through a combination of meritorious acts of service and the luck of being in the right place at the right time. Such was the case with Parquin, who was fortunate enough to have Marmont nearby to vouch for him when he asked Lefevre-Desnoëttes, the colonel of the *Chasseurs de la Garde*, if he might join that regiment. As Parquin comments, these were popularly known as *guides* when in the field.

Thanks to his service in these two regiments Parquin is able to furnish accounts of many of the battles of the period 1803–14. He is observant and does not miss the telling detail, but where he is remote from the historic incident he does not pretend to have witnessed it. There is a natural development in his accounts; as a chasseur at Jena he experiences the bewildered sense of being an infinitesimal, insignificant part of the battle; as a captain in the campaign in France with a mission given him by the Emperor himself, his view is much broader. Yet it remains a personal view; he confines his account to his own observations and thoughts without recourse to other authorities after the event. This naturally enhances the genuine tone of his writing, but it also produces those minor errors of detail which are inevitable in a highly personal account, particularly when it is set down some thirty years after the happenings which it describes.

This is occasionally true when Parquin gives Napoleon's movements, in spite of the fact that for the last years covered by the memoirs he was never far from the Emperor. Parquin's sequence of events at Leipzig correctly starts on 16 October 1813 with the battle of Wachau. For the next day he gives the Imperial headquarters as being in a windmill and tells of the death of Lieutenant Henneson, one of his friends. He has in fact omitted the second day of the battle and is writing of 18 October. According to Parquin, Napoleon on the night of 17 October slept at the Black Eagle Inn before bidding the King of Saxony farewell at 6 a.m. and crossing the Elster at 7 a.m. In fact, Napoleon stayed at the Arms of Prussia hotel on the night of 18 October and visited the King of Saxony at between 7 and 9 a.m. before crossing the Elster by the Lindenau bridge. This bridge was blown deliberately after him, not unexpectedly as Parquin implies. On the other hand, although Napoleon had abdicated before 11 April, Parquin can justifiably give this date as the negotiations leading to the abdication on the 7th were protracted and tortuous.

Some of the names given by Parquin display orthographical eccentricities. This is understandable when it is remembered that he was recalling places and men he had known many years previously. Certainly it is not difficult to verify in the majority of cases that men were indeed present at places where Parquin mentions them and his own *état de service* corroborates his account of his own movements. Parquin does not deal exclusively with his own exploits, however. He skilfully introduces into his narrative the accounts of others such as his friend Henry and the hussar Guindey who earned immortality when he killed Prince Louis of Prussia at Saalfeld. This historic incident has been described by many writers, but Parquin had the advantage of hearing the story from Guindey himself when they served together, and his retelling of it is likely to be accurate.

One may entertain some doubt about Parquin's claim that he retells these stories word for word as he originally heard them, just as it is difficult to believe that the considerable amount of dialogue which appears in the memoirs is a completely authentic re-creation of what was really said. Here one must accord a certain licence to the author for this use of dialogue renders the memoirs far more lively and entertaining than an earnest recital of events in the style of Marbot. The passages of conversation moreover have a spontaneity which brings the speakers to life. Indeed, behind this personal tale by a frank, unpretentious soldier lies a polished skill which is reminiscent of Mérimée. There is little fine writing for its own sake, but occasionally evocations such as the all-pervading winter gloom at Eylau and the menace held by the forest of bayonets glinting in the sun at Wagram are impressive in their impact. Parquin's use of images is strictly limited and is sometimes overworked. For him cavalry charges are usually brilliant and meals excellent, and the use of a few foreign words like *boyar* and *alcalde* tends to replace more elaborate description. Nevertheless, the pace and balance of the overall presentation do not allow the memoirs to become a monotonous sequence of ill-defined events.

Much light relief is afforded by the non-military side of these memoirs and Parquin's amorous adventures are neatly interspersed among the historic actions which form the main theme of the work. In these adventures there is very little that would shock the modern reader, although the introduction to the imposing *Souvenirs* of 1892 apologetically explains that certain cuts have been deemed necessary since the *aventures de garnison* are subsidiary to the main theme and the book is meant to be read by anyone. Few readers would now be offended by the manner in which the adventures are related and they provide a felicitous balance to the more violent and historic episodes. They also serve to cast more light on the interesting character of the author.

Modest though his family background was, Parquin clearly had certain contacts with a more influential world. His entry into the 20th Chasseurs, a regiment of considerable repute which was already up to strength, was due to his father's friendship with the colonel of the regiment, and it seemed quite normal to him that as an ordinary chasseur he should be invited with his father to dine with the officers when the regiment came to Versailles. Despite his family's disapproval of his chosen career there was never a moment's doubt in his mind about the correctness of his choice. His dreams of promotion and decoration recur frequently and this was not unnatural at a time when rapid advancement through merit or through the removal of one's superiors in battle was common. There is more than a hint that Parquin was dissatisfied with his own rate of progress and though this is largely attributable to his burning ambition, there is also the impression that he felt he deserved more because of his social origins. He is never malicious and rarely condescending, but he does appear sensitive about social status. Many of Napoleon's generals were of humble origin, but Parquin can still find room to comment at length on Moreau's rise from the position of a lowly clerk. On the other hand he takes pride in mentioning his 'old and close' friendship with Sourd, 'who later became a general and a baron', and his contacts with Captains Moncey, Oudinot and Lauriston, all sons of marshals, are stressed. Not surprisingly, Parquin does not subscribe to the exaggerated accounts of the latter's valour at Amstetten in 1809; Lauriston *fils* was one of the peers who sentenced him in 1840. Nevertheless, while promotion was open to all, men like Parquin's friend Guindey, who came from peasant stock, won it by sheer bravery, and his vulgar behaviour at Prince Esterhazy's estate, as related by Parquin, did not indicate a very high intelligence.

Parquin himself displays courage and initiative, but no great intellectual powers. He shows little interest in art or literature and what he remembers is doggerel in the style of Corneille and the popular songs of the day; the cultural associations of the Esterhazy estate impress him less than the prince's wealth and the thought that he can give the château as his address. Parquin would not be capable of writing, as did his contemporary de Brack, a detailed work on light cavalry tactics. He nevertheless appears as a man of great charm and complete loyalty. His charm is most obvious in his relationships with women when the amorous adventure is one that is enjoyed on both sides. He is never excessive in his attentions and treats each conquest with genuine respect. Admittedly a certain vanity is present when he recounts these exploits, but he is faithful to the memory of the women of whom he writes and maintains a discreet silence as to their identities. In its more manly form this charm made him quickly accepted by his comrades and he in his turn gave himself fully to the regiment. He does not hesitate to defend with his sabre the honour of the corps and when one of the sergeant-majors loses his troop's pay it is Parquin who organizes a collection to replace the lost money. Sometimes what appear to modern eyes to be questionable inconsistencies intrude. How is it that Parquin can pride himself on being the leader of the French prisoners in Vilna, and yet leave them when the opportunity comes to stay in a comfortable private house? But he is also capable of a host of generous acts. He is always ready to share what he has with his comrades and in Spain, unlike most of the French army at the time, he treats captured guerrillas as human beings.

Above all, it is his unswerving loyalty to the Emperor that stands out. Like so many others he identifies his own fortunes with those of Napoleon and with the army he responds wholeheartedly to the favoured treatment given by the Emperor. To be in the service of the Emperor is a way of life where conditions, though harsh at times, are better than those at a corresponding level in civilian life. It is an army which a British memoirist like Thomas Morris, perhaps not from entirely altruistic motives, can admire for its reward of merit. Nor are Parquin's memoirs punctuated with the floggings which characterize the memoirs of Morris or of Costello. After reading Parquin one is left with the impression that here was an enjoyable life where hardships were made tolerable by a binding sense of purpose. Parquin is not blind in his devotion to Napoleon; he can criticize him for the divorce of Josephine and he can bemoan Napoleon's indifference towards the army in Spain. But he remains a loyal member of a well-tempered fighting force whose prowess stemmed in large part from its devotion to the Emperor.

Napoleon's concern for his cavalry had come none too soon. After the Revolution its standard had fallen badly, largely because of the loss of its upper-class officers through purges or emigration. Napoleon quickly appreciated the significance of cavalry and he was determined to organize it as an effective force which would have parity with any enemy. As a start he imbued his mounted troops with his own ideas of the way in which they should fight: 'Cavalry needs audacity and practice; above all it must not be dominated by the spirit of conservatism or avarice.' He made the distinction, which had not been observed previously, between heavy cavalry, cavalry of the line and light horse. The cuirassiers and carabiniers of the heavy cavalry and the dragoons of the cavalry of the line appear in passing in the pages of Parquin, but it is the hussars, the lancers and more especially, the *chasseurs-à-cheval* of the light cavalry who occupy the central place. The light cavalry formed the largest part of the French mounted arm and its reputation for bravery and application while on service, and for bravado and an uninhibited *joie-de-vivre* when not, was rapidly established; their brilliant uniforms exemplified the panache with which they lived and fought. Parquin's mention of Napoleon's personal orders concerning such a minor detail as an article of uniform shows how aware the Emperor was of the small factors which give a unit pride in itself. When, in 1803, Parquin joined the 20th Chasseurs, the process of creating an unbeatable force was well under way.

The *chasseurs-à-cheval* were armed with sabre, carbine and pistols and they were expected to fire from the saddle when in the skirmishing role, but undoubtedly their preference was for the sabre. The increasing importance of these units is shown by the fact that although the term *chasseur* was in general use in 1760 it referred only to *élite* mounted infantrymen attached for their shooting ability to hussar and dragoon regiments. By 1812 there were, nominally at least, thirty-two regiments of *chasseurs-à-cheval*, the 20th having been raised in 1793. Their functions were varied and arduous. Because of their mobility they were particularly suited to reconnaissance duties and often formed part of the advanced guard, the rearguard and the flank screens of the army. Their task was to harass the main enemy force and impede his manoeuvres so that he gained no advantage for his confrontation with the French main force. They were trained to change rapidly from column into line and to change front and fall on the enemy's flank. After the battle they had to cover any retreat or pursue the enemy to complete the victory. 'After Jena,' Napoleon remarked, 'the light cavalry capitalized the victory all on its own', when it drove the Prussians all the way to the Baltic, capturing fortresses and thousands of prisoners. Parquin participated in that pursuit, but his is the view from troop or squadron level. For him little tactical subtlety is involved; he delights in the heady excitement of the charge *à outrance* and any variation is considered highly ingenious, as when at Wagram Colonel Castex inclined his charge away from the square of infantry given him as his target, to charge, with complete success, a square which had just discharged its muskets.

In battle the French cavalry tactics were of course based on the shock action of massed mounted charges. These charges started at a trot and the pace would quicken into a gallop at some 150 yards from the enemy; it was only over the last 50 yards that the full impetus of the charge developed. To achieve the desired result it was vital not to start the final dash too soon, or tiredness and loss of formation would lessen the impact. Lack of discipline among the troopers moreover could lead to their overshooting the target. Thus when General Lepic led his men in an irresistible, but over-impetuous charge against the Russians at Eylau he found himself in the enemy's third line with only a handful of survivors and was extremely fortunate to escape. Support was necessary too from both infantry and artillery in certain conditions, for obstacles such as fortifications or a well-disciplined square were almost invulnerable to cavalry.

However, properly used, cavalry represented a decisive weapon in the battle of this period, especially when it possessed the spirit of Parquin and the 20th Chasseurs. It was a burning, aggressive desire to be in the thick of the action, a desire which gave rise to an attitude which scorned as *une tactique si peu brillante* the refusal by Wellington to give battle in the Peninsula without the likelihood of victory. The efficacy of such tactics could be recognized, but the prolonged avoidance of the head-on clash was conduct alien to the temperament of the French cavalry. The driving force of the cavalryman was *l'Esprit Cavalier* which held for certain the view that in battle he who struck the first blow would always triumph. Having decided what his object should be, and having weighed the risks involved, the cavalryman pursued that object and ran the risks without allowing himself to be distracted from his chosen course of action. Above all, he would not passively submit to the will of the enemy. If he received a blow his only thought was of making the riposte; if he suffered a setback his urgent concern was immediate retaliation.

Drawing inspiration from the Emperor himself the French cavalry eagerly and confidently sought battle and in its violence experienced an almost mystical exaltation. It was not difficult for certain chroniclers to compare the Napoleonic cavalryman with the legendary knights of the *Chansons de Geste*. On a more practical level this idea is given expression by de Brack in his work on light cavalry tactics and training, *Avant-postes de Cavalerie Légère:*

The Cavalryman charging, is a being actuated by one all-pervading feeling, which is almost intoxicating. Take care not to weaken this sentiment, which is both subtle and fleeting.

This driving compulsion was still present in those cavalrymen who fought with such skill and determination in the campaign in France—the final section of Parquin's memoirs. Defeat was coming to Napoleon with the inevitability of the dénouement of a classical tragedy. No doubt those serving him were conscious that the end was near, and yet none of their instinctive verve and dash deserted them. Men such as Parquin measured up to de Brack's requirements:

A man must be born a Light Cavalry soldier. No situation requires so many natural dispositions, an innate genius for war, as that of an officer of light troops. The qualities which render a man superior, intelligence, will-power, ought to be found united in him.

Left constantly to himself, exposed to constant fighting, responsible, not only for the troops under his command, but also for those which he is protecting and scouting for, every minute finds employment for his mental and bodily faculties. His profession is a rough one, but every day affords him opportunities for distinguishing himself; a glorious compensation which repays his toils so much the more, as it shows so much the sooner what he is worth.

(From *Light Cavalry Out-Posts*, a translation for Field-Marshal the Marquis of Tweeddale, 1876.)

Parquin did not achieve the high rank reached by some of his comrades; his military career after 1815 was not outstanding and he died in disgrace. Yet in his memoirs he hints at the vision he has glimpsed. If, in his search to find that vision again in a world far removed from the glorious Empire with a nephew who had not the greatness of the uncle, Parquin was guilty of foolishness and bad judgment, this should not detract from his earlier achievement. The natural telling of his story reveals an attractive, frank cavalryman who, for all his charm, is happiest where the action is. This is the man of whom the state prosecutor could say in 1840:

'Il s'est peint devant vous en quelques mots quand il a dit qu'on ne l'appelait pas au conseil, mais qu'il était un homme d'action.'

B.T.J.

Acknowledgements

I wish to thank Brigadier Peter Young for his guidance and constant interest in the preparation of this work. I am grateful to Antony Brett-James and David Chandler for much helpful advice; the latter has kindly allowed me to draw upon his work *The Campaigns of Napoleon* for details of Napoleon's cavalry and of the cavalry charge.

I am also indebted to Mr W. A. Thorburn for information relating to the organization of a Chasseur regiment.

B.T.J.

Chronological Table

THE PRINCIPAL STAGES IN PARQUIN'S CAREER AS RECORDED IN HIS MEMOIRS

1803

1 Jan.	Joins 20th Chasseurs as volunteer at the age of 16
	Service in France
28 June	Member of picquet guarding First Consul at Abbeville

1804

1 May	Corporal in the 20th Chasseurs
June	Seriously wounded in duel at Lannion

1805

1 Dec.	Service in Holland

1806

1 May	Quartermaster in the *compagnie d'élite*
20 Sept.	Leaves Holland for campaign in Prussia
14 Oct.	Battle of Jena

1807

8 Feb.	Battle of Eylau
15 Feb.	Wounded and captured near Königsberg
9 July	Treaty of Tilsit. Released from captivity
15 Oct.	Rejoins regiment at Stolp

1808

	Service along Baltic coast

1809

1 Jan.	Leaves Prussia for Frankfurt
2 Feb.	Sergeant
Mar.	Army moves to Bavaria
30 Apr.	2nd Lieutenant
6 May	Wounded by pistol shot at Amstetten
15 June	While commanding town of Oedenburg in Hungary receives personal order from Napoleon
6 July	Battle of Wagram

1810

10 Feb.	Returns to France
1 May	Ordered to Spain as part of special detachment

1811

5 May	Wounded at Fuentes de Oñoro
June	Staff officer at Marmont's headquarters

1812

Apr.	Captures Portuguese standard
15 July	Defeats English officer in single combat
22 July	Wounded at battle of Salamanca
Oct.	Returns to France

1813

27 Feb.	Transfers as lieutenant to 13th Chasseurs

10 Mar.	Lieutenant in 1st Regiment of *Chasseurs à cheval de la Garde*
6 Apr.	Receives cross of the *Légion d'honneur* after personal request to Napoleon
26 Aug.	Battle of Dresden
16 Oct.	Battle of Leipzig
30 Oct.	Wounded in face by bayonet at battle of Hanau
21 Dec.	Captain in 2nd Regiment of *Chasseurs à cheval de la Garde*
1814	
1 Jan.	Returns to Paris
6 Feb.	Leaves Paris for campaign in Eastern France
3 Mar.	Given mission by Napoleon. Leads attack against Oulchy-le-Château
5 Mar.	Slightly wounded by Cossacks
20 Mar.	Leads charge against Russian guns. Praised by General Sébastiani
31 Mar.	Arrives at Fontainebleau
20 Apr.	Witnesses Emperor's farewell to the Guard

Charles Parquin

Napoleon's Army

I

On the eleventh day of Nivôse in the eleventh year of the Republic [*1 January 1803*],[1] I alighted from the Paris coach at Abbeville together with one of my friends, a certain Monsieur Fournerat.

Having been directed to the residence of Monsieur Idoux, the quartermaster captain of the 20th Regiment of *chasseurs à cheval* which was stationed in that town, we asked to see the captain so that we might enlist in the regiment. Monsieur Idoux pointed out to us that the regiment was fully up to strength, that in any case my friend was not tall enough to be taken into the regiment and that probably I had not reached the required age for signing on. I was barely sixteen at the time.

'You are perfectly right, but would you be so good as to look at this,' replied Monsieur Fournerat, handing him a note from Colonel Marigny whom we had seen in Paris before we left. The note was an authorization for us to join the regiment and after it had been read, all objections were removed. At the time I was five feet six inches tall and I was eventually to grow to five feet nine. If necessary, my height was more than enough to compensate for the amount by which Monsieur Fournerat fell short of five feet two, the minimum height required by the regiment.

We each had to contribute 27 francs to the regimental funds. This was expected of all newcomers and we were happy to comply with the custom. Then a chasseur who was on duty at the quartermaster's house took us to the barracks. We had asked to join the 6th Troop and our request had been granted. This troop was commanded by a friend of my father, Captain Lavigne, whom we had seen in Paris at Colonel Marigny's house. The captain had promised my parents that he would look after me. It is a fitting tribute to his memory to recall that he kept his word right up to his death at the battle of Jena [*1806*].

When we arrived at the barracks the regiment was mounted and in full dress. It was about to be inspected by the *commissaire des*

[1] In 1793 it was decreed that a new era should be considered to have begun with the foundation of the Republic. There were to be twelve months of thirty days each, with five days at the end for festivals. The system was abolished by Napoleon with effect from 1 January 1806.

guerres[1] who was responsible for the administration of the regiment. I was struck by the fine appearance of the regiment which was considered to be one of the best in the army and which had just taken part in Moreau's highly successful Rhine campaigns. General Richepance, whose brigade included both the 11th and the 20th Chasseurs, never failed to observe as he engaged the enemy that with the 31st he was certain to be victorious.

The regiment's dress was as follows: the chasseurs wore a shako made of black cloth and from the top of its elegant shape there hung a flame of golden-yellow cloth which came to a point in a tassel of the same colour. When full dress was worn, this cloth was allowed to hang down open and a black and red plume was attached to the top of the shako.

The length of the queue was four inches, of which one inch was bound with a band of black wool to leave the last inch of hair projecting. Two long thick tresses hung down the cheeks and were bound at the ends with small bands of lead. The hair, including the tresses, was pomaded and powdered.

The green dolman [*jacket*] had golden coloured facings and piping, white woollen braid and five rows of convex buttons. The riding-breeches also had white woollen braid. The riding-boots were creased at the instep. The green and gold sash which we wore was eight inches wide and had tassels of the same colours. The final touch to this brilliant uniform was provided by the gauntlets which we wore. Each chasseur had a sabretache which hung down about two feet on his left side and was attached by three straps to the sabre belt. This sabretache was used by the chasseurs when they were orderlies for carrying letters and also for carrying their handkerchief if they possessed one.

The regiment had the most beautiful horses. The first squadron had black horses, the second bays, the third chestnuts. The fourth squadron, the trumpeters and the band had grey horses.

My friend and I were overjoyed to be members of such a fine regiment but I must confess that we were impressed most by the band.

'Only one thing upsets me,' I said to my friend, 'and that is having such short hair.'

[1] An official, whose creation dated back to the seventeenth century, empowered to inspect military units in order to prevent false claims on the state by regimental commanders in respect of non-existent men. The post was abolished after the Restoration.

'That is true,' he replied, 'but it will grow with time and within six months we shall have splendid queues like the other chasseurs.'

We learned by experience that we needed a year.

The next morning the corporal of our section took us to the clothing stores where we were issued with all the items of our uniform. Then, when we had returned to the barracks, our corporal discreetly told Fournerat that it was the custom for each new recruit on joining the regiment to put something into the section funds. My friend and I each gave a louis to be used for purchasing extra meat and our contribution marked our acceptance into the regiment. The corporal thanked us for our generosity and thereafter we were thought of as good fellows by the others in the troop.

The soldier's profession is a hard one to follow, especially in the cavalry. It is true that an honourable rank may be the reward for an exacting apprenticeship, but a true sense of vocation is needed if a man is to pass through the early stages of the apprenticeship without being too disheartened.

The sergeant of our troop was a most interesting person. He was between twenty and twenty-two years of age and it was said that he had been an *enfant de troupe*,[1] He was a handsome man and a good soldier who was strict but fair. He ultimately reached the rank of *maréchal de camp*[2] and no doubt he would not have stopped there if the Restoration had not forced him to languish for nineteen years as a lieutenant-colonel on half pay. Monsieur Lacour, for this was his name, took a liking to me and I can honestly say that it was he who made a soldier out of me. I had been in the troop for five months when one Sunday, as he was looking us over before the main inspection, he stopped in front of me. After eying me from head to foot he said:

'Parquin, your uniform looks fine, your weapons are well kept and you handle them well, but you are not a soldier, damn you! Be more confident and look me straight in the eye! Frighten me if you can, damn you! Remember you are a soldier now!'

I obeyed him instantly and thereafter he never had cause to give me further lessons of this sort.

My barrack-room corporal's name was Tisse. He had been awarded

[1] The sons of soldiers, serving or dead, could be educated at the state's expense with a view to their eventual entry into the army.

[2] This title, which was in use from the seventeenth century until the Revolution, reappeared after the Restoration and was finally abolished in 1848 when it was replaced by *général de brigade*.

a *carabine d'honneur*[1] for releasing three hundred French infantrymen and capturing the two companies of Hungarian grenadiers which were guarding them. This was how he would recount his exploit:

'While Moreau was winning the battle of Hohenlinden I had to remain all morning at the rear having my horse shod by Robin our farrier. When we tried to rejoin the regiment we became lost in the forest as we rode towards the sound of the guns. We reached one of those large clearings which are so common in forests in Germany and where vast quantities of game of all sorts come to graze. There we saw, without being seen ourselves, about three hundred disarmed French prisoners with an escort of Kaiserliks.[2] We had a flash of inspiration and, galloping forward, we rushed on the column firing our pistols and crying: "Forward! Follow us! Take no prisoners!"

'The enemy soldiers were taken completely by surprise and thought they had fallen into an ambush. They halted, but were slow to fire. The French prisoners leaped at their muskets and seized them. In a moment the tables were turned. The French now made the Hungarians their prisoners and under our orders led them off to our headquarters.'

Several other men in the regiment had won *armes d'honneur*. Captain Lavigne had won his with the Army of the Rhine during Moreau's retreat when, although only a captain, he had commanded the regiment for a whole day. By skilful manoeuvres and well-timed charges he had succeeded in extricating the regiment from an almost hopeless position and had so greatly helped the whole army.

Captain Kirmann, the commander of the 3rd troop was also the possessor of a *sabre d'honneur*. The blunt request for it as made by Colonel Lacoste, the regiment's commanding officer when it was part of the Army of the Rhine, gives the clearest idea of the bravery of this officer. The request was couched in the following terms: 'Captain Kirmann has so worn out his sabre by indefatigably striking down the enemy that the Government cannot but give him another.'

'Granted!' was the First Consul's reply. I should not omit to mention here that the winner of an *arme d'honneur* received double pay.

Among the heroes of the regiment there was also a corporal of the

[1] *Armes d'honneur* were instituted by the First Consul in 1799 and were given for feats of outstanding bravery. They bore an inscription showing the details of the action for which they were awarded. The system ceased when the *Légion d'honneur* was created.

[2] A term used by the French soldier for German soldiers in general and sometimes applied by extension to French émigrés.

compagnie d'élite who, when he was only fifteen years old, had captured one of La Tour's [*Austrian*] Dragoons.[1] He was attached as trumpeter to the skirmishers one day when he came unseen upon this enormous dragoon. Placing his pistol against the dragoon's throat, he cried, 'Surrender or die!' At these violent words the dragoon gave up his sabre and was made prisoner. When he was taken back to the supporting troop of chasseurs, they began to laugh and to mock the dragoon, a Hercules who had allowed himself to be captured and disarmed by a mere boy. The Austrian suddenly changed his tune.

'I was not captured, I deserted,' he said.

'What, Henry, do you mean to say that you did not take him prisoner?' asked the chasseurs.

The trumpeter's answer was to turn to the dragoon and say, 'So, I didn't capture you! Well, get on your horse and take your weapons. I am going to recapture you for it would seem that the first time does not count.'

But the chasseurs did not want a repetition of the encounter and the Austrian remained a prisoner.

I became very friendly with Corporal Henry whom I first met in the *salle d'armes*; he was my own age and he gave me much good advice. His death, which came at the battle of Raab in Hungary in 1809 after he had become an officer in the regiment, was a grievous loss to us.

Among the more daring members of the regiment there was also Corporal Popineau who had won his *carabine d'honneur* during the famous retreat which General Moreau so skilfully carried out through the Black Forest back to the Rhine. Popineau's fine feat of arms recalled a bygone age of chivalry.

Colonel Schwartz was the commander of a force of 600 hussars of Archduke Charles's army. The men were the best available in the Austrian army for the colonel had the right to recruit from among the most skilled horsemen in every unit. He had, moreover, a completely free hand in the conduct of his operations. He had been harassing the rearguard of our army, capturing convoys, cutting the column of route, releasing prisoners, attacking whenever a suitable opportunity arose, moving by night rather than by day; in short, he was a redoubtable exponent of guerrilla tactics.

He had had several clashes with the 20th Chasseurs and the Austrian hussars had frequently experienced the exceptional bravery

[1] La Tour (1737–1806) was of French extraction although he had been born in Luxembourg.

of Captain Kirmann. As Colonel Schwartz had heard of the captain's brilliant feats, he decided one day to measure his strength against him. He therefore appeared at the regiment's camp under a flag of truce and challenged Captain Kirmann to meet him in single combat with the sabre. He was informed that the captain had been shot in the right arm the previous day and was in the field hospital. Following his display of bravado Colonel Schwartz turned his horse and was about to return to his own camp when Corporal Popineau—who was in Kirmann's troop at that time, although he was later to be promoted to the *compagnie d'élite* when it was formed—galloped his horse forward and rode up to the colonel, saying:

'My captain was slightly wounded yesterday and is unable to fight. He will greatly regret missing the chance to meet you in combat, but if you would care to cross swords with his corporal, I am ready to give you satisfaction.'

'I like your spirit,' said the colonel, drawing his sabre.

He had no sooner said this than the two combatants wheeled their horses and slashed at each other with their sabres. A parry by Popineau came just in time to save him from a blow from his opponent and the latter immediately received a slash across the face from a rapid counter by Popineau.

'Go and have your wound treated, Colonel,' said the corporal, 'and when you have recovered I will give you a second chance to fight me. It will be on foot in front of the regiment and I shall kill you so as to teach you how to live.'

'I never fight twice against the same person,' said Schwartz as he left the field of battle.

'As you wish,' said Popineau, wiping the blade of his sabre.

This deed, which was witnessed by the whole regiment, together with other equally honourable exploits, won a *carabine d'honneur* for Corporal Popineau.

There was also a certain sergeant named Filhatz in the *compagnie d'élite* who had received a *sabre d'honneur* while serving in the Army of the Rhine, but I cannot remember exactly the nature of the feat which earned him such an honourable award. Monsieur Filhatz was a very brave soldier who became a major in the regiment and an officer of the *Légion d'honneur*. He retired from the army after the disastrous Russian campaign during which his feet were badly frost-bitten.

At the beginning of the eleventh year of the Republic, France was at peace with the rest of Europe, but it was not difficult to foresee that England, who claimed that her commercial interests had been harmed, would soon break the Peace of Amiens [*27 March 1802*].

Thus it was that at about this time the First Consul came to inspect the Channel coast and to choose the site of the camp at Boulogne where, a year later, the army which was to carry out the invasion of England established itself.

Everyone knows the facts which prevented the invasion from taking place and which in turn led to this magnificent army's crushing defeat of the Austrians and Russians during the famous Austerlitz campaign.

On 1 June 1803 the regiment unexpectedly received orders to go and carry out escort and communication duties along the road from Amiens to Saint-Valéry. When the First Consul arrived, he slept at the house of the mayor of Abbeville [*28 June*]. I was a member of the dismounted picquet which was to guard General Bonaparte. I still recall with what joy and pride I did sentry duty outside the apartment he was occupying and how great was my happiness at his acknowledgement when I presented arms to him as he was returning to his apartment. I little imagined then that ten years later I would be made a captain in the Emperor's *Guides*. I do not think I have ever known a finer experience than my sentry duty outside the door of the man on whom the eyes of all Europe were already fixed.

Throughout the First Consul's journey, triumphal arches were erected everywhere. I remember how at Rouen on 1 July when the regiment was going from Abbeville to take up garrison duties at Caen, we read the following lines on a triumphal arch:

Diogène, jadis, sa lanterne à la main,
Cherchait partout un homme, et le cherchait en vain;
Le Cynique ne put en mettre un sur sa carte,
Et, les larmes aux yeux, rentra dans son tonneau;
Mais qu'eût-il fait s'il eût rencontré Bonaparte?
Le philosophe alors eût éteint son flambeau!

Indeed the great Corneille[1] himself, whom the Emperor would have made a prince if the poet had lived in our times, would not have disowned these lines by a fellow-citizen two hundred years after him.

On our arrival at Caen we relieved the 10th Dragoons. This regiment had not been on good terms with the lively young men of the

[1] Pierre Corneille (1606–84) was born in Rouen. In his plays the grandeur of his style and the exaltation of man's freedom and strength of will made a great appeal to Napoleon.

town who were always keen to practise their skill with weapons. There were more than one hundred fencing-masters in Caen.

The 43rd Infantry Regiment had been involved in many duels and the regiment had been assailed from all sides and forced to move outside the walls of the town. The Minister of War replaced the colonel of this regiment and several young men of the town who had been concerned in the affair were severely punished. On the orders of the First Consul the 43rd Regiment re-entered the town with drums beating and colours flying; a deputation from the town met them outside the gates and escorted them back into the town.

We arrived in the midst of these events. Colonel Marigny, who had a great liking for young people, organized a tournament to which all the young men in Caen as well as the fencing-masters in the town were invited. The tournament took place in the fine surroundings of the Café Labassée on the promenade. An event, which in itself was regrettable, nevertheless did much to ensure that the inhabitants of Caen took to us immediately.

A dreadful fire had suddenly broken out in one of the villages near to the town. General Laroche [*-Dubouscat*], who commanded the [*14th Military*] district heard of the fire just as he was arriving for the tournament. As he was near the cavalry barracks occupied by our regiment, he rushed into the guard-room and shouted: 'To horse! To horse! There is a village on fire!'

Turning to the duty sergeant, he asked: 'Where is the duty trumpeter?'

'I have just given him permission to go to supper, sir.'

'Where is his trumpet?'

'Here it is, in the weapons rack.'

The general seized it and, in the middle of the courtyard, sounded boots and saddles. All the other trumpeters took up the call and within a few minutes the whole regiment had mounted. I should mention here that General Laroche had been a boy trumpeter and he had not forgotten his former rank. Once the regiment had assembled, the general placed himself at the head and led it at the gallop to the blazing village.

Its help came just in time and it saved the houses which the fire had not reached. Thanks to its action, the damage was not extensive—as it would certainly have otherwise been in this district where most of the houses had thatched roofs.

This splendid response in such circumstances by the regiment and the highly successful tournament which took place afterwards made things turn out perfectly for us. Not only did the young men put on a tournament for the instructors in return, but they also provided a vast amount of punch which did much to cement good relations. These good relations continued for the short time we spent in Caen and several wealthy young men of good family joined the regiment; not only did they make the customary contribution, but they also equipped themselves and provided their horses at their own expense. It was thus that Messieurs de Gonneville, de Vomel, d'Infreville and Lethermillier joined the regiment as chasseurs. The first of these became a colonel and was in charge of the remounts at Haguenau in 1830; the second and the third died gloriously face to face with the enemy and the fourth died while serving as the colonel of a light cavalry regiment.

Our stay lasted only two months and when we left on 1 September we were escorted for a league beyond Caen by the young men of the town who bade us look after those of their companions who had joined us. As I have indicated, all four of them were to distinguish themselves in their military careers.

The regiment passed through the town of Bayeux where it spent the night. This is an area which is well known for its beautiful women and to tell the truth, I must admit that it was indeed there that I saw the most beautiful women in Normandy.

We continued on our way through Avranches, Coutances and various other towns until we finally eached Rennes where the depot was to be established under Major Castex, our senior riding instructor who had just joined us. This officer, who had risen from the rank of chasseur in the 24th Chasseurs to that of *gros major*[1] in our regiment (this rank was then the equivalent of a presentday lieutenant-colonel), was fanatical in the execution of his duties. In winter he would have classes on their horses from four in the morning until ten at night. He had had lanterns installed inside the riding school and they lit up the place as brightly as daylight. The major himself often rode there on his own young horse called Breton. He was determined to train it perfectly, especially as he was an excellent horsemen. One day the instructor captain remarked that the skittish horse was frightened by the lanterns and that there might be an accident.

'A major in charge of riding,' answered Monsieur Castex, 'does not fight with the army; he should be killed in the riding-school, for it is in this way that he dies at his post.' His words were said in a Gascon

[1] The term *major* usually indicated a senior officer in charge of some form of training or administration, or of medical services.

accent which made his speech sound so peculiar that no one could restrain a smile.

The first time that he saw action with the regiment at the battle of Jena on 14 October 1806 he was made a colonel. We shall see later the nature of the brilliant feat which won him this promotion. At the battle of Eylau on 7 February 1807 he was made an officer of the *Légion d'honneur*; at the battle of Friedland [*1807*] he became a commander of the order and a *baron de l'Empire* and was awarded 4,000 francs; at the battle of Wagram [*1809*] he won his general's epaulettes; in the unfortunate Russian campaign of 1813 he was made a major-general; in 1813 he transferred with this rank to the mounted grenadier regiment of the Guard as senior instructor; finally in the campaign in France he was made a grand officer of the *Légion d'honneur*. Under the Restoration he was made a viscount; he commanded the 5th Military District and he remained in this post until the 1830 Revolution, in which he took no part. Few other soldiers gained greater promotion than this and certainly none was more knowledgeable and brave than our intrepid Major Castex.

On 1 May 1804 the major called me to his office to inform me that I had been made a corporal on the recommendation of Captain Lavigne and that I would be confirmed in the rank at the Sunday parade the following day. He told me, moreover, that I would be sent in my new rank as one of a detachment which was going to join the patrols stationed on the Atlantic coast. My troop was at Lannion and was responsible for communications between this little town and Morlaix.

The headquarters of Marshal Augereau, the commander-in-chief of the *Armée de l'Océan*,[1] were at Brest. Colonel Marigny, the staff and the first squadron were at Saint-Brieuc; the remainder of the regiment was spread along the road to Rennes to link up with Major Castex who, as has been seen, commanded the depot at Rennes.

On 15 May I was given a friendly reception when I arrived at Lannion, but I had to stand my fellow corporals a dinner at the Arbre Vert hotel to celebrate my stripes. Eight meals at 3 francs apiece put me very much in favour with my new comrades who swore me their friendship—and who kept their word. It was not long, however, before I noticed that my stripes had caused some jealousy in the troop.

A month after my arrival I was on duty and was inspecting the rooms. I noticed in the weapons-rack a sabre which was not up to the

[1] *L'Armée des Côtes de l'Océan.*

required standard of cleanliness and I reprimanded Chasseur Hayer to whom it belonged. He retorted that only a newcomer would have the nerve to criticise an older member of the troop and that if I would like to try out my sabre against his, he would prove that he was the better man.

At this unexpected insubordination I did not give the chasseur four days punishments as I should have done; instead, I accepted the challenge and a quarter of an hour later I was waiting outside the barracks for my opponent. He was not long in coming and the duel took place immediately. We drew our sabres and after exchanging several blows which were parried on both sides, I lunged forward and pierced my opponent's shirt under his right arm with the point of my sabre. As I withdrew to resume my guard, Hayer caught me on the foot. I was wearing light shoes and I received a deep wound on the instep. Blood gushed out of the wound and I fell down on the spot. Four chasseurs came and picked me up and then carried me to the civilian hospital in Lannion which was run by the Sisters of Charity.

My wound was so serious that I might have had to have my foot amputated or at least be forced to walk with a limp for the rest of my life. My extreme youth and the purity of my blood saved me.

After putting my foot on a plank to keep it upright and so aid the binding together of the nerves and muscles which are so numerous in this part of the foot, the surgeon placed my leg between two sheets which were bound as tightly as possible. For six weeks I remained on my back without moving. When the doctor finally removed the appliance, he found my wound to be in the best possible condition. He assured me that I would not have a limp, but added that I would have to stay another month in hospital. In order to strengthen the nerves in my foot, I would go, whenever the hospital butcher killed an ox or a cow, to let the blood from these animals flow over my wound. This treatment, which I continued even after leaving hospital, worked wonders for me.

A few weeks later I had fully recovered and I was discharged from hospital. It is not difficult to imagine how delighted I was, but I had no idea that the first of my amorous adventures would date from that day. Heaven granted me this as a reward (or so at least I thought at the time) for the incredible suffering which I had so bravely borne. This incident from my youth is one of those which I still remember with the greatest feeling when I look back over the years.

A male nurse from the hospital came and suggested that he should accompany me back to the cavalry barracks. He had time to spare as it was his day off. I did not really need his aid, but I did not wish to deprive him of the tip that he was probably after and so I agreed.

I took my leave of the good sisters at the hospital, promising that I would return and visit them.

'Yes, yes, yes, we shall be so glad to see you!' they all called. 'But make sure that you are in good health this time!' added Sister Seraphina, the Mother Superior.

I thanked them as best I could and on 1 September I left the hospital. I set off with the male nurse, but after we had gone a short distance along the rue Kérempont he said to me: 'Corporal, would you care to call on someone who has been most interested in you since the day you were wounded and taken to hospital?'

'Who is this kind person?' I asked him in astonishment.

'It is Mademoiselle Marguerite, a beautiful girl who is the laundress at the hospital. This is where she lives,' he added, pointing to a door. He went up to it and knocked. The knocker had scarcely fallen when a window on the first floor was opened. A pretty face appeared and Mademoiselle Marguerite, for she it was, said quietly to my companion:

'I am coming down, Michel.'

A moment later the door opened and a beautiful woman appeared to greet me. She was quite tall and must have been between twenty and twenty-five. She said to me: 'You need not come up, sir; there is a room downstairs where we can go.'

We went into this room and to get rid of Michel as quickly as possible, I gladly gave him 20 sous—to go and have a drink, as the expression is.[1]

'Mademoiselle Marguerite,' I said to the beautiful young girl, after taking the seat she had offered me, 'I have come to thank you for all the concern you have shown for me and to entreat you to continue this concern.'

By starting in this way, I immediately put her at her ease and spared her all the embarrassment that generally accompanies first meetings.

'Oh sir, you are so deserving of that concern. It was a serious wound for one so young. I was at my window when you passed by on the stretcher which the four chasseurs were taking to the hosptial. Heavens! you were so pale!'

'I had lost a great deal of blood.'

[1] The expression *pourboire*, which dates from the middle of the eighteenth century, still had a very literal meaning at this time.

'Since I am allowed in the hospital at any time during the day because I run the laundry there, I hurried on ahead so as to be there when you arrived. You cannot imagine how the good sisters were frightened by your terrible wound.'

Then suddenly she stopped and said: 'Heavens! you must excuse my thoughtlessness; you have been so ill and I am making you talk without thinking of offering you anything. Do have a cup of coffee.'

I could not dream of refusing and immediately Mademoiselle Marguerite began setting up a small table on which she spread a white cloth; then she brought some coffee and some fruit which she had previously got ready in anticipation of my visit.

While she was doing this, I took the opportunity of looking more closely at my new acquaintance. She was a beautiful, tall, dark-haired girl, simply dressed but strikingly neat in appearance. The room was not luxurious but it was immaculately clean and tidy. When the coffee had been poured out, we sat down and took the refreshments.

'Sir,' she said, 'would it be indiscreet to ask you the cause of your duel? Was it over some lady?'

'Not at all, Mademoiselle, for to be sure, I had had no time to think of such pleasures, having only just arrived from the depot. The incident took place as a result of an argument over a military matter so you can imagine it does not make very entertaining telling. I would rather, with your permission, talk of something more interesting. If you do not mind, let us talk about you.'

'Of course,' replied the charming girl.

'You seem to be on your own in this house.'

'Oh no sir; I have with me Marianne, an elderly woman who helps me with the housework.'

'Yes, but I meant that you have no family.'

'Alas, my father was in the army and he died on service before Lille[1] when I was eleven. My mother, who would never remarry, looked after me until I was twenty, but then I lost her. She had run the hospital laundry for ten years and, as you can imagine, I had helped my dear mother in her work. When my mother died, the Mother Superior, who was fond of me, kindly let me take over the work. I have four women working for me down at the river.'

When Marguerite had finished speaking, I said to her: 'You are a most worthy and loyal daughter; your father paid his debt to his

[1] In 1792 Lille was successfully defended by 7,000 National Guardsmen when it was besieged by 34,000 Austrians.

country and your mother paid hers to nature. I am sure that heaven will help and protect you, for you deserve happiness, Marguerite.'

'I hope so; when a person is honest and earns a living by hard work, what more is there to ask for or to fear?'

The table had been cleared a good hour when I took my leave of Marguerite, asking as I did so if I might come again to see her. I said that I had to call on the good sisters the following Sunday. Could I call on her when I came by?

'Of course, sir. That would be admirable for Sunday is the only day when I do not work. At what time will you be calling at the hospital?'

'After the two o'clock roll-call,' I answered.

I rose and took my leave of her, assuring her that I would not forget her kindness, her touching concern and her generous hospitality. Then I started back to the barracks, not without looking back frequently to see if I could catch a glimpse of her at her window, but my curiosity was disappointed.

When I reached the barracks I was warmly welcomed by my comrades, my superiors and the chasseurs in the troop, including my opponent who was one of the first to come and ask me how I was. As he cut such a comical figure apologizing to me, I said to him with a smile:

'If you had done that before our fight I would not have been two and a half months in hospital and you a fortnight in prison. But since we cannot relive the past, here is my hand and let us think no more of it.'

He seemed very grateful for my attitude and I subsequently learned that my action was highly thought of in the troop. I did not, however, escape a severe reprimand from my captain when I reported to him the next day. He told me that had I not suffered so much from my wound, he would have given me a fortnight in prison, for I deserved the same punishment as Chasseur Hayer for having drawn swords with him when he was my subordinate. Then he asked me about my health and gave me a louis, which was the equivalent of a quarter of the allowance which my father made me. This was not a lot, but my father, although not poor, was not rich. His income came from trading in spices, preserved foods and imported wood. He had a big family to raise for there were seven children. My mother, who was fortunate enough to remain in good health until her death at the age of eighty-three, had considerable influence over my father and had never been willing for me to become a soldier. According to her, I had taken up a career for idlers, but it will be seen whether such a career at that particular time was deserving of that description.

As for my sergeant, Monsieur Lacour, he shook my hand heartily and said affectionately: 'Parquin, you have paid dearly for your stripes; you fought well, but from now on you will avoid any similar incidents. In any case, I will see to that!' he added as he left me.

Monsieur Lacour could not blame me in the same way as Captain Lavigne; all the regiment knew how the sergeant had fought a duel with Jary, the quartermaster sergeant, at Abbeville. This affair was so unusual that it deserves to be recounted.

Jary was a very witty but sarcastic young man. While the two of them were playing billiards, at which they were equally skilled, an argument arose. They decided to settle their differences outside. The quartermaster was very brave; Monsieur Lacour was no less so, but he was also much more accomplished at handling a sabre. He had therefore agreed to the duel suggested by Jary only so as to give the latter a lesson by leaving a souvenir of the duel across his face. When they were on guard, the sergeant struck with his sabre at his opponent's foot. This was only a feint and while the quartermaster was trying to parry, Lacour grazed his face with a thrust. Jary's pipe, which was in his mouth, was shattered. Immediately the quartermaster stopped fighting and in all seriousness said to his seconds:

'Gentlemen, I am postponing this duel until tomorrow; then, I shall be careful to wear a mask, for the gentleman facing me is a clumsy oaf who could end up putting out one of my eyes.'

This witticism made everyone burst out laughing. The bad feeling immediately disappeared and the two opponents embraced each other.

At the battle of Eylau Quartermaster Jary had his head blown off while he sat smoking his pipe; I am sure that if he had still been able to speak, he would have said that this was a joke in extremely poor taste.

But to return to the barracks. There I was astonished to notice two four-pounder guns and two ammunition wagons which I had not previously seen.

'It is the artillery which arrived this morning,' one of my comrades told me. 'The regiment is going to learn how to fire guns.' He told me that there was an allowance of 4 sous a day per man for this training and this news pleased me as much as it did my comrades.

Since the captain had excused me from duties for a month, all I had to do was to look after my weapons and whiten my leather equipment which greatly needed this attention when I drew it from the stores where it had been kept during my absence. My horse, however, I found in fine condition, for one of my friends had taken care of it while I was in hospital.

From the Thursday I came out of hospital until the following Sunday, which was to be the day of my future visits to the rue Kérempont, time passed slowly for me. At last the longed-for day arrived. Since I was a corporal, I had obtained the captain's permission to have a uniform of superior cloth made at my own expense. On my dolman were my stripes, which should have been made of wool, but which in fact were made of very white goat hair. Riding-breeches and light well-made riding-boots should have completed my uniform, but my wound did not allow me to walk out in riding-boots. I therefore put on shoes and, since to my great regret I could not wear my breeches, I had to go out in overalls made of good quality cloth. My hair had grown during the eighteen months I had been in the regiment and I was able to wear the regulation pomaded and powdered queue and tresses, but to my grief, my moustache had refused to grow despite constant encouragement with the razor.

In short, such as I was, I was fairly presentable to go visiting the pretty, tender-hearted girl in the rue Kérempont. In my simplicity I liked to think that I would favourably impress Mademoiselle Marguerite, especially when I heard my comrades humming all day long:

Voulez-vous être aimé des belles?
Engagez-vous dans les chasseurs.

So I set out for Marguerite's house and soon I was there.

If I had been careful over my appearance, the girl for her part had neglected nothing to make herself even more pretty. She was wearing a round bonnet and its raised part at the front had a lace fringe. Her ebony-black hair was perfectly smooth on her white forehead and it was gathered into two bandeaux with a parting in the middle. I still remember how her hair seemed to escape from the back of the bonnet and fall in an enormous chignon on her long and beautifully white neck.

She was wearing pear-shaped earrings and had a little gold cross hanging from a velvet ribbon around her neck. Her dress in a dark-blue thick material was very short, as was the fashion then, and it revealed a blue ribbed stocking which fitted smoothly over an elegant leg. A sash of pink watered silk with ribbons on it emphasized her pretty waist. Finally, on her very dainty feet she wore shoes with quite high heels which were covered with ribbons. It was enough to turn the head of the most reasonable of men, and I have never been reasonable in these matters!

'I have been waiting for you,' she said, holding out her white hand which I hastened to kiss. 'Please sit down, sir.'

When I was seated, she asked with concern about the state of my wound. She asked me if I had suffered much, if I had been glad to see my comrades again and if they had welcomed me back. All these questions were inspired by a genuine interest and they touched me deeply. I replied to them with feeling for, as I told her, they made me very happy. After spending an hour chatting of one thing and another and saying those sweet nothings which a young man and a young girl always say to each other, Marguerite suddenly exclaimed:

'Heavens! How silly of me! Here I am, not thinking of warning you that there is no visiting at the hospital after three o'clock. The good sisters would be really hurt if you did not visit them today as you have promised.'

'What, Marguerite, do you want me to go already?'

'You could come back when you have been to the hospital,' she said, blushing slightly.

'Of course—and I will spend the evening with you if you will let me.'

I could see by her smile that she was agreeable to this and I took my leave.

At the hospital my arrival was quite an event. The porter, the male nurses and particularly Michel, showed such a concern for me that I was quite touched. I thanked them and went over to the Mother Superior's rooms. On seeing me, Sister Seraphina let out a great cry, tugged on the bell and the five sisters came running up and surrounded me. The Mother Superior made me sit down. Everyone showed the greatest interest in my health and asked what I had done since leaving the hospital. The good sisters were especially anxious to learn if I had made my peace with the chasseur whom I had fought.

'You know,' they said with that admirable simplicity which is the mark of a truly religious person, 'it is a bad thing not to love one's neighbour.'

'I have made my peace with him,' I answered, 'but I have not become friends with him, for he has never been other than a fellow-soldier with whom I wish to live in peace.'

I had to keep up a prolonged conversation with these excellent people and I am sure that I would have had to go far to find myself such a centre of attraction. Are not all women, even including nuns, the daughters of Eve? Nevertheless, I was on tenterhooks, for the time I was there seemed terribly long. The thought of my charming Marguerite was ceaselessly running through my mind and making my heart beat strongly for her. After an hour I could wait no more and I rose to take my leave, saying as an excuse that duties which I could not avoid called me back to the barracks. Thereupon the sisters ran out, only to return with sweetmeats, marzipan cakes, chocolate and a jar of preserves which they made me take for, seeing that I was going to refuse, they themselves put these things in my sabretache.

'Here is an elixir of long life,' said the Mother Superior, handing me a glass of Malaga wine.

'To your health, sisters,' I said, drinking it. 'May God grant you a long life so that humanity may benefit from it.'

This toast brought me endless thanks. I was at a loss to know where to put the jar of preserves for the clothes I was wearing had no pockets in them. I took from my sabretache the best handkerchief that I had, wrapped it around the pot and held it in my right hand. Fortunately I had not far to go before I could dispose of it.

My visit to the hospital had taken longer than I had intended and yet the sisters seemed so happy and pleased to see me that I almost reproached myself for not making my visit last longer than an hour. When I arrived at Marguerite's house, she said with a charming little pout: 'I thought the sisters were going to keep you until the six o'clock bell, sir.'

'They were delighted to see me,' I said, putting down the jar of preserves and asking Marguerite to accept it. I then took from my sabretache all the other delicacies and offered those to her as well.

As she took them she said: 'I will accept them only on condition that you do not refuse the modest supper I have prepared.'

'Of course I will not refuse; I can stay with you until ten o'clock.'

'But sir, it is too dangerous to be out these days at ten o'clock on a Sunday when the inns are all full. There are often drunkards in the streets. You should leave earlier for we will have finished supper by seven o'clock.'

'What! Is it so unpleasant with me that you want me to leave so early?'

'Oh, that is not the reason, sir. It is just that I would fear for your safety.'

'You may set your mind at rest, my dear girl. I have Jacqueline to protect me and she will make anyone who wants to be a nuisance on the way back keep his distance.'

At the name of Jacqueline, which she took to be a woman's, I perceived that she blushed. Without seeming to understand all of my words, she said quite sharply: 'Who is this Jacqueline?'

'She is the only rival you have to fear,' I answered. 'She is the blade of my sabre.'

'That is just as well,' she said.

We sat down. The supper was good for, despite what she had said about it, she had taken much trouble over it. There was some excellent roast veal, very fresh sea-fish, a salad, apple fritters which she made particularly well, cider and a bottle of Bordeaux. The dessert was provided by the delicacies which the sisters had given me. When the supper was over, I gently chided her for giving me the excellent Bordeaux when she had not drunk any of it herself.

'I must admit,' she told me, 'I did not buy it especially for the occasion. It was from the cask which we bought when mother was ill. I think there are still about fifty bottles left, so you see sir, you have no grounds for reproaching me there. In any case, as a convalescent, you should drink wine.'

She swiftly cleared the table and we sat down by the fire. I was still so young that my emotions on being near to such a pretty girl made me strangely self-conscious. I remember that to put myself more at ease I asked her to sing; without hesitation she did so in a very pleasant voice. She sang a song which was very popular at the time. Its refrain went:

Love, respect and friendship
Travel the same road together.

'That is truly the picture of the happy life which I hope to lead with you,' I said, carried away with delight. The wine had clearly dispelled my shyness. Suddenly I kissed Marguerite. She pulled a face and said:

'Come sir, that was very naughty of you.'

'Oh, if you are annoyed at me Marguerite, give me back my kiss immediately and then you will not hold it against me.'

'There sir,' she said, holding out her hand, 'let us be friends. I forgive you.'

I complimented her on her fine voice and thanked her for her kindness in letting me hear her sing.

'Oh, please do not thank me; I love to sing, especially when there is someone who enjoys listening to me.'

'My dear Marguerite,' I said, 'there is one thing that I would like you to do for me.'

'What is that?' she asked.

'I would like you to use my christian name instead of being so formal by calling me sir every time you speak.'

'What is your name?'

'Charles.'

'Well, I have to tell Charles that the half-hour has just struck at the hospital. It is therefore half past nine and he needs half an hour to get back to the barracks.'

'Alas, that is true. Time flies when I am with you, Marguerite. When may I see you again?'

'On Sunday of course, Charles; and if you will have supper with me then, that will be proof that you have enjoyed supper this evening.'

'Most certainly I will,' I said eagerly, taking her hands.

'You do understand,' she added, leaving her hands in mine, 'that I have to work all the week and Sunday is the only day when you can see me and come to my house. Also, Charles, you must be very discreet.'

'Have no fear, Marguerite: if there is one quality which I possess, it is discretion and you will be able to judge this for yourself.'

I drew her to me and this time the charming young girl did not resist my long kiss.

I had word from her regularly twice a week by means of Marianne; on Mondays when the old woman came to collect my washing and on Saturdays when she returned it.

It is not my intention here to go into further details of my affair with Marguerite. In any case I promised my discretion and even forty years later I am keeping my word. It is enough to say that the six months which my troop spent at Lannion were a time of great happiness for me and I still cannot think of that time without feeling very moved.

In the troop everyone set about learning to handle the guns and after a few months we were all capable of serving a gun. It should however be mentioned in passing that we never had the opportunity of using the talent which we acquired.

Lannion was only a very small garrison town, but life was very pleasant there. I remember how one day when out walking beyond the town with one of my friends, we met Captain Lavigne who was returning from a carriage-ride in the country with some ladies. My companion, who had some reputation as a wit, observed: 'Have you noticed how the ladies of Lannion seem to prefer Lavigne [*the vine*] to le vin [*the wine*]?'

Indeed, Captain Lavigne was not only a very pleasant person, but also one of the most handsome officers in the regiment. I am sure that when we left the town, he was one of those who were most missed.

As might be expected, there were also many tears when I left my dear Marguerite. She was later to marry, on 15 August 1805, the hospital gardener. He had sought her hand at the time when my wound confined me to bed, but Marguerite had refused to marry this young man who was a good worker, but who had no savings with which to set up house. I also think that I was partly responsible for the refusal.

On his name-day [*15 August*] the Emperor gave a certain number of dowries to be distributed in all the departments of France among marriageable young girls whose fathers had died in battle leaving no inheritance. The Mother Superior, Sister Seraphina, was fond of Marguerite and the gardener and she easily arranged the marriage with the help of the mayor of the town. Under the terms of the award each couple received the sum of 1,200 francs to set up house. Thus Marguerite was able to marry the gardener, who from that day on had a very pretty flower indeed to tend.

The tour of duty was not, however, enjoyable for everyone. There was, for example, Chasseur Fournerat who had enlisted with me. He had no cause to regret leaving the town for he had suffered a mishap which I feel I should relate.

One day towards the end of autumn as he was walking on the outskirts of the town, he noticed some fine lady-apples in an orchard. He climbed over the surrounding hedge and, without further ado, started to eat some of the tempting fruit. The previous day the Breton farmer who owned the orchard had lost all the apples from one of his trees which had been completely stripped by thieves.

He thought that Chasseur Fournerat was one of the perpetrators of this galling theft and so he crept up quietly and lashed out with a flail which struck Fournerat in the face and fractured his jaw. The chasseur was knocked out and had to be carried back to the barracks. Thus, while Marguerite and I were peacefully partaking of the forbidden fruit in the garden of the Hesperides, some very common fruit was bringing nothing but pain and misfortune to my friend.

II

After leaving Lannion on 1 December the troop spent the night at Guingamp, a pretty little town on the road from Rennes to Brest. The next day it moved on to Saint-Brieuc where the regiment had its headquarters. I was left behind at Guingamp with four chasseurs for escort and communication duties. I stayed there for one month and during this time nothing worth relating happened, apart from an incident which occurred when I and my detachment went four leagues down the road to Brest to act as escort to Marshal Augereau. He was on his way to Paris where he was going to take over the command of the army corps which was in the Tyrol during the glorious Austerlitz campaign.

While I was escorting the marshal's carriage I had occasion to dismount. I did so, knowing that I would easily make up the distance lost by my stop and, indeed, I was at the head of my escort when we entered the town. As we went past an infantry picquet which presented arms I gave the order to draw sabres, but when I tried to draw my own sabre it was no longer at my side. My mortification can be easily imagined! I had left my sabre on the road at the spot where I had dismounted. Fortunately it was raining at the time and since I, like my chasseurs, was covered by my cloak, no one noticed that my sabre was missing.

After receiving 20 francs which the marshal generously gave me for my detachment and after handing over to the corporal who had come with four chasseurs to relieve us as the marshal's escort, I wheeled my horse around and galloped off to the place where I had dismounted. To my great despair I could not find my sabre and footprints at the spot told me clearly that someone had picked it up. In vain did I question the few travellers whom I met on the road for I obtained no satisfactory information. I went on as far as the next village down the road, but was no more successful. I returned to Guingamp feeling thoroughly discontented. I tried to buy a sabre in the town, but there were none of regulation pattern to be had. I was at a loss to know what to do.

The five of us were all billeted in private houses and our horses were stabled at one of the inns in the town. The house where I was staying was in the main square of Guingamp and belonged to Monsieur M. who was a respectable citizen of the town. On Sundays he was kind enough to invite me to dine with him and his family. So it was that one Sunday when my dejection was obvious to all present, he said to me after the table had been cleared and we were alone having coffee:

'You are sad, Corporal. I have no right to ask you about your private affairs, but if I can help you in any way, do not hesitate to ask me.'

'You are very kind, sir, but unfortunately my sadness results from a situation which your kindness is unlikely to be able to remedy.'

I then told him in detail why I was so upset. My host immediately replied: 'You have not tried all the means available to recover your sabre. Allow me to offer you some advice; if you follow it and still do not find your weapon, then you can really mourn your loss.'

'Please sir, tell me what to do! I shall follow your advice immediately, I assure you!'

'Ask the priests in the four parishes where you were when you lost your sabre to announce your loss during their sermons at the main mass next Sunday. Offer a reward of 6 francs for the finder if he brings it back to you.'

When I heard this suggestion, hope came back to me. Monsieur M., who knew the area well, was extremely kind and made four identical circulars which I sent to the priest of each of the parishes named by Monsieur M. The following Sunday my sabre was found and brought to me before the day was out. I was only too glad to give the promised reward to a tailor's employee who had found my weapon on the road.

I thanked Monsieur M. for his excellent idea and to repay him for his generosity to me on several occasions, I invited him to dinner at the inn where the chasseurs and I usually had our meals. The dinner was a very merry affair. Monsieur M. sang us several songs, including one in praise of General Moreau. Monsieur M. and General Moreau had both been born in the town of Morlaix and my guest had known the general particularly well before the Revolution when he had worked with him in the office of Monsieur Frenières, the public prosecutor at Rennes. I remember one of the verses of the song composed in honour of the victor of Hohenlinden. It went thus:

Gloire au guerrier magnanime,
Au conquérant de la paix!
Moreau, ton talent sublime
A fait l'honneur des Français.

Eh bien, sous l'ancien régime,
Moreau, ce grand général,
Aurait été caporal.

It can be seen that this song refers to Moreau's humble origins. Indeed, notwithstanding the example of General Chabert and a few others, it must be admitted that but for the Revolution, Moreau might never have been called upon to reveal his great talents. But why, alas, did he later have to tarnish his former glory![1]

On 1 January 1805 I was ordered to take my detachment back to the regiment at Saint-Brieuc. When I arrived I gave the squadron sergeant-major a report on the period during which I had been in charge at Guingamp and then I hastened to find my friend Henry, the corporal of the *compagnie d'élite*, and to take him to dine with me at the Hôtel de l'Ecu.

When we reached the hotel, we sat down to eat, but I wanted to find out what had happened in the regiment while I had been away for eight months.

'Well, first of all,' said Henry, 'your humble servant had an unpleasant experience six months ago. Major Watrin was given a young wolf as a present by the local countryfolk and the major used to walk around the town with the animal—which was said to be completely tame. One day when I was coming back from the butcher's with a chasseur who was carrying the meat for the section I met Major Watrin coming through the barracks. The wolf, which as usual was with him, was probably attracted by the smell of the fresh meat, for the animal leapt upon it and started to devour it in no uncertain manner.

'The chasseur who was carrying the meat on his back was terrified and dropped it in spite of my repeated cries that the animal was tame. The only effect of my cries was to make the wolf increase its efforts. When I saw this I rushed at the animal to make it release the meat, but it turned on me furiously, opening its enormous mouth. I immediately drew my sabre and slashed through the animal's hamstrings, much to the displeasure of the major who has disliked me ever since.'

On 1 February the regiment left Saint-Brieuc for Pontivy, which at that time was called Napoléonville. It remained there for two months

[1] Moreau (1763–1813), after his victorious campaigns in Germany became a political rival to Bonaparte. After conspiring with the Royalists he was forced to go into exile in America. He returned to Europe and was killed at Dresden, fighting against his own country.

and during this period my captain attached me to the quartermaster's stores. I wrote a good hand and I was quite pleased to learn book-keeping. On 5 April the regiment left Napoléonville for Versailles where it arrived on 1 May. My father came to see me the same day that we arrived, and Captain Lavigne invited us both to dine with the officers.

I remember that on the following Sunday three of my friends and I were given leave until the next morning. We decided to go to the theatre in Paris for Talma,[1] the famous actor was appearing in a play that day. At that time there were neither *gondoles*, that is, public coaches with a large number of seats, nor trains for travellers going to Paris. The only vehicles available were *coucous* which were drawn by two horses and which took passengers as far as the Place de la Révolution, the presentday Place de la Concorde. The four of us boarded one of these vehicles and so as not to be late in reaching Paris, we took no other passengers. Consequently, we had to pay double fares.

We urged on our driver who was going at a very leisurely pace, but our words had no effect on him. One of us had the bright idea of offering him 4 sols for every private carriage which he could over-take and as it was a Sunday, there were many of these on the road. The driver agreed and whipped up his horses. One of us noted down each carriage which we overtook and this novel way of making pro-gress kept us amused the whole of the journey. When, however, we reached the Place de la Révolution, it transpired that we had over-taken forty-four private carriages and we had to add 8 francs 80 centimes to the 10 francs for the fares, which made a total of 18 francs 80 centimes. We had not counted on this happening and when we had paid the driver we did not have enough money for the return fare. We had to give up our splendid idea of going to the theatre and instead, we had to spend the evening in the Café des Aveugles at the Palais-Royal.

There we saw a man dressed as a savage beating a big drum to-gether with a large number of other musicians and this spectacle had attracted a big audience. For us, this savage, his band and a few bottles of beer had to take the place of Talma and Mademoiselle Raucourt.[2]

[1] François-Joseph Talma (1763–1826) was the leading tragic actor of his day. He was one of Napoleon's intimate circle and was greatly admired and generously rewarded by the Emperor.

[2] The early life of Mademoiselle Raucourt (1756–1815) was marked by scandals and debts. She fled to Russia, but after three years returned to France under the queen's patronage, only to be imprisoned during the Terror.

Our regiment stayed at Versailles for five months until 5 October 1805 when we were ordered to Paris. The 20th Chasseurs were quartered in the Bellechasse barracks in the Saint-Germain district.

The following Sunday there was a mounted parade when the regiment was reviewed by Prince Louis,[1] the Emperor's brother. The Paris garrison consisted of only two infantry regiments. In the one, the men wore green uniforms and were called the *Gardes de Paris*. In the other, the men wore red uniforms and had the same title, but the street urchins of Paris called them the 'lobster guards'.

The troop of Mamelukes[2] was a great novelty for us. I little thought then that they would one day come under my command together with the troop from the Young Guard which I was to command during the campaign in France. The Mamelukes, when they rode past the saluting base, charged forward without keeping any dressing. Then they would pull up their horses abruptly on the spot; it was just like a flight of pigeons taking off from one field to fly to another. Later they were to perform this manoeuvre in a more conventional manner.

At this date the Emperor was in the field with his army and was winning his famous victory over the Russians and the Austrians at Austerlitz. This period was one of great glory for France beyond her borders, but within the country all was quite peaceful; there were only 3,000 soldiers in Paris and very few others in the departments.

During the time which the regiment spent in Paris I frequently visited my father's house. My parents had thought that the first years of army life would suffice to turn me against the career which I had adopted despite their wishes, for they wanted to see me follow them in the family business. In fairness I must say that my father now saw that my choice of career would not be changed and he no longer tried to interfere. My mother, despite her grief, continued to show me the same kindness that I had always received from her.

Our regiment left not only Paris but France itself when it was ordered to Holland. On 1 December 1805 we reached Nijmegen. From there we went on to Deventer and then to Arnhem where we learned, more to our profit than to our loss, that units sent to Holland

[1] Louis Bonaparte (1778–1846) was King of Holland from 1806 until 1810. He married Hortense de Beauharnais and their son was to become Napoleon III.

[2] Bonaparte had used these troops in Egypt for scouting duties and some of them returned with him. In 1804 he formed a squadron of Mamelukes which included other nationalities besides Egyptians. Nearly all of them were massacred in their depot at Marseilles during the White Terror which followed the Restoration.

received double pay because of the high cost of food. From there the 20th Chasseurs moved on to Amersfoort, one of the prettiest little towns I have ever seen in Holland. From Amersfoort the regiment went to Breda, where I experienced my second amorous adventure.

The regiment was billeted among the citizens of the town while the barracks, which were in a bad state, were being repaired. I was acting as quartermaster and after billeting the members of my troop throughout the town, I took my billeting order and made my way to the house at which I was to stay. In the street shown on the order I expected to see a fairly respectable-looking house for it is the custom for the quartermaster to have an officer's billet for himself.

However, I found myself in the crowded working-class district and I discovered that I was billeted on a dyer and his family. I am sure he was a most worthy fellow, but his rooms were filled with cloth, dyes and furniture; there were also half a dozen children who were obviously enjoying themselves for they were all either laughing or crying. The good dyer himself told us that he had only a small room to offer us and this was next to the room where the infernal din from his numerous family was going on. 'Do not worry yourself about food,' he said to me, 'you are welcome to share our meals.'

Although I was touched by his kindness, I nevertheless went back to the town hall to ask for another billet. It was closed and I would have had to wait until the next day before obtaining another address if I had not noticed a certain woman in the office at the town hall that morning. She was about thirty years old, spoke French perfectly and seemed to be giving orders to the clerks and acting as an interpreter. I had asked her what her name was and where she lived.

Mademoiselle Van V. lived in the main square of Breda and not only worked as a clerk at the town hall but also ran a drapery and fancy goods shop. I entered her shop and walked through it to the back room where I found her dining with two other young ladies. I later learned that they were her two sisters.

'Mademoiselle,' I said, 'I must apologize for disturbing you.'

'What is the matter, sir? Please sit down.'

'Mademoiselle, I have little to say, so please allow me to stand. That is moreover what I normally do when I am speaking to ladies.'

Then I told her how I had gone to my own billet after billeting the whole troop. Now, however, I had come to ask her to change it for me because the only furniture that I had found had been six children who made an infernal noise.

'The good fellow on whom I was billeted,' I added, showing her my order, 'did in fact invite me to eat with him. I must admit in fairness that he was most hospitable, but I prefer a quiet clean room to all the food in the world.'

'Sir,' she said, 'this is an error which I will correct immediately,' and she began to look through a sheaf of billeting orders.

'Did you want rooms for two persons?'

'Mademoiselle, if you have accommodation for only one, I can leave my chasseur with the dyer since we are going into the barracks in a few days time.'

'Well Corporal, since you say you want somewhere quiet, I can offer you a room in my own house. Your regimental quartermaster-sergeant arrived this morning and he came to reserve the whole of the first floor at forty-five francs a month for Monsieur Margueron, your quartermaster captain. He will not be here for a fortnight, so I can accommodate you until he comes.'

I thanked Mademoiselle Van V. most sincerely and asked her if she would allow me to go and inform my chasseur of what was happening so that he could bring around my belongings.

When I returned an hour later Mademoiselle Van V. herself came to help me settle in the room which had been reserved for the quartermaster captain. There was every possible comfort for me. She had even been so thoughtful as to bring up some bread and butter and cheese as well as some pipes, which are the first concern of every good Dutchman. Mademoiselle Van V. also had the kindness to invite me to supper at six o'clock.

During the course of the meal I learned that the house was occupied by three sisters; Mademoiselle Van V., the eldest, who ran the house, Mademoiselle Henriette, who was about twenty years old and a charming little girl of about twelve. They had a brother who was away in the army. He was serving as a cadet in an artillery regiment at The Hague. There was one servant who did the cooking and cleaned the rooms. The shop was a very smart one which stocked all sorts of millinery and fancy goods.

Sergeant-Major Boissard, the senior instructor's secretary, had fallen ill and Monsieur Castex took me to replace the sergeant-major while the latter was away for a month. During this time I did not have to be present at the roll-calls; I merely had to be present at the major's office from nine until four. I had only to note the names of any callers and to open a few letters which I could answer if they concerned service matters.

My evenings were free and I had time to cultivate the pleasant company of my hostess. This lady, who was exceedingly kind to me, allowed me to stay at her house until the quartermaster captain arrived. Mademoiselle Van V. had a fine figure. She was fair-haired and had an admirably fresh complexion. When she laughed, as she often did, she showed thirty-two immaculate white teeth. She was thirty years old! Is that not the age when women are at their most attractive to a young man of twenty? Not surprisingly, I was not to look upon such an attractive woman without further consequences. . . .

It was at this time that an unpleasant incident took place within the regiment. Colonel Marigny was accused of certain malpractices by a majority of officers and was placed under close arrest until the matter had been investigated. This order was given by Major-General Michaud.[1] As our colonel was guarded by two sentries from the 65th Regiment which was commanded by Colonel Coutard, a friend of Monsieur Marigny, it was easy to arrange for the colonel to be able to slip out of his quarters one day. The rumour immediately went around that he had broken out and had deserted, for at Breda we were only three leagues from the Prussian lines. The story was completely untrue: Colonel Marigny had quite simply taken the post-chaise to Paris in order to go and see his powerful protector the Grand-Duke of Berg [*Murat*] whose aide-de-camp he had once been.

I have not yet spoken of the colonel and this is a suitable moment at which to do so. He was a pleasant-looking man of between thirty and thirty-six years of age who always dressed most smartly. He was not well versed in the art of intrigue, but was known for his kindly disposition. He was reputed to be very brave, but was considered to be much more suited to being on the brilliant staffs of Prince Murat and the Prince de Neufchâtel [*Berthier*] than at the head of a regiment.

He was a fine shot with the pistol and a great gambler. When fortune was kind to him the regiment was sure to receive something, such as new gauntlets or plumes, from him. He often cancelled punishments and was very popular among the non-commissioned officers and men. The majority of the officers, however, were against him and they had charged him with selling privileges. Major Castex adopted a very wise middle course during this conflict and for the six months that the colonel was absent, it was he who commanded the regiment.

When Sergeant-Major Boissard had recovered he returned to his post and I had to go back to my troop. Major Castex gave me proof of his satisfaction when on 1 May 1806 he appointed me quartermaster

[1] Commander-in-Chief of the Army of Holland.

of the *compagnie d'élite* as the position was vacant after Quartermaster Jouglas had been promoted to the rank of sergeant-major within the same troop. It is not difficult to imagine how happy and flattered I felt at this appointment when I was not even twenty years old. As quartermaster to the *compagnie d'élite* I was able to rejoin my friend Henry. In fact, I became senior in rank to him, but he was never jealous about it.

On about 10 August we had to leave for The Hague where the new King of Holland, Prince Louis Napoleon, was staying. This was the same brother of the Emperor who had reviewed us eight months previously in Paris. As we arrived in the middle of the summer we set up camp in the beautiful woods near the palace. The non-commissioned officers and men were in excellent tents and the officers, apart from those on duty, had quarters in the town.

On 15 August, which was the Emperor's name-day, the regiment was reviewed by King Louis. With one accord, all the chasseurs moved inwards from the flanks and formed a circle around the king. Then six hundred voices cried in unison:

'Long live the Emperor! Long live King Louis! Long live Colonel Marigny! We want our colonel! We want him back!'

'You shall have him, my friends,' replied the king.

Then the regiment formed up in its correct order and rode past at the gallop. The next day we were due to return to Breda. I was particularly anxious to return without delay as I had left someone very dear to me there.

On 15 August our camp was visited by Queen Hortense who was already so famous for her beauty, her charm, her intelligence and especially her kindness. She was in a barouche drawn by six horses. With her were two other ladies. One of them was looking after a child of about three years of age; this was the prince who, a little later, was to be carried off by croup to the great despair of all his family and of the Emperor especially. The other lady was younger than the queen, who seemed very fond of her. I subsequently learned that this was a childhood friend who had been with the queen in Madame Campan's school. She was Mademoiselle Cochelet, Queen Hortense's companion.

Captain Lavigne, who was orderly officer, was warned of the visit in good time and he paraded the regiment. He had the happy idea of bringing the band up to the centre of the line where the queen's carriage had halted. Our band, which was a very good one, began to play the popular tune of the day, *Partant pour la Syrie*, and as everyone knows, the music was composed by Queen Hortense herself. She seemed very touched by this thoughtful gesture and was anxious that all punishments should be excused. Captain Lavigne told her that they had already been excused since it was the Emperor's name-day.

'Then I am sure you will recognize that my intentions were well meant, at least,' the queen said to Captain Lavigne. Before the carriage left, the young lady sitting opposite the queen beckoned to Javot, our bandmaster, to come forward. On behalf of the queen she gave him 20 napoleons for the band.

If at that moment I had said to one of my friends, to Henry for example: 'You see that young lady in the queen's carriage, leaning forward to give some money to the bandmaster; one day she will be my wife,' he would have thought that I was mad. And yet I would have been speaking the truth. . . .

The carriage drawn by six horses conveyed the queen back to The Hague. That evening there was a banquet followed by a ball at the court and Captain Lavigne, who had been relieved as orderly officer, was fortunate enough to go. He even had the great honour of being invited by the chamberlain to dance a quadrille with Queen Hortense. This was to thank him for the courtesy shown to her at our camp.

On 16 August our regiment set out to return to Breda, whence we were to move to Cologne on the 20th of the same month.

Leaving a town where one has been stationed is always the same; the mutual sadness, the endless promises to think always of each other, never to forget each other, to write and so on. Mademoiselle Van V. wanted me to take something by which I would be able to remember her. She had seen that I smoked and so she said: 'Charles, I want to give you that fine pipe which is in the display-case. I cannot do it openly, so buy it from my sister when she is in the shop. And she slipped 48 francs in my pocket. I must confess that I was delighted to be given the beautiful meerschaum pipe which had tempted me more than once, but which I never really thought of buying because of its price. Nevertheless, I was reluctant to accept such a gift.

'What! Charles,' said Mademoiselle Van V., 'you will not take a souvenir from a friend! I find that most hurtful.'

I hesitated no longer and expressed my very real gratitude to her for the gift.

As Mademoiselle Henriette was busy in the shop with several customers when I left, I said to her: 'Please do not sell that particular pipe. I shall purchase it from you tomorrow. It is 48 francs, I believe?'

'Yes sir,' she said with an obvious look of pleasure which I put down to the satisfaction of having sold the pipe.

The next day when I entered the shop at midday, I found Mademoiselle Henriette at the counter. Immediately she said:

'I am so glad to see you before my sister returns from church. Here is the pipe—she had already wrapped it in tissue paper—it is a present from me. I do not want any money for it; I can pay the 48 francs from my savings.'

I did not want to accept it for the whole situation was extremely embarrassing. If I told Mademoiselle Henriette that her sister had given me the money for the pipe, I would be betraying a secret. If I told the elder sister that her younger sister wanted to give me the pipe as a present that would be another secret—only more so. Without further ado I took the meerschaum pipe from Mademoiselle Henriette and, to show my gratitude, I kissed her. It was none too soon for the regiment to leave Breda; otherwise I would have been obliged to carry on my affair on two fronts and this would soon have revealed to Henriette the nature of my association with her elder sister who, in turn, would have realized what a threat her sister represented.

Before the regiment left Breda we were ordered to cut off our queues and tresses. This order upset us greatly and it was only when the officers pointed out the very good reasons for the order that it was obeyed. They told the men that a campaign was about to start and that it would be much cleaner and distinctly more convenient not to wear queues and tresses when on active service. Moreover, Major Castex insisted on it and so greatly was he respected in the regiment that the order was carried out.

This then was the reward for all the effort and care that I had taken to encourage the growth of my hair which, if I may say so in all modesty, gave me a queue and tresses which were as fine as any in the troop.

'Come then,' I said to my friend Henry, 'if we have to sacrifice then, cut away! In any case I need some hair to set in a ring and to make a fillet on which to hang a locket.'

'Well, if that is the case . . .' said Henry and he started on his task.

I bought a locket, had a fillet made of my hair and attached a gold clip. Then I had a lock of my hair set in a pretty ring. These purchases cost me more than 60 francs, but I did not want to be outdone by the two sisters. The day before our departure they invited me to take some punch with them and before I took my leave of them I discreetly handed each one her little present. At four o'clock the next morning as I rode past the house where these charming sisters lived, a window on the second floor opened. With tears in her eyes Mademoiselle Van V. waved her handkerchief to me in farewell. I waved back and then the delightful girl disappeared for ever from my life.

The regiment left Holland via Nijmegen and then made its way up the left bank of the Rhine as far as Cologne where it arrived on 1 September. A camp was established at Brühl and here the operational squadrons were organized; afterwards we moved on towards Mayence [*Mainz*]. The Rhine was crossed on 20 September and the following day we were in Frankfurt.

Great was our astonishment when, as we rode along the main street of Frankfurt, we caught sight of Colonel Marigny in full dress, standing beside Marshal Augereau on the balcony of the Hôtel du Cygne. Cries of 'Long live Colonel Marigny!' burst out from the head of the column and ran down its whole length as the regiment rode past. It was clear to the chasseurs that their colonel was back and that his troubles were over; Prince Murat had indeed taken an interest in the fate of his former aide-de-camp.

The Emperor, who had learned of the regiment's demonstration at The Hague on his name-day, had said: 'A colonel who is as popular as this with his regiment should be given back to his regiment.'

He quashed all the legal proceedings, saying that it was right that regimental officers should be aware of the shortcomings of their colonel, but that he had no time for those who denounced others. Then he ordered the colonel to resume command of the regiment when it arrived in Frankfurt.

The next day we went forward into Germany, passing through Aschaffenburg and Wurzburg. This latter town was the seat of the brother of the Austrian Emperor, the Grand Duke Ferdinand, who, despite this fact, was a member of the Confederation of the Rhine.[1] This was the prince whom Napoleon, while on his way to Jena, asked if he was satisfied with the conduct of the troops who had crossed his states under the command of General Vandamme. The Grand Duke's reply was complimentary to the officers and men of the corps, but not to their general.

'What is your complaint against him?' asked Napoleon.

'Sire, I am not complaining about the expenses he has caused me, but rather about his incivility. He made me pay 500 francs a day for his food and yet he never allowed me to dine with him.'

[1] This league of German rulers had placed themselves under Napoleon's protection in 1806.

The Emperor appeared to be visibly annoyed and said to the grand duke: 'If I had two General Vandammes in my army I would have one of them shot, but as I have only the one whom you know, please allow me to keep him despite all his faults.'

After crossing the Rhine we became part of the 7th Corps of the *Grande Armée*. The regiment was delighted to have its colonel back, but it was very sad to lose Major Castex. He had been ordered to Bonn, a little town on the Rhine near Cologne, for the depot which we had left at Brühl had been moved there. The major's disappointment can easily be imagined; he would even have preferred a less senior rank if he could have remained with the army. He begged and entreated Marshal Augereau to use him in any way that would allow him to take part in the coming battle. Our regiment had been brigaded with the 7th Chasseurs for a few days. Now this regiment had crossed the Rhine without a colonel or a major to command it. Major Castex pointed this out to the marshal and was given authority to command the 7th Chasseurs until Monsieur Lagrange, its colonel, arrived. The latter did not in fact arrive for the whole of the campaign and since Colonel Marigny was killed during the battle of Jena, Major Castex was, as will be seen, appointed to be colonel of the 20th Chasseurs the day after the death of Colonel Marigny.

Since crossing the Rhine we had moved as part of a brigade. The 7th and the 20th took turns to form the vanguard of the 7th Army Corps and rode at the head of the column towards Saxony.

On 10 October, when crossing the Saal at the little town of Saalfeld, the 3rd Corps under Marshal Lannes had the first encounter with the enemy in the shape of a Prussian infantry corps commanded by Prince Louis of Prussia,[1] the king's nephew. This infantry gave way before our troops and withdrew in disorder through a ford across the Saal. Prince Louis with a few hussars of his staff tried to rally the fleeing men. Suddenly, a French sergeant-major from the 10th Hussars named Guindey cut him off and, pointing his blade at the prince, he cried: 'Surrender, General, or you die!'

The prince retorted: 'What! Surrender! Never!'

Brushing aside Guindey's weapon, the prince struck the sergeant-major a blow across the face with his sabre. He was about the strike a second time when Guindey countered and ran him through the chest. Killed instantly, the prince fell from his horse. The prince's aides had seen him engaged in single combat with a French soldier and they

[1] Born in 1772, Prince Louis was the brother of Frederick II. An attractive and intelligent leader, he was one of the most implacable opponents of Napoleon.

came galloping across. They would certainly have captured or killed Guindey if a hussar from the 10th had not arrived at the gallop crying: 'Hold on, Sergeant-Major!'

With his pistol he shot dead a Prussian hussar, whereupon the prince's aides took to their heels.

When the French army learned of the death of Prince Louis of Prussia, the event gave rise to the following song, which proves that the battlefield does not always inspire melancholy:

C'est le Prince Louis-Ferdinand
Qui se croyait un géant
Ah! l'imprudent!
Un hussard, bon là,
Lui dit: N'allez pas si vite,
Ou bien, si non ça,
Je vous lance une mort subite,
A la papa!

Being badly wounded, Guindey could not hold out with only one hussar, so together they fell back to the troop which was supporting the skirmishers. On reaching it Guindey reported to the lieutenant in charge:

'Sir, if you will go forward with me a thousand yards down to the river, we will find the body of a general whom I have just killed. It was he who gave me this wound across my face. We shall be able to take possession of his sabre and his grand cross if the enemy have not reached him first.'

Guided by the sergeant-major, the officer galloped forward with his troop and arrived at the spot where two hussars of the 9th, who were brigaded with the 10th, had already come upon the body of the prince.

'I was the one who killed him,' said Guindey, 'his blood is still on my sabre. He should have the mark of my thrust in his chest. Take his purse if he has one; you are welcome to it. But give me his sabre and his grand cross so that I may deliver them to the marshal.'

The hussars from the 9th gave Guindey the items he requested and he bore these trophies away to the marshal. At the same time as he arrived at the 3rd Corps headquarters some Prussian prisoners were revealing that Prince Louis-Ferdinand of Prussia, their general, had just been killed by a French hussar. This information was so important that the marshal passed it on immediately to the Emperor.

Guindey was in the field hospital having his wound treated and so the marshal could not send him to the Emperor's headquarters. He therefore sent one of his aides with the sabre and the grand cross to ask for a reward for Guindey. The Emperor awarded him the *croix d'honneur*, saying: 'I would have made him an officer as well if he had taken the prince alive.'

Before he left Saalfeld on the morning of 12 October the marshal went to see Guindey in the hospital where he gave him his decoration and of course reported the Emperor's remarks.

'It was not my fault, sir. You can see what he did to me,' replied Guindey, showing his wound. 'I can assure you that he was in no mood to surrender.'

The worthy sergeant-major requested, and was granted, permission to stay in the rear for a fortnight so that he might recover fully.

He kept his hussar orderly with him so that he might be looked after properly. He remembered that on the 9th the regiment had halted some leagues before Saalfeld in a pretty village of some size to the right of the main road. The regiment's staff had stayed in the château there. He thought he would go to this château and ask for hospitality for himself. In return, he would offer his protection to the place during the period of his convalescence.

When, therefore, the corps had moved out of Saalfeld, leaving behind only the field hospital and the body of Prince Louis of Prussia laid out in a church where I myself saw it, as did the whole of the army, Guindey immediately went to the château and asked for hospitality. He was made welcome by Baroness W. who saw the advantages of having someone to protect her home in such troubled times. Her husband was away, probably serving in the Prussian army, and she felt, moreover, that she could trust anyone from the regiment which had just spent two days in the village without giving any cause for complaint.

Guindey was therefore very well treated as a guest. He had had the foresight to warn his orderly not to drink excessively, not to gossip and above all not to mention the matter of the prince's death and how the sergeant-major had come by his wound.

'Fritz,' he had said, 'we are the only Frenchmen in this village and things could go badly for us if you were to say anything.'

Fritz, the hussar, promised that he would follow all the sergeant-major's advice, but how well he kept his word will be seen.

After putting his horse in the stables Guindey was taken up by the housemaid to a fine room which was situated above the stables. This suited the hussar perfectly as he was able to keep an eye on the horses. The house was occupied by the baroness who was about forty years old, two young girls of between sixteen and eighteen and a son aged twelve. There were also numerous servants of both sexes.

Once he had settled in, Guindey sent for Fritz who brought up his travelling-case with a change of clothing. The orderly then helped him to treat his wound. The baroness had been kind enough to send up some lint and some eau-de-Cologne, for the only treatment that there gimental medical officer hadprescribed was eau-de-Cologne well diluted with water. A pad of lint soaked in this solution had to be applied to the wound in the morning and in the evening. When he had dressed, the sergeant-major went down to the drawing-room as invited; there the whole family had gathered. The ensuing conversation was sad and subdued and was wholly about the horrors of war. Guindey was hopefully suggesting that these horrors would soon be past when the steward came to announce that dinner was served. The baroness immediately offered her hand to the hussar, who escorted her into the dining-room. When she was seated he sat down on her right. The others took their places and the meal began.

The baroness spoke French well; Guindey was young, charming and well educated. The dinner, which had lasted an hour, was nearly over when the steward who had originally announced the meal entered, looking most agitated. He bent over to murmur something to the baroness, but had not said more than a few words when the latter uttered a cry, covered her face with her hands and rushed from the room.

At this cry, this gesture and this sudden exit, the whole family rose from the table and followed the baroness, leaving a very surprised Guindey all alone in the dining-room. He was about to return to his own room, wondering what he had done to deserve such treatment from his hosts, when the baroness came back. She was holding a handkerchief and was obviously most upset.

'Sir,' she said, 'I have come to ask you to forgive me and my family for our incivility towards you. Please be good enough to come into the drawing-room for a moment so that I may explain.'

Guindey hastened to comply with her request and, in the drawing-room, he sat in the armchair which the baroness pointed out to him.

The baroness sighed, wiped her eyes and explained her conduct thus:

'Sir, yesterday dire rumours were circulating about the fate of our army. In particular there was talk of a calamitous happening which we simply could not bring ourselves to believe. It was said that Prince Louis of Prussia, who before the campaign started had lived here with us for six weeks while his forces were billeted in the district, had been killed. I have just learned that it was you who killed him!'

She broke down in tears and could not go on.

Then Guindey said: 'That is only too true, Madame; but it was in self-defence that I did it, for the prince had first wounded me.'

He then asked her permission to withdraw and when he had left her he sent for his orderly. 'Fritz,' he said to him, 'saddle the horses as quickly as possible for we must leave.'

'What!' said the orderly, 'leave the château?'

'Yes. Take my travelling-case; we must mount without delay. I will explain once we are on the way.'

Guindey quickly wrote a short note for the baroness, telling her that he understood her grief, that he wished to respect it and that he would go elsewhere. As he was mounting to leave he handed the note to a servant and told him to deliver it to the baroness. A quarter of an hour later on the road to Saalfeld he said to his orderly: 'Who could have told them that Prince Louis is dead and that I killed him? Have you been talking when I told you not to talk?'

As Fritz did not answer, he continued: 'Speak up, for the harm has been done and I want to know the truth now. Come along, speak up!'

The orderly answered: 'To tell the truth sir, I must admit that I did say that the prince had been killed and that you were the one who had killed him. But I could not prevent myself from saying it. This was how it happened: while you were upstairs dining with the baroness and her family, I was downstairs dining with the servants. While I was peacefully eating my dinner and drinking my beer just as you had advised me, one of the servants, the porter, a great boastful rogue, started taunting me, saying how good the Prussians were. "Have you not seen how they have dealt with your companion?" he said, meaning you sir!

'I was tempted to put him in his place, but I remembered your instructions, so I said nothing and drank another glass of beer to help me keep my temper. But there was no stopping him by turning the other cheek. He still kept up his taunts. Drinking glasses of beer achieved nothing, for my temper came to the surface in the end and I told him straight that if his prince had wounded you in the face, he would not be wounding anyone else because you had run him through with your sabre. That was how it all came out. But I am truly sorry sir, for my words have caused you to lose some splendid quarters.'

As can be imagined, Guindey quickly relented towards his orderly and after merely reprimanding him he said: 'We shall go back to the hospital at Saalfeld, but we shall spend as little time as possible there for I am anxious to rejoin the regiment.'

'I am as anxious as you to rejoin it,' said Fritz, 'and I swear on the blade of my sabre that the first Prussian that I meet on the battlefield will answer for that great loud-mouthed porter.'

The fight with the prince and the incident at the château were recounted to me by Guindey himself. I knew him well when he was assistant adjutant of the mounted grenadiers of the Old Guard and it was while he was holding this position that he died bravely at the battle of Hanau in 1813.

But to return to 13 October 1806, the eve of the battle of Jena. By a series of forced marches the regiment had reached its appointed position. That day we bivouacked in the fields near the village where the marshal's headquarters had been set up. There was also an infantry division in the village and this division was to occupy an important pass through which the army was to advance the following day, 14 October, in order to reach the field of battle at Jena where the whole Prussian army had assembled.

Because of the proximity of the village of Gera we were able to have supplies of sheep and geese for these are raised in great numbers in Saxony. Our encampment was in a potato field and we dug up the potatoes with our bayonets. The regiment had just been issued with these new weapons, but this was the only use we made of them; in fact, we threw them away before we went into action. Needless to say, we were made to pay 7 francs 50 centimes for them at the end of the campaign, but we had rid ourselves of a cumbersome weapon which we found useless.

On 14 October 1806 at dawn, which comes quite late at this time of the year, the 1st Division of the 7th Corps attacked the position which we were to hold. This was a pass which had to be captured, and the enemy defended it strenuously. At seven in the morning we stood to arms and our brigade, led by General Durosnel, who had become one of the Emperor's aides and *Gouverneur des Pages*,[1] started to move forward. The road was already covered with bodies.

'Someone has caught it around here,' commented the chasseurs, meaning that there had been a fierce exchange of fire in the area through which we were passing.

I took advantage of a brief halt to go up to my former captain and

[1] Napoleon had revived the practice of having a corps of pages at court.

pay him my respects. Monsieur Lavigne showed his pleasure at seeing me and offered me a drink which I gladly accepted. The dull reverberations of *le brutal*, as we called the cannon, could be heard, producing that uneasy feeling which all soldiers know.

As I was showing some impatience at not moving forward, the captain said: 'Be calm, Parquin; even if they start without us, they will not do everything. There will be something for everyone.'

The column started to advance and I took my leave of Captain Lavigne. Alas! I had spoken to him for the last time.

When we had gone through the pass and reached the plain, Colonel Marigny, who was at the entrance to the pass and who was shouting and gesturing to urge on the men more quickly as we went forward in fours, said to me:

'Quartermaster, have you a good horse?'

'Yes sir.'

'Well stay close to me. You will be my orderly for the rest of the day.'

Sergeant-Major Isnard who had been with him had just been struck down by a cannon-ball. So it was that I remained with my colonel, feeling very proud of my new position which I preferred to my normal position of serrefile at the rear of the *compagnie d'élite*.

I was not yet twenty years old and had been in the army for four years. This was the first time that I had seen the enemy. I had the worthy desire to distinguish myself in action and I was pleased to have my first opportunity in front of my colonel.

When the *compagnie d'élite* had reached the plateau beyond the pass, the colonel ordered Captain Fleury who commanded it to take up position on the left of the 7th Chasseurs and to maintain the proper distance between the two regiments on the field of battle. Then he said to me:

'Quartermaster, stay near the pass and tell Captain Sabinet of the 5th Troop to proceed at a trot to his position to the left of the *compagnie d'élite*. Pass on the same order to all the troops down to the last one. Then come back to me at the gallop; I shall be at the centre of the regiment.'

The colonel left and I carried out my task. While I was so engaged many wounded came past me on their way to the field hospital. I shall always remember a sergeant of the 5th Hussars, a man of truly martial appearance, whose white pelisse was completely covered in blood. He had just had his left arm shattered by a cannon-ball and yet he did not cease telling the chasseurs of our regiment whom he met as they advanced up the pass: 'Come on, my brave chasseurs! The Prussians are not all that bad!'

These words probably meant: 'Before *le brutal* hit me, I got among the enemy with my sabre.'

When the seventh and last troop of the regiment had come through the pass, I galloped off to rejoin the colonel who gave the order for capes to be rolled and worn in bandoleer fashion. He appeared happy and proud to see his regiment drawn up in line of battle and to know that each of the six hundred men was determined to acquit himself well that day. The weather was fine; the fog which had lingered on had now completely disappeared. It was eleven o'clock and the plain seemed to be alight as the whole length of the line fired. The fire was largely cannon-ball and grape-shot, and the hares, which are particularly numerous in Saxony, caused great mirth and cheers in the ranks as they were chased in all directions across the vast plain. From time to time, it is true, some cannon-balls did reach us, but they are scarcely worth mentioning.

One of General Durosnel's aides galloped up in search of the colonel. He had no sooner said a few words to him than the colonel said to the chasseur who was behind him: 'Chasseur, dismount. I can feel my saddle slipping. Tighten the girth a little for we are going to charge.'

The chasseur jumped from his horse, put his arms through the reins of his own horse and gripped the saddle-girth with his teeth. The colonel had raised his left leg to make the task easier. At that very moment Monsieur Marigny was struck by a cannon-ball and was decapitated.

My shock and grief were overwhelming. The colonel's horse, no longer feeling the hand which had been controlling it, set off at a gallop straight towards the enemy. As for the chasseur, he quickly remounted and I went back to my post with the *compagnie d'élite*, stopping only to inform Major Watrin of the fatal blow which had robbed us of our colonel.

'I saw him fall,' the major told me.

At least ten minutes went by before the regiment received any new orders. This was doubly unfortunate; for us, as we were still subjected to the enemy gunfire, and for the 7th Chasseurs, who had charged headlong against the Prussian army and had broken the first and second lines. As they were not supported by our regiment they lost the fruits of one of the most daring charges that was made that day.

Our former senior instructor, Monsieur Castex, who was then commanding the 7th Chasseurs and who had executed the charge so brilliantly, did not consider it wise to return by the way he had come for the Prussians who had lain down and over whom the 7th had ridden during the charge, had reformed. He therefore charged back through a Saxon regiment which was instantly brushed aside and thrown into disorder.

One of my friends, Sergeant Bucher of the 7th Chasseurs said to me that evening as he showed me his blood-stained sabre: 'Smell it Parquin, and you will notice a musty smell.' What he had done was to cut off some of the queues worn by the Saxons. The Saxon cavalry, as we had formerly done, pomaded and powdered their queues which they wore half-way down their backs.

When Major Castex brought back the 7th Chasseurs he had lost half of his strength, that is, some 300 men. This loss was more than outweighed by the damage which he had inflicted on the Prussian army.

General Durosnel came to order our regiment to retire out of the range of the enemy cannon and we carried out this manoeuvre in fours at the trot. At that moment it was my sad lot to see Captain Lavigne fall and I remembered how that morning he had said, to calm my impatience: 'Parquin, there will be something for everyone.'

The regiment and the army suffered a great loss with the death of Captain Lavigne and I was to miss him greatly. I did not learn until the evening that he had not survived the amputation of an arm and that he had been buried on the field of battle with Colonel Marigny. They had not got on well together in life, but by chance death had united them for ever.

The whole day long the brigade manoeuvred in the face of heavy gunfire which caused considerable losses. However, the regiment did not strike a single blow and, as has been seen, nothing resulted from the charge which the 7th Chasseurs made. Consequently, it was the infantry and the artillery which carried off the honours of the day.

I can still see the 16th and the 7th Light Infantry Regiments and the 14th and the 27th Regiments of the Line advancing on the enemy in spite of the terrible hail of grape-shot and musketry fire. The flageolets which sounded above the music played by the bands did not miss a single note. The gaps caused by the cannon-fire were instantly filled. Wherever these brave soldiers went with bayonets levelled the enemy infantry and artillery surrendered.

A column of captured Prussians, led by their band was marching past the regiment when the bandmaster was recognized by the chasseurs in spite of his efforts to conceal himself.

'It's Javot!' shouted the chasseurs and indeed it was. Javot had once been the civilian bandmaster of the 20th Chasseurs. He was an excellent composer and also played the horn beautifully. When Colonel Marigny had temporarily left the regiment in Holland, Javot who had often received substantial personal gifts from the colonel, decided not to remain with the regiment and he had gone to Prussia so as to employ his talents in Berlin. There a colonel had made him an attractive offer and he had enlisted in the colonel's regiment; now the whole regiment had been taken prisoner.

Major Castex, after returning from his charge with the 7th, had assumed command of the 20th following the death of Colonel Marigny, and now he claimed Javot, who was immediately handed over. Javot was made to take off his Prussian uniform and to put on our regimental uniform. We had lost enough men for us to find him one that fitted. Javot entered Berlin at the head of the regiment a week after being taken prisoner and only three weeks after leaving there at the head of a Prussian regiment.

The evening following the battle we set up camp in the suburbs of Weimar where I spent a melancholy night after meeting Lieutenant Lavigne. He was mourning the loss of a beloved brother who had also been my father's friend and my protector.

The next day I went foraging to obtain supplies from a nearby village. When I returned in the evening I was astonished to learn through a bulletin which had come late that day that we had won a great victory the previous day; fifty thousand Prussians killed or captured, three hundred cannon taken, sixty standards taken and so on. I must admit that I had not expected this. It was true that we had lost a great number of men through gunfire, but the regiment had not made a single charge, had not struck a single blow and had not taken one prisoner.

'The other regiments must have performed better than we did,' I said to Henry.

'Have no fear,' he answered, 'our turn will come.'

Not all the army took part in the battle of Jena. The Guard cavalry had not arrived in time and the 1st Hussars had acted as the Emperor's personal guard. Prince Murat did not arrive with the cuirassiers until the evening, but they contributed to our success by their unrelenting pursuit of the enemy who was already in flight at all points when they arrived.

We remained three days in this camp and during this time the appointment of Major Castex as colonel of the regiment was confirmed to the great satisfaction of everyone. After the charge made by the 7th the Emperor had sent for him and had said: 'You are a brave man, Colonel. Tell your men that I was confident that they would prove themselves better than the Prussians and Saxons.'

On the 18th we resumed our advance and by the 25th we were on the heights around Berlin, having marched by stages without meeting a single enemy soldier. What had become of the fine Prussian army which had but a short while previously waited so proudly for us at Jena? What had become of this army in which even the most modest officer thought that he was another Frederick? This army had been partly destroyed, and what remained had sought refuge inside fortresses; it would not be long before these too fell to the might of the French army.

III

On 25 October we spent the whole morning on the heights above Berlin so as to give the corps under Marshal Davout the honour of being the first to enter the city. This honour had been won by the corps with its fine performance at Auerstadt where it had fought the Prussians under their king. Although less than half as strong in numbers as the Prussians, the corps had completely defeated them. The Emperor decreed that Marshal Davout should take as his title the name of the battlefield where he had been victorious and the marshal became the Duc d'Auerstadt.

Our brigade, following the 3rd Corps, entered Berlin at two in the afternoon. It was a fine autumn day. The city was beautiful, yet it looked depressing. All the shops were closed and no one was at the windows. In the streets there were few people and no carriages at all. The only sound to be heard was the rumble of our guns and wagons.

We merely passed through the city before going on a few more leagues to occupy several villages beyond it. In the village which we were occupying the inhabitants had deserted their houses. There was ample fodder for the hay had just been gathered in, but supplies such as meat, bread, beer and brandy, as well as oats, had to be obtained from Berlin itself.

The day after we arrived there was a trumpet-call for the quartermasters to assemble. They were to go to Berlin to draw supplies for four days. Regimental Sergeant-Major Mozère was in charge of the party which consisted of the troop quartermasters and their duty orderlies. After we had acquired some carts, we set off.

The subdued and depressing Berlin which we had seen the day before had a completely different appearance now. It was exactly like a small version of Paris. Everyone was going about his business and the regimental sergeant-major intended to go about his pleasures. He came over to me as we were entering the city and said:

'I shall be away for a while and since you are the quartermaster of the *compagnie d'élite* you will take charge during my absence. It will take about three hours to issue the supplies for we are not due to be served until after the artillery and the 7th Chasseurs. It is now midday. Go to the stores with the party and let the men have their meal and feed the horses there. Then, when it is your turn, take charge of the issue. Here are the tickets and the details of what each troop and headquarters are entitled to. I am going off to dine at the Black Eagle Hotel which is nearby.'

'I understand, sir,' I said, taking the tickets from him before he quickly went on his way.

I led the party straight to the stores. I had been there an hour and the artillery units had finished drawing their supplies. The 7th were about to take their turn when a messenger arrived with a letter for Mozère. As I was acting for him, I broke the seal and opened the letter. It was an order not to draw any supplies but to tear up the tickets and to return as quickly as possible with the troop quartermasters as the regiment was moving to Neustadt. I immediately told the men that we were not going to draw any supplies and ordered them to prepare to leave. I sent a messenger to the Black Eagle to warn the regimental sergeant-major of what had just happened and to inform him that I had started back with the others.

Just as I was about to tear up the tickets, the Jew who was issuing the supplies said to me:

'Quartermaster, is the R.S.M. in charge of the party here?'

'No. I am acting for him.'

'Have you the tickets?'

'Yes, of course.'

'What are you going to do with them since you are not taking your supplies?'

'What a question! I am going to destroy them.'

Then the little Jew came over to me and said:

'You will probably want to do what the R.S.M. of the 7th has done, sir. You could arrange things with me as he did.'

'What do you mean?'

'I gave him 100 gold fredericks for the tickets.'

'How can you prove that?'

He showed me the tickets which the 7th should have used; so, wasting no time, I struck a bargain with him and the exchange took place without delay. Each frederick was worth 21 francs.

The party had mounted and we set off immediately, following the route given in the colonel's orders. We had been going at a walking pace for two hours when the R.S.M. caught up with us. He took me on one side and anxiously enquired what I had done with the tickets since no supplies had been drawn.

'You will probably be angry with me, sir, but I exchanged them for 50 gold fredericks.'

'You have acted quite wrongly,' said Mozère, 'they were worth more than that.' And he took every one of the 50 coins that I showed him.

I had been wise to make sure of my share when dealing with someone so righteous and yet so sharp, for he did not see fit to give me a single frederick. I was none the less delighted to be relieved of all responsibility while still having my money-belt full.

The next day we arrived at Neustadt. The regiment had already settled in and was encamped beyond the town. Running along the left side of the camp there was a canal leading to the Oder and on it there were numerous boats containing all sorts of provisions which had obviously come from Berlin. From these boats the chasseurs had seized small casks of Bordeaux wine, barrels of sugar and crates of lemons. These trophies were immediately borne off to the tents. I remember that it was not possible to go a few yards without coming across a small cask from which one end had been removed and in which four or five sugar loaves and some lemons had been thrown. There would be a chasseur stirring the mixture with a big stick and you can imagine what a splendid drink resulted.

When I found my friend Henry I showed him my money-belt and told him that he could help himself.

'Thank you very much,' said Henry, 'but I do not need any as the Prussians have already supplied my needs.'

'Indeed?'

'Yes; feel my money-belt.'

Mine was tiny compared with his. I was astounded and asked him to explain how he had come by such good fortune.

He made me tell him about my expedition first and then he said:

'You really are too simple; you ought to have twice the amount. There was no need to give 50 fredericks to the R.S.M. You should have told him that you had torn them up. He would not have gone back to Berlin to see if it was true!

'I also had some dealings with a Jew when I made my money, but it was not by selling tickets. I merely had to close my eyes in the middle of the night and you know how I like to sleep! I was on duty at one of the outposts when up came a little Jew who asked me nicely not to take any notice if he opened the lock gates to let through his boat which was ahead of the others on the canal.

'I had not had orders to watch the boats. My instructions were to post my mounted sentry during the day on a hill-top some thousand yards away and at night to post him half-way up the hill. So I let myself be won over and I allowed the lock to be opened and the first boat to pass through. For this the Jew handed over 200 fredericks to me. Since all this took place at night no one else is likely to find out about it.'

I complimented Henry on the profitable night which he had spent.

'In five days time,' he said, 'I shall be on duty again by the canal and if there is no change of orders and the Jew returns, I shall strike the same bargain with him. It really is a splendid stroke of luck, do you not agree? There is profit without risk.'

The regiment remained a week in this encampment and it seemed that this time was advantageously employed, for the chasseurs acquired large numbers of fredericks during it. The day before we left, the remaining boats on the canal suddenly disappeared.

The rumour spread that the price of their release had been 60,000 francs, but it was obvious that ordinary chasseurs and N.C.O.s were no longer involved when such a sum was at stake. This was a figure which was much too high for our rank. At Tilsit, after the campaign in Prussia had ended, Colonel Castex published the following order:

'Chasseurs, I know that you have acquired a great deal of gold. No matter how you have acquired it, it is yours to keep. But look after it, for there will be no more to be had in the same way. We are now at peace!'

On 2 November the regiment passed through Posen [*Posnan*] on the road to Warsaw. We were marching against the Russians. We halted for a fortnight in a village ten leagues from Warsaw. We were in a poor region of Poland, but the regiment had much gold and the inns did good business.

One evening in one of these inns kept by a Jew, for in Poland a Jew may undertake any employment, an argument over something quite unimportant broke out between the hussars of the 8th and the chasseurs of my regiment. I happened to be there at the time. Popineau, a corporal from the *compagnie d'élite* and the senior fencing instructor in the regiment, raised his voice and demanded to know if there was a fencing instructor from the 8th Hussars present so that they might settle the argument. A trumpet-major wearing the decoration of the *Légion d'honneur* rose and announced that he was the senior fencing master of the 8th Hussars. Thereupon all argument ceased.

Popineau beckoned to me to follow him and when I had gone outside with him he said to me: 'The honour of the regiment is at stake; I am counting on you, Quartermaster. If I should be worsted you will not allow the regiment to be dishonoured.'

'You may rely on me,' I answered.

The trumpet-major's second and I took lanterns for it was dark and we lit the way to a meadow behind the inn.

The preliminaries did not take long and were confined to measuring the weapons which were both standard military sabres. Both men saluted and the fight began. There were no wild swings, but thrusts and parries were made in such rapid succession that it was quite clear that two champions were facing each other.

After several attacks had been skilfully delivered and parried Popineau was too late in countering a blow which fortunately did not injure him seriously but which nevertheless rendered him incapable of continuing. I immediately took off my coat and demanded that I should be allowed to take his place. Popineau took the lantern from me for, although he was in pain, he was still able to hold the lantern for us while sitting on the ground. I had carefully studied the trumpet-major's style while he was fighting Popineau. He was left-handed. With such an opponent one must always attack inside his guard. Consequently, we had no sooner faced up to each other than, feinting to disengage outwards, I lunged on the inside. The point of my blade entered his left breast.

The trumpet-major fell. For a few moments we feared that the wound was a mortal one, but fortunately this was not the case. I told him to cough and he did so without experiencing any pain, although his wound started to bleed profusely. The regimental medical officer was sent for and when he arrived at the inn he treated the two wounded men. The 8th Hussars left the next day, but the trumpet-major remained with us and we gave him every attention possible. Later, he came with us to Warsaw where the regiment arrived on the 10th; from there he went on to rejoin his regiment. I was to meet him again seven years later when I was serving in the Imperial Guard Chasseurs.

The army crossed the Vistula on 6 December and did not encounter the Russians until the crossing of the Bug when, on 24 December, the Mamelukes fought an engagement with them. Their dress caused much surprise and alarm among the Russians who thought they were being attacked by Turks. The Mamelukes executed a brilliant charge against twelve guns, which they captured.

On 1 February 1807 the whole army started to advance. One morning five days later I was almost a victim of my own rashness when I was in a party of chasseurs who had volunteered when the colonel had called for skirmishers. I wanted to get to close quarters with some Cossacks for this was the first time that I had seen any.

With my pistol ready I galloped forward across the plain towards a group of Cossacks. Ten yards from them I fired and immediately one of them fell. All had gone well until that moment, but when they in their turn charged and I was obliged to turn about and return to our line of skirmishers, my horse, which was badly shod, slipped on the snow and fell under me. I would certainly have been captured or killed, but my coolness in the situation saved me. I quickly got from beneath my horse which had risen and, putting my arm through the reins, I aimed my pistol steadily at the nearest Cossack who was threatening me with his lance. I succeeded in holding him off until Monsieur de Beaumont, an officer of the 3rd Hussars who was looking for his regiment on the battlefield, very fortunately came to my aid. Thanks to his courageous intervention I was able to remount quickly and gallop away, leaving behind my colpack which had fallen off.

Once I had reached our lines I shouted to the Cossacks, who had put my headgear on the end of a lance, to sell it back to me. They agreed and I gave them a gold frederick. This was rather an expensive bargain, but it was the Jew in Berlin who was footing the bill.

The action at Mohrungen where the Russians attacked us and were everywhere repulsed and the skirmishes at Bergfried, Waltersdorf and Deppen were a prelude to the battle of Eylau. Our brigade formed the vanguard of the 7th Corps which fought the whole of the day of 7 February to capture the cemetery at Eylau and the famous plateau. In the evening, as the men pushed aside the snow to light fires made of shattered doors, they also had to push aside dead bodies. That same evening I piled some straw on one of the dead Russians and out of him I made a pillow for my head before sleeping soundly all night.

The next day, 8 February, at daybreak our brigade was mounted and on the move, led by our general. We were going towards the town when Marshal Soult sent his aide-de-camp to General Durosnel to tell him not to move on from his present position but to halt and to deploy his forces until further orders came. The general replied that as the brigade was part of the 7th Corps he had received orders from Marshal Augereau to move on to Eylau and the brigade resumed its march.

Then Marshal Soult himself came up at the gallop to the head of the column and announced to General Durosnel:

'In the name of the Emperor I order you to go no further. I will take responsibility for halting your brigade and I am sending an aide-de-camp to the Emperor immediately to inform him of what I have done.'

'And I, sir,' said General Durosnel, 'am sending an aide-de-camp to Marshal Augereau to inform him of what has happened.'

The marshal positioned the brigade in front of the artillery park of his corps. As we were deployed, the regiment had a battalion in square of the 27th Infantry Regiment on its right and drawn up behind us were the 7th Chasseurs. The whole morning we were subjected to enemy gunfire, but it was so badly aimed that few of the cannon-balls reached us.

It was on the right and in the centre that the fighting was the fiercest. It was not very cold, but what was hard to bear was the thick snow which the north wind blew so violently in our faces that we were blinded by it. The pine forests around the edge of the battlefield made it even more cheerless. Moreover, the overcast sky, in which the clouds were barely higher than the tree-tops, shed a gloomy light over the whole scene. It was impossible not to remember that we were hundreds of leagues away from the clear skies of France. . . .

At about two o'clock in the afternoon an enormous mass of cavalry started to come forward at us at walking pace. The snow and the marshy ground made this the only pace possible. As the enemy cheers rang in the air Colonel Castex asked if the carbines were loaded. When told that they were, he ordered; 'Take aim!' Then he ordered the officers to fall in with the men and did so himself. The enormous mass of dragoons was still coming at us at walking pace, but the colonel remained unmoved.

When it was six yards away he ordered sharply: 'Fire!' The regiment carried out this order with drill-like precision. Consequently, the effect of the volley was terrible. Almost the whole of the enemy front rank was struck down. The enemy hesitated a moment, but soon the dead and wounded were replaced by the second rank and a mêlée developed.

Without the presence of mind of Captain Kirmann, the regiment would have been seriously threatened, for a group of Cossacks had come round to attack us from the left and so catch the regiment between two fires. Captain Kirmann's timely order for one of the squadrons to face to the left thwarted the Russian plan.

This mass of cavalry was unable to break our line and finally it turned back, but not without having inflicted heavy losses upon us. More than a hundred men of the 20th Chasseurs were killed or wounded. The enemy left at least three hundred dead on the field for the battalion in square of the 27th Infantry Regiment caused great losses among the Russians by its well-aimed fire when the enemy retreated.

The Emperor had taken up a position which overlooked the whole battle and his eagle eye did not miss a single phase of it. He had seen the critical position of the 4th Corps artillery park and he had been delighted to see the Russian cavalry cut down, smashed and put to flight. He immediately despatched one of his generals who was acting as an aide-de-camp to congratulate the 20th. When the general arrived the chasseurs greeted him with cries of 'Long live the Emperor!' and brandished their blood-stained sabres.

The day of 8 February 1807 at Eylau was a glorious one for the whole army and the regiment eagerly took the opportunity to make up for the involuntarily passive role that it had played at Jena.

When the aide-de-camp sent by General Durosnel to the corps commander arrived, he found Marshal Augereau seriously wounded. He was sent on to the Chief of Staff to make his report on the order whereby Marshal Soult had held back the brigade.

When the aide-de-camp had finished, Marshal Berthier merely commented: 'Good.' Then he added:

'Captain, I want you to stay on here for an hour or two; I may have need of you.'

It was nearly three o'clock. The aide-de-camp was Captain Laffitte, whom I subsequently knew well when I was serving in the Guard Chasseurs where he was a major, and he personally described what happened at Berthier's headquarters:

'There was a widespread rumour at the headquarters that the Russian army which was fleeing before us when hostilities were resumed on 1 February had suddenly changed its mind and had turned to face us in order to give battle. Their Commander-in-Chief, Bennigsen, had made this sudden decision after reading despatches which had been found on an aide-de-camp of the French Chief of Staff. This officer had been carrying the despatches to Marshal Bernadotte and had fallen into enemy hands. The despatches had revealed that the Emperor did not have the whole of his army at hand. The Russian army, which was fully assembled, therefore had a good chance of success if it attacked immediately.

'The battle was joined at daybreak along the whole of the line and Marshal Augereau worked wonders with his corps which, from 20,000 men in the morning, was reduced to 3,000 men by the evening. Nevertheless, he held the key position which he had taken the previous day.

'At exactly three o'clock it was clear that the enemy was trying to cut our line of battle in two. To achieve this end a column of 15,000

Russian grenadiers with bayonets levelled charged our centre without firing in spite of the terrible fire from forty cannon of the Guard Artillery which had been sited on the plateau of Eylau. Nothing could stop them and they still came on at the same pace.

'The Emperor, surrounded by his staff, kept his glass trained on this forest of bayonets and said to Marshal Berthier: "What courage! What courage!"

' "Yes," replied the marshal, "but perhaps your Majesty has not noticed that such courage has brought the range down to one hundred yards."

' "Murat!" cried the Emperor. "Take all the cavalry available and wipe out that column!"

'There were nearly seventy squadrons, including twenty from the Guard, commanded by Marshal Bessières and it was he who led the charge which immediately followed the order. The great mass of infantry was laid low like a field of corn which is swept by a violent hurricane.

'General d'Hautpoul, who was commanding the cuirassiers, was killed. General Dahlmann, who was commanding the Guard Chasseurs, was killed. It was thought for a short while that General Lepic, who was commanding the Guard mounted grenadiers, had been killed or captured for he did not appear at the head of his regiment when it rallied and the roll was called. Followed by only a few of his men, his eagerness had carried him into the third Russian line. A Russian officer, who spoke perfect French, had then advanced on him with a squadron and had almost completely surrounded him.

'He addressed the general thus: "Surrender, General. Your courage has carried you too far. You are in our rear lines."

' "Take a look at these faces and see if they want to surrender!" answered the general and shouting to his grenadiers: "Follow me!" he set off at the gallop back through the Russian lines.

'Half of those who followed him were killed by the Russian fire.

'The Emperor was delighted to see the general return and greeted him saying: "I thought you had been captured, General. I was most worried."

' "The only report of me that you will ever receive will be that of my death, Sire!" answered the fearless commander of the Guard mounted grenadiers.'

The next day, 9 February, the army pitched camp on the battlefield. It was a sad place to see; it was even more sad to have to live there. Our regiment had lost many men who had been killed or wounded. The sergeant-major of the *compagnie d'élite* had been seriously wounded so I called the roll. Out of the hundred men who had been present in the morning we had lost twenty-seven, killed or wounded. Lieutenant Saint-Aubin, who had been with the troop only a week, had been killed by a pistol-shot fired by a Russian officer at point-blank range.

On the 10th the brigade was combined with the cavalry commanded by Prince Murat. On the 15th, with the help of an infantry battalion which had cleared a wood on our right, we took up position in the village of Trunkestein. We could see the towers and steeples of Königsberg [*Kaliningrad*], the second capital of Prussia. We were counting on reaching this city and reorganizing there for this had become imperative. However, the brigade was destined to suffer a setback.

The next day at about three o'clock the advanced guard which was posted ahead of our encampment was attacked not only from the front, but also on the flanks. The infantry battalion which had secured the wood the previous day had withdrawn and abandoned the wood without warning us.

The enemy had been able to bring his troops unseen through this undefended wood round to our right flank and they began a fierce attack on several points simultaneously. The advanced guard, ordered back to the village at the gallop, raised the alarm. The brigade mounted as quickly as possible, but within the village some fifty men were killed or captured. I was among these latter. My horse was killed under me and as I lay on the ground I was wounded five times by lance-thrusts. It was in this clash that Lieutenant Sourd of the 7th Chasseurs, who later became a general and a baron, was wounded and captured. Our long-standing and close friendship dates from that day.

Among my wounds was one in the thigh which made me limp, but which did not prevent me from walking, albeit slowly. The Cossacks pulled me from beneath my horse and searched me. They took away my belt in which they found a few gold fredericks. The greater part of my wealth was in the collar of my coat or transformed into buttons. My friend Henry had taught me this way of concealing from the enemy what little wealth I had. Since we had left Holland our uniform had changed. Long coats, overalls and half-boots had replaced the dolman and riding-breeches. Our new uniform was such that there were a good number of buttons for which fredericks could be substituted and consequently I was able to keep some forty of them after my capture. Whenever I had need of money I simply undid the stitching of my collar or removed a button.

IV

The Cossacks took us half a league behind their forward positions and their hetman[1] came to inspect us. As soon as he saw my uniform he asked me if I belonged to the regiment which the dragoons and the Cossacks had charged at Eylau. I told him that I did indeed belong to that regiment. In good French he complimented me on being a member of such a brave regiment. He furthermore expressed his admiration by giving me some excellent French brandy to drink and some very tasty white bread to eat. As I was finishing off my meal, the like of which I had not had for two weeks, he unfolded a map of France which showed the departments and, pointing to the departments in La Vendée and Brittany, he asked: 'Are these not areas which do not supply men or money to Bonaparte?'

'With all respect, sir, you are completely wrong as far as the money is concerned. As for the conscripts, they are so few because many of the soldiers in the army have volunteered before the age of conscription. In fact, it will be a year before I reach that age myself.'

When the hetman left me he made a comment which truly reflects the integrity and unshakable determination of the Russian spirit: 'The Russians have still much to learn from the French, but one day they will equal their masters!'

It was night time when we arrived at Königsberg and we were herded together in a large unheated church where we found a little straw to lie on and some dry biscuits to eat. About fifty of us from the brigade had been captured. The officers were treated better than the men. Then they were separated from us and we did not see them again.

However, the next day the wounded were examined and I was moved into hospital, but I stayed there only a few days because of the approach of the French army. In the next bed in the hospital was a young officer of the 14th Infantry Regiment who had been wounded and captured on the 16th. He told me that only a fortnight previously he had been at the Opéra in Paris. He had passed out of the Military Academy at Fontainebleau[2] on 1 February and had left that same day

[1] Originally denoting a Polish military commander, the term was retained by the Cossacks.

[2] The Military Academy was founded at Fontainebleau in 1803. In 1808 it was transferred to St-Cyr on the Emperor's orders so as to remove the cadets from the distractions of court life.

to join his regiment in Poland. Sadly for him he died of his wounds while in the hospital.

Sledges were brought to take us to Vilna. I remember that on the first day of the journey the front of our sledge broke and the horses went on, leaving the sledge behind with four wounded prisoners in it. It took an hour to make good the damage and we suffered terribly from the cold. I think I suffered more at that time than I have ever done in the whole of my service. I was only twenty years old, I was a prisoner of war and I had sustained five wounds, including a very deep and painful one in my side. In addition, my right foot was very swollen and I was suffering greatly from the wound which I had received years previously.

I was truly thankful when, a few days after crossing the Nieman, we arrived at Vilna. We were put into a large church which had been converted into a hospital and which was situated beyond the town on the right bank of the Dvina. We had not been there more than a few days before I started walking with the aid of crutches and taking advantage of what little sun there was.

One day when I was taking my usual rather depressing walk, I noticed a very smart sleigh in which two ladies who were wrapped up in enormous furs were sitting. They were accompanied by a footman as well as the driver. When the sleigh reached the hospital gates it stopped and one of the ladies beckoned to me in a most friendly manner. This was so unlike the treatment I had been receiving for the previous few days that I went over to them as quickly as I could, although my progress was still slow because of the wound in my thigh. I was quite taken aback when I reached the locked gates to hear a French voice sympathetically enquire after my condition and that of my companions. The good ladies asked my age, my rank and what part of France I came from.

The very real interest which these kindly visitors showed in us was not confined to these questions. On learning that there were three hundred of us Madame Drémon, for this was her name, asked if there were any officers among us. When I told her that there were none, she asked me to take 1,000 roubles in notes (the equivalent of about 1,000 francs) which she handed me in a small wallet, and to share them among her fellow-countrymen. I gratefully undertook to do this and was so bold as to ask her where she had been born. I learned that she was from Lorraine, that she and her husband had lived for some time in Nancy and that they had settled in Vilna some years before. Her husband was away on business in St Petersburg and Moscow.

'Were it not for that,' she said, 'he would already have come to help you.'

Madame Drémon, who came thus to us like a ministering angel, left the hospital after readily giving me this information and promising to return after mass on the following Sunday. It was on a Wednesday that she paid her first charitable visit.

When I went indoors I asked one of my colleagues from the regiment to help me and we went around the wards to distribute the money. When we had left Königsberg there had been three hundred of us, but on the day when I gave out the money there were only two hundred and eighty of us left. I gave each man 3 roubles and, adding the 16 left over to the 3 due to me, I shared these between two of the prisoners who were very badly wounded and needed the money more than the others.[1]

The following Sunday our ministering angel did not fail to come, just as she had promised. She arrived in the same sleigh. After exchanging greetings I gave her an account of how I had used the money with which she had entrusted me. When she had listened to the details

[1] Here, as elsewhere in his memoirs, Parquin's method of calculating seems a little obscure.

she expressed her surprise at the fact that I had kept nothing for myself.

'I am not as poor as the others, Madame, but if you will allow me to keep the empty wallet, then I shall be the happiest of all those whom you have helped.'

'Of course you may keep it if that is your wish,' she said.

Then, after a pause, she added: 'Would you care to visit the town?'

'Madame, if I were to visit the town, it would be so that I could come and thank you on behalf of my companions for your generosity.'

'Sir, I am but doing my duty as a Frenchwoman. Would you like to come and stay at my house? I am sure that my husband will approve of my actions if you do accept my invitation.'

'Madame, I cannot refuse such a kind invitation. I am deeply grateful to you, I assure you.'

'I have brought clothing and footwear,' said Madame Drémon. 'Please be so kind as to have it distributed to your companions in distress. It comes from the French colony in Vilna as did the money which I gave you last Wednesday.'

The footman brought me a large bundle of stockings, shirts and shoes of various sizes. I called over two other prisoners who picked up the bundle and I assured Madame Drémon that the clothing would go first to those who had greatest need of it. The hospital bell had just rung so I took leave of our benefactress who, before I left, said: 'What is your name, Quartermaster? I know your rank, but what is your regiment?'

I was glad to give her the details which she requested. Then she added: 'I shall see what I can do; I am hoping that General Korsakov, the governor, will allow me to let you stay at my house in the town.'

I thanked her sincerely, although I doubted whether her request would be granted. Madame Drémon left me with a promise to return three days later on the following Wednesday.

I went back inside the hospital and with the help of some of my companions in distress I gave out the stockings, shirts, shoes and other items of clothing to the prisoners who needed them. I was the youngest prisoner in the hospital and yet circumstances made me their leader. They begged me to convey their deepest gratitude to the charitable souls who were doing as much as they could to relieve our wretched situation.

On Wednesday, as promised, Madame Drémon arrived in her sleigh, but only her servants accompanied her this time. There was no other lady with her. I was waiting for her and I had made myself as presentable as possible in the circumstances. I had taken a bath, put on a white shirt and washed my hair. Madame Drémon was some distance away when she caught sight of me and she joyfully waved the piece of paper which she was holding.

'Look!' she said when she reached me. 'This is a document which you must show to the hospital superintendent and to the guard commander. It is your pass to leave the hospital and to come to see the general with me. I will wait for you while you arrange matters and then I will take you to the general's headquarters where I hope to obtain permission for you to come to my house in the town.'

I was so taken aback that I almost forgot to thank Madame Drémon. I went as quickly as my limp would allow me to the superintendent's office and to the guardhouse to show my welcome document to the appropriate authorities. It had the desired effect. I collected my few belongings and the guard commander accompanied me to the sleigh where Madame Drémon made me get in beside her. Then she instructed the driver to take us to the governor's residence.

'I am afraid,' said Madame Drémon, blushing slightly, 'that I had to tell a little lie to obtain permission for you to move to my house. I said that you were a relative of mine, although you come from Paris and I come from Nancy. But after all, it is possible to be distant cousins, isn't it?'

I was pouring out my thanks to her for her great kindness when we arrived in the main square of the town and passed in front of a very smart drapery and fancy goods shop. Madame Drémon pointed to the shop and said: 'That is where I live, but we have to see General Korsakov first.'

Some distance from the square the sleigh stopped in front of a large gateway which was guarded by two sentries. This was the governor's residence. We got out of the sleigh and a footman took us up to the first floor where we found the governor sitting by a roaring fire. He stood up when he saw Madame Drémon enter, enquired politely after her health and offered her a chair. I remained standing, leaning on a chair and supported by my crutches.

'This is my young relative,' said Madame Drémon to the general. 'I mentioned him to you yesterday when Your Excellency did me the honour of visiting my shop.'

'Well Madame, what do you want?'

'I should be most indebted to you, General, if you were kind enough to allow him to spend the time he needs for his recovery at my home. There he would be able to have all the attention which he needs.'

'Madame, you know that I am too human and too chivalrous to refuse your request,' said the governor.

Then, turning to me, he asked: 'How old are you, young man?'

'I am twenty.'

'What! You have not even reached the age for conscription.'

'I anticipated it by four years when I volunteered,' I answered.

The general continued to put questions to me and he asked me where in France I came from, the name of my regiment and where I had been wounded and captured. When I told him that I had been taken prisoner near Königsberg a week after the battle of Eylau, he exclaimed:

'Ah! That was the battle which Bennigsen won over your army.' I could have retorted: 'In the same way as General Suvorov won the battle of Zurich[1] over Massena.' But my position caused me to be rather more non-committal, so I merely commented: 'I thought it was the other way about, sir.'

Madame Drémon rose and bade farewell to the governor who hastened to give her his arm as far as the door. I bowed and offered my arm to my pretty make-believe cousin so as to go down the stairs and into the sleigh.

During the short time that our visit had lasted I had taken advantage of the chance to study General Korsakov. He was a handsome man who at the time seemed to be about fifty years old. He was extremely smart in appearance, his uniform was perfect on him and his elegant, aristocratic manner gave no grounds for doubting the role in which history has cast him as one of the most appreciated of the favourites of Catherine the Great.

When we reached Madame Drémon's home we alighted from the sleigh. As we went through the shop I noticed in it several young ladies who, I later learned, were Polish and German. It was a very large shop which sold millinery, chinaware, glassware and other similar things; in short, it was an important centre for the retail of the sort of goods produced in Paris. An assistant who spoke German, Russian and French was in charge of the sales staff.

The room which Madame Drémon had been good enough to prepare for me in her home was small but well furnished. She had thought it better for me to occupy this room on the ground floor rather than a larger one which was available on the third floor. I was grateful to her for her thoughtfulness for I still had a limp.

The doctor whom she called declared that I needed much rest and

[1] Massena had defeated the Russians at Zurich in 1799.

that I must refrain from going out on foot since an accident at this time of the year would greatly retard my recovery. I was far too happy in my new lodgings to look for entertainment elsewhere. I could not, however, refuse to go out in the sleigh once or twice a week in answer to the invitations from the French merchants in Vilna which came as a result of my being at Madame Drémon's home.

There was a small colony made up of some ten families. These worthy merchants had been approached for contributions by Madame Drémon when our convoy of prisoners had arrived in Vilna. This excellent woman, in the absence of her husband who would certainly have undertaken the task for her himself, had circulated a list on which contributors entered the amount of their donation. She had taken care to put herself down first for 100 roubles and in a single day she had seen the collection rise to a total of 1,000 roubles and this was a source of great joy to a person as generous as she. This was the sum which she had asked me to give out on the occasion of our first meeting.

I spent ten weeks in her home and not once did we fail to go to the hospital on the Sunday to distribute money and gifts which had been collected by the French colony. It can easily be imagined how happy and proud I was when, every Sunday after mass—which we never failed to attend—we would travel out to the hospital where my fellow prisoners were living. Madame Drémon's representations to the governor had helped us greatly for he had requisitioned clothing for us in the town and as a result all the prisoners were properly clothed. I am truly glad to be able to record here our gratitude to General Korsakov.

I never wanted any part of the gifts donated by the French colony, but in fact I was more than rewarded for my disinterested attitude as Madame Drémon devised a means of compensating me handsomely. Her shop was patronized by the wealthiest people in Vilna and whenever it happened that a customer hesitated over a purchase because of the price, Madame Drémon would say: 'The profits on the sale are for a good cause; they are for a French prisoner.'

Thereupon any debate over the price would cease and in this way my own little fortune doubled during my stay in this hospitable home. I was, however, quite unprepared for the charming thoughtfulness shown by my minstering angel in anticipating my needs after I left Vilna. Not only did the shop assistants replace all my clothes apart from my uniform—which I did not want to leave off despite its patches—but Madame Drémon had had the foresight to prepare soup tablets which I found most welcome when I was travelling. In short, everything had been thought of by these good ladies; they gave me personal articles and food in such quantities that I was forced to decline much of it.

How I regret not taking part in the Russian campaign, disastrous though it was, for then I would have been able to see my charming benefactress again! But I was serving in Spain with the part of the regiment which was there from 1810 to 1812. Nevertheless, my thoughts and memories were always turned to Vilna at this time. The misfortunes of war may have afflicted that hospitable house and those of our other fellow-countrymen who so generously aided us in our distress. The date for our departure from Vilna was 1 June. I left Madame Drémon and the other French residents with tears in my eyes. My 'cousin', who had ensured that I would lack nothing on the journey, handed me a small parcel and said: 'Here are two books; do not lend them to anyone until you have looked through them. You will find them helpful and entertaining.'

'You may be sure that as always I shall do as you tell me,' I said and, sad at heart, I took my leave of Madame Drémon, never to see her again.

The group of prisoners set out for Kovno. When we completed the first stage we had done almost eight leagues—thirty-seven versts by Russian measurements. We stopped in a village where we were billeted in groups of four or five on local peasants. We slept on straw and were able to buy milk and potatoes. At this first halt my thoughts were turned to Vilna and it was not long before I opened my travelling-case and took out the two books which Madame Drémon had given me. They were Caesar's *Commentaries* in French and in Latin. Great was my surprise when I saw between the opening pages of the first volume ten one-hundred rouble notes. This meant that there was a total of one thousand roubles, the equivalent of one thousand francs. I must confess that this delicate way of supplying my needs during my captivity made me think even more highly of the charming Madame Drémon. I would none the less have liked to have had a note from her as a souvenir. But this was ingratitude on my part, for I still had the small green wallet which she had given me on the occasion of our first meeting and it was into this wallet that I put the money.

While I had been living at Madame Drémon's house I had not had to take a single button from my clothes to use as money. The thousand roubles which had just been given me so discreetly meant that I would be able to obtain all that I required during the time that I was to remain a captive.

As prisoners of war we received only bread of inferior quality. Each soldier was paid 2½ sous and as I was an N.C.O. I received twice this sum, 5 sous. I must admit that orders concerning us were characterized by a certain humanity, and if our suffering was considerable, it was due to the climate, the poverty of the country and our wounds, and certainly not to the harshness of the Russian commanders.

On the second day of our march I took aside four prisoners who were chasseurs from my regiment and I addressed them as follows:

'The five of us will form a mess. Every day one of you will go on ahead of the main body by two hours in order to purchase three pounds of beef and some vegetables at the place where we are due to halt. He must then set about preparing the dinner so that we shall find it ready when we arrive. I warn you that I shall be the only one not to do these duties, but I shall be the only one to pay. Every day I shall give 5 roubles to the man who goes on ahead.'

Then I immediately gave the 5 roubles for the next day's expenses. The chasseurs were delighted with the proposal which they gratefully accepted. The weather was fine, but for us it was too hot. Fortunately we would start early and complete the stage by ten o'clock.

Between Vilna and Kovno we met the Emperor Alexander who was travelling to join his army and he inspected our detachment of prisoners. I marched at the head of the column as I was the only N.C.O. present. He spoke with us in a kindly manner and asked if we had any complaints about the way in which we were being treated. Since we had no complaints to make, the Emperor seemed very satisfied and he gave me sufficient money for each prisoner to have a ducat apiece. I thanked him on behalf of my companions in distress and he continued on his way.

On the same day when we were two hours from Kovno we met two regiments of Bashkirs.[1] Their main weapon was the bow and arrow and because of this our soldiers called them the 'Cupids' of the Russian army. I do not think that these troops could have successfully measured up to ours. I remember that when I returned to my regiment, they were still joking about a chasseur who was the only man to be hit by an arrow shot by a Bashkir soldier.

'If your nose were not so big and so long,' said the other chasseurs, 'Cupid's arrow would have missed completely.'

At Kovno, after our modest meal, we went for a walk and during

[1] A once nomadic people who had settled between the Volga and the Urals.

it we noticed a convent. I do not know what prompted me, but I suggested to the two chasseurs with me that we should visit the convent and we went into the parlour. We stated that we were French and we were made most welcome. All the nuns came running to the parlour grille.

Among these ladies there was a young girl of good family who spoke French perfectly. She was merely staying temporarily in the convent and her lay dress showed that she was not even a novice. When I asked her if it was her intention to cut herself off from society when she seemed endowed with all the qualities needed to succeed in it, she confessed that she was leaving in a month's time when she had completed the period stipulated by her parents for her stay in this convent, which was a very pleasant one and much frequented by the Polish aristocracy.

Thanks to this charming interpreter we were able to make ourselves understood by the sisters who seemed quite vexed that we had already dined. However, as we were staying another day at Kovno, we promised to return the next day.

So it was that the next day at noon the five of us sat down to eat in the refectory. We were given meat soup, beef, bacon, sauerkraut, potatoes, beer and brandy in liberal quantities. We thanked the good sisters whom, it is true, we had impressed when, before we had unfolded our napkins, one of us had risen and recited grace in Latin.

The next day we continued our march towards Minsk and Smolensk. We stayed a week in Smolensk which had been a fortress within the old borders of Poland. Among the chasseurs who were messing with me was one who had a very fine voice. It was he who had said grace at the convent at Kovno. This fact was to involve us in a very pleasant adventure. A few days after our arrival in Smolensk we were strolling on the ramparts above the town as we regularly did after eating at midday. We met few people, although the place was used as a promenade by the inhabitants of the town, for there was a broad avenue with fine trees on both sides. At that particular moment there was no one in sight. The chasseur who had the fine voice took advantage of the silence about us to start to sing the *Marseillaise* and we all sang the chorus of this hymn of liberty.

A carriage which was approaching at a trot slowed down at some distance from us and the two people in it, an elderly gentleman and a young man, seemed to derive much pleasure from hearing us and we supposed that these gentlemen understood French.

Indeed, when the song had ended, the carriage stopped. The young man stepped down, came over to us and said in good French: 'Gentlemen, would you be recently arrived prisoners?'

When we answered that this was true, he pointed to the elderly gentleman who had remained in the carriage and said: 'If it is not a tactless request, my father would like you to write out the words of the song which you have just sung so admirably.'

We all went over to the carriage and Emery, our singer spoke to the young man's father and promised him that we would be on the promenade with the *Marseillaise* the next day at the same time—two o'clock in the afternoon.

'Our quartermaster has a fine hand and he will probably write it out if I dictate it,' he added.

'I shall be glad to do so,' I said.

'I shall come here on my horse tomorrow at the same time to collect the copy from you since you have been kind enough to agree to do it,' said the young man.

After saying this, he gave us a friendly wave and the carriage set off at a trot and disappeared from view.

The next day was a Sunday. We were on time for the meeting, but as there were more people on the promenade we did not think it wise to sing the *Marseillaise* as we had done the previous day. I had written the words out neatly when Chasseur Emery had dictated them to me and now he had the copy in his pocket.

The young man, riding a fine grey horse and followed by a liveried servant, arrived promptly at the place on which we had agreed the previous day. After we had greeted each other he dismounted and took the song which I gave him, for Emery had insisted that I should give it. In exchange the young man asked me to accept 5 ducats, adding that it was a small collection made by his family who were very happy to possess our national anthem.

'I hope, sir, that you will accept this gift which is gladly offered by a Polish family, for otherwise I would be greatly upset. You must know how much we admire the French nation.'

I was sure that my companions would approve of my action so I accepted the ducats and said: 'You have shown us such consideration that we have but one regret—that we shall not make the acquaintance of such a charitable family as yours. Would you kindly convey all our thanks to your family, sir.'

'I have another task for my father,' the young man added. 'I have to ask you if you are free to spend tomorrow at our home which is two leagues from here.'

'Sir,' I answered, 'we have to be present at the roll-call in the morning, but we are free for the rest of the day, provided that we are back in town before the gate closes at nine o'clock.'

'I am delighted that my family's wish to see you can be satisfied without causing any difficulties, for the last thing we would wish to do would be to bring you further trouble. You already have the misfortune to be prisoners of war far from home.'

He remounted and promised to be back the following day, Monday, at noon to take us out by carriage to his home.

The next day we were waiting for him. I had been careful to warn Emery: 'Be prepared to do the honours today. Make sure you remember the words of the songs you sing best. That will be a very convenient way for us to repay the hospitality which they have been so kind as to offer us.'

Of the five chasseurs in our group, Emery and I were the only ones not to be embarrassed at moving in society. Our three companions were not very polished fellows, it must be admitted, but I was sure that they would not be out of place at the table of a Polish baron, especially if the food was good, as we hoped it would be, and as indeed it turned out to be.

When we saw the young man approaching exactly on time, we were careful to go through the town gates on foot and not to enter the carriage until we were some distance outside.

If our uniforms were not in a very impressive state, they were at least clean and nothing better could have been expected of us as poor prisoners of war. Moreover, our uniforms had seen active service; we had slept in them in bivouacs and they were impregnated with gunpowder.

The carriage had been travelling for an hour along the road when we turned off into a forest. After going through it for about half a league we entered a long broad avenue. At the end of it the carriage stopped and we alighted at the foot of a flight of steps leading up to a large country house beyond which was a sizeable village.

The first person who appeared was the old gentleman whom we had seen in the carriage on the occasion of our meeting on the ramparts at Smolensk. He welcomed us warmly. When we reached the entrance-hall at the top of the steps he led us into a vast room hung with portraits of his family and it was easy for us to see that our host had been a soldier. In one painting he was shown in uniform with his sword at his side and wearing a silver sash, which, in all armies except the French, denotes high rank.

We had been there a few minutes when a lady who was about forty years of age and a young girl of between sixteen and eighteen entered and were introduced to us as Madame and Mademoiselle L . . . ki. We bowed and answered the many earnest questions which we were asked. There was a third lady present, a companion, who spoke French very well. I think she might even have been French, but as she did not give her name we were not so indiscreet as to question her on this point.

The baron and his son spoke French and made themselves quite easily understood. The young lady, however, did not say a word. I had the impression that she had been taught to be reticent in this way when in the presence of any foreign soldiers whom she might chance to meet. It is a well-known fact that all well-bred young Russians and Poles are familiar with our language. At all events, Mademoiselle L . . . ki was extremely beautiful, having those fine looks which are typical of women from the north, especially from Poland, and which make such an impression on the imagination. Silent or not, she was undoubtedly the most beautiful adornment of our gathering.

Before dinner it was suggested that we should take a stroll in the park. We had already accepted when the young man, who was my own age, asked if there was anyone in our group who would measure swords with him in the *salle d'armes*. I was the only one who could reasonably engage in a bout so I agreed, albeit regretfully, for I would have preferred to go for a walk with the ladies.

The baron followed his son to the *salle d'armes*. Emery and one of the chasseurs accompanied the baroness and her daughter while the other two chasseurs remained with me. We went to a large room which had a pinewood floor and in which the walls were decorated with gloves, masks and foils.

Once we had positioned ourselves and made the customary salute I saw that I was facing an amateur of considerable ability. I was not unskilled, but a fencer needs constant practice and I had not touched a foil for two years. Consequently, in the very first exchange I was hit. Soon, however, I had the measure of my opponent, but, wishing to give him a good bout, I let him hit me quite often. Nevertheless, when we finished with the best of three hits, I took care to make two of them.

The baron and his son complimented me and swore that they had never yet met anyone of my ability. They insisted that I must be a fencing instructor, but I assured them that this was not at all the case.

In fact, I consistently refused the post of regimental fencing instructor although I was often urged to accept the appointment.

The ladies had returned from their walk and we were informed that dinner was served. For my part, I was very glad to learn this, for our contest had given me a healthy appetite. We went into the drawing-room where our hosts had gathered in evening dress. We apologized for our worn travelling clothes and our apologies were accepted with kindly understanding by the family. I offered my hand to the lady of the house as my position as head of the group required. I would have preferred to offer it to the charming young girl, but she took her brother's arm and the others followed us into the dining-room. At the table I was on the right of the baroness and the baron was on the left of his wife. The baron's son and daughter and the companion sat opposite us and Emery and the others occupied the remaining places. Behind us stood numerous servants. I have forgotten to say that before we went into the dining-room the lady of the house had glasses of brandy served to us from a silver tray. This is an old Polish custom.

The meal was an excellent one with as much beer and claret as we wanted. Our hosts were attentive to our every need and were especially anxious to see that our wine-glasses were kept full, but I had warned my companions to be very moderate so as to create a good impression. We spoke at length about France and Poland and about our Emperor for whom the Poles professed the highest admiration.

The baroness said that she had been told that Emery had sung the *Marseillaise* remarkably well, and charmingly asked if he would kindly let her hear this song which had such stirring words and music. Emery, as can be imagined, needed no urging and he sang it so well that he drew the compliments of everyone present.

When we had returned to the drawing-room for coffee Emery, who had noticed a piano there and had guessed that the young lady played it, asked her if she would play. The baroness did not give her daughter time to answer, but said: 'Marie, if you are not too tired after your walk, you could sing an Italian air.'

Mademoiselle Marie sat down at the piano which suddenly came to life at the touch of her skilful fingers. It was the introduction to a sparkling Italian air to which we listened, but which we did not understand since none of us knew Italian. The music, however, gave us great pleasure.

A day so pleasantly employed was bound to pass quickly. Soon seven o'clock struck and we had to think about leaving in order to return to Smolensk. The baron had kindly had the carriage brought round to the front and his son insisted on accompanying us back, saying that in this way he would be able to enjoy our company longer than his parents would. We could not refuse a wish which was expressed with such delicate courtesy.

We took leave of our kind hosts, asking them to accept our thanks and our regrets for, since we were moving on the following day into Russia itself, we would probably never have the pleasure of seeing them again. We promised them that we would never forget the beautiful day which we had spent in the country thanks to their generosity and here in my memoirs thirty-five years later, I am happy to show that the promise has been kept.

The next day we left Smolensk after being there for a week which, as has been seen, included one exceptionally pleasant day.

We were to march to Kaluga, passing through Volmir on the way. Once beyond Smolensk we left the hospitable soil of Poland and entered Russia where we immediately noticed a great difference. The genuine interest, the assistance and the sympathy to which we had been accustomed in Poland no longer came from anyone except the boyars,[1] that is, the local noblemen.

All the soldiers were away with the army after vast levies had been raised in this enormous empire for the campaign of 1807. Often, because of the lack of soldiers, we had women as our escorts and these were usually as old as possible, although still able to travel the distance from one village to the next. At this time of the year every peasant, young man, woman and child old enough to work was busy in the fields.

I am always ready to talk about the fair sex, no matter what class its members come from, but to tell the truth, these old women spoke to us only to insult us in their own language, which was half Tartar, and they often struck us with their sticks.

We had already completed several stages from Smolensk and we were only one day's march from Volmir when, during the hour-long halt which the prisoners usually made at the halfway point, a carriage bearing a Russian nobleman and his family stopped on the road.

This nobleman asked the Russian officer in charge of the column if he could speak to one of us. The officer beckoned to me and I approached the carriage. The boyar was sitting on the left side of the back seat. He asked me in French from what part of France I came, in what arm I was serving and where I had been wounded; in short,

[1] This title had been abolished by Peter the Great a century previously.

all the usual questions which are prompted by curiosity. I had no sooner answered him than a very pretty young woman who was sitting on his right and whom I took to be his wife or daughter, said to me: 'Sir, is there a French grenadier among you? I would so like to see one!'

'Madame,' I replied, 'your wish is soon granted for I am the quartermaster of the *compagnie d'élite* of my regiment and as such, a grenadier.'

I immediately perceived that the lady was greatly surprised and she quickly commented: 'What sir! You are a grenadier and you do not have a big moustache!'

'Madame, in the French army, grenadiers are chosen by their courage and their stature.'

'Obviously,' she said, 'and by these standards you must be one.'

'If you had had any doubts, Madame,' I said to her, pointing to my forage cap where a hunting-horn was flanked by two grenades, 'here is the proof.'

'I had made up my mind that I would give a ducat to the first French grenadier that I met. I should be glad if you would take it.'

'I will indeed take your ducat, Madame,' I said, 'but only so that I may give it to the sort of grenadier whom you were expecting to see.'

Thereupon I signalled to a grenadier of the 14th Regiment of the Line, the possessor of the finest moustache in the column, and I handed him the ducat.

'This good lady has offered this ducat for the prisoner with the finest moustache.'

The soldier thanked her for her generosity and as I was about to take my leave of the Russian family, the lady called me and gave me two ducats, saying: 'These are for the two grenades on your cap.'

'Thank you, Madame. It will not take me long to grow the moustache.' I said with a bow.

Our column set off again and the nobleman's carriage went away in the opposite direction. From Volmir, where we spent the night, we continued our march and in a few days we reached Kaluga, a town some fourteen leagues from Moscow.

I remember that we arrived early in the day, so a friend and I went into a church where we were surprised to find priests who spoke perfect French. One of them told us that some of the priests attached to the church were in fact French. It was not difficult to recognize them as Jesuits by their curt manner of speaking. They did not even offer us a pinch of snuff.

One of them, however, went further than this. He met one of our number, a young drummer-boy, in the market square of Kaluga. The lad was out for a walk and was carrying a walking-stick when the priest approached him and asked to borrow the stick.

The drummer-boy had no idea what the priest wanted to do with the stick and willingly handed it over. The Jesuit no sooner had it than he proceeded to beat the drummer-boy with it. The latter, although very young for he was still a boy-soldier, would have struck back, but this would have aroused the local population who would have made him pay dearly for striking a priest. He therefore preferred to leave his stick in his assailant's hands and to take refuge in the barracks where we all were.

The next day we continued our march and reached Vladimir where we stayed for four days. We were due to go on to Kazan and from there to Siberia, but Vladimir was to mark the end of the journey for news that peace had been made had just reached the town. The Russian officer in charge of the column told us that we would return as far as Smolensk by the same route as the one by which we had come. From Smolensk we would be sent to Mittau [*Yelgava*] in Kurland which was a Russian province. Afterwards, each of us would find at the Prussian border orders concerning the direction he was to take. Our return took us through Kaluga, but our drummer-boy who had been so roughly treated by the Jesuit was not anxious to meet him again and this time he refrained from strolling about the streets with his stick.

When we arrived at Smolensk my companions asked me to call on the baron and to apologize for their not coming as they were tired after much travelling and they were continuing their journey very early the next day.

I was pleased to undertake the mission. I hired a carriage and two hours later I was at the baron's home. There I found the ladies alone; the baron and his son had gone shooting for a few days. I expressed my regrets at not being able to meet them again, but I did not hide my pleasure in seeing these delightful ladies once more. The baroness wanted me to stay to dinner, but I could only pay a brief call so I refused politely and half an hour later I took my leave of them, assuring them of our gratitude for the generosity they had shown when we had first passed through Smolensk.

I returned early to the town and conveyed to my companions the friendly messages which the ladies had sent in the absence of the baron and his son. We left Smolensk for Mittau on 15 September 1807. We had received permission to make our own way there. I calculated how much money I had left and discovered that I was rich enough to pay for post-horses and food and lodgings for us along the way. Between Smolensk and Mittau nothing worth recalling happened, except that a few stages from Smolensk our carriage, which in reality was merely a cart with some bales of straw acting as seats, caught fire because of the great speed of our four Polish horses. The hub of one of the wheels burst into flames and the fire spread to the straw. This accident forced us to go on foot to the next staging-post.

The day on which we former French prisoners of war entered Mittau happened to be exactly one month after the departure of an illustrious exiled French family. At the instigation of the Russian government this family had been obliged to leave the continent to go and live at Holyrood in Scotland. It was to return from across the sea and sit upon the throne of France seven years later.[1]

From Mittau we made our way to Warsaw and after resting there for a few days we set out for Pomerania where our regiment was stationed. The regiment's headquarters were at Stolp and the squadrons were billeted throughout the countryside as far as Kolberg, a port on the Baltic. On 15 October we arrived at Stolp after an absence of eight months. When we reported to Colonel Castex, he had just finished lunch.

'Ah!' he exclaimed. 'My children have come back to me. Well, how are you? Have you suffered much?'

I replied: 'Anything we have suffered was forgotten the moment we had the joy of rejoining the regiment with Colonel Castex at its head.'

'Really?' said the colonel in his Gascon accent and he permitted himself a small smile of satisfaction. 'I thank you for your kind thought.'

Then he dismissed us after informing us that we would each return to our respective troops and I would resume my post as quartermaster of the *compagnie d'élite*, for I had never been replaced. My duties had been carried out by Sergeant Jouglas who had been the quartermaster before me.

It can easily be imagined how happy I was to resume my post. Moreover, in the regimental paymaster's office I found letters from my family as well as 200 francs from my father. I had written to him from Vilna and the glossy paper on which I had written, together with the seal on the envelope, had made my parents think that my position as a prisoner was fairly comfortable since I could send such an elegant letter and especially since I did not ask for money.

[1] As the Comte d'Artois, the future Charles X spent part of his exile in Scotland.

My greatest joy was to be reunited with my friend Henry. He had just been decorated and as I was congratulating him he said: 'It was Schipska (his mare) who won my decoration for me.'

'Really!' I said. 'Tell me about it.'

'You can hear the story when you have told me how you spent your time as a prisoner and not before.'

The next day at dinner I gave him a detailed account of all that had happened to us and when I had finished, Henry told me of all that had happened to the regiment since 15 February, the day when I had fallen into the hands of the enemy. Henry went on:

'You were most unfortunate, Parquin, for the day after you were captured the regiment returned to its base where the squadrons re-formed and the losses of men and horses sustained in the Prussian and Polish campaigns were made good. After we had spent three comfortable months there the army started moving forward again with renewed vigour.

'We had daily encounters with the enemy at Spanden, at Momiken, at Altkirch and at Wolfsdorf. At Guttstadt there was a bloody engagement. The regiment was part of the division commanded by General Lasalle and we were constantly in the enemy's fire. Our position covered flanking movements on both sides by an infantry division which reached the woods and turned the enemy's left. The regiment had been harassed all day by a band of Cossacks. Our chasseurs had charged them, but could not get to grips with them because the Russian tactics were to withdraw at the gallop to the cover of their own artillery and we lost many men when their guns were suddenly brought into action.

'Our colonel was extremely annoyed by these tactics which were causing us heavy losses, so he took advantage of a moment when our infantry had gained control of a small wood to our right to order Captain Bertin to take a squadron around the wood. From the other side of the wood he was to issue forth into the plain against the enemy as soon as he heard a volley fired by a troop and he was to charge headlong against the enemy in the direction of his own lines. Captain Bertin had not been gone five minutes before the colonel galloped over to Lieutenant Capitant and gave him the following orders:

' "You will take your troop at the trot to a distance of ten yards beyond the edge of the wood there," and he pointed to a spot some three or four hundred yards away. "Your front rank will take aim with their carbines. The enemy opposite you will charge in a body, but you will not give the order to fire until they are six yards away. They will return to the charge and you will be battered, unhorsed and cut down. But you will not withdraw. I shall be watching you."

'These orders were carried out with the same precision as that with which they had been given and when our troop was charged by the enemy we opened fire at point-blank range. At that moment the squadron under Captain Bertin emerged and charged the Cossacks who were taken from the rear by Captain Bertin's move and attacked again by our troop. They were cut down and run through from all sides and were completely routed. They lost many prisoners and left the field covered with their dead.

'I must admit, Parquin, that day at Guttstadt brought a handsome revenge for the one at Trunkestein when you and so many others were captured.'

'But tell me,' I said to Henry, 'how did you win your decoration? you modestly say that it was thanks to your horse. I would like to see that remarkable animal.'

'But that is the truth,' said Henry. 'You may judge for yourself.' And he gave me his account of what had happened.

'On 12 June, the day of the murderous battle at Heilsberg, I was attached to Prince Murat's staff as an orderly. You know the prince. He is the commander-in-chief of all our cavalry, but he always wears the uniform of a drum-major and wields a sabre as well as any of his men.'

'Yes,' I said, 'I know the one you mean.'

'Well, at about two in the afternoon, Prince Murat rode over to the Emperor who was with the grenadier division commanded by General Oudinot. The Emperor and General Oudinot were standing on a rise and the Emperor was observing the enemy through his glass. Prince Murat dismounted and gave me his horse to hold. He bowed to the Emperor and shook hands with Oudinot to whom he began to talk. Suddenly a cloud of dust rose in front of us. The Emperor immediately focussed his glass on the spot and asked Prince Murat what it was.

' "Nothing, Sir."

' "What do you mean, nothing? Go and see more closely." Saying this the Emperor gave a vigorous blow with his whip across the flanks of the prince's horse which the prince had already remounted. General Oudinot wasted no time in begging the Emperor to enter one of the squares where he would be safer, in view of the movement on the plain.

'The prince, his suite and I set off at the gallop. As the prince rode past Colonel Déry who commanded the 5th Hussars he called out:

' "Follow me with your regiment. We shall charge that rabble which is coming towards us."

'In a moment we were to grips with them, but we had no sooner struck the first blow than the prince's horse was hit by a cannon-ball. I immediately jumped from my horse and, holding my own horse's reins under my arm, I helped the prince to extricate himself from beneath his horse. His left boot came off and remained in the stirrup.

' "It is nothing. Give me a horse!" said the prince.

'I offered him my own and the prince mounted it, wearing only one boot. He had not taken my horse to withdraw from the danger around him; on the contrary, he had taken it in order to hurl himself once more into the midst of the enemy, shouting:

' "Forward! Forward! Long live the Emperor!"

'In a quarter of an hour the three or four thousand Cossacks who had taken possession of the centre of the plain had been swept from it like dust.

'I had returned to the prince's headquarters with his saddle and I can assure you that it was no light task for there was more gold than iron on the saddle.

'The prince sent my horse back to me with a request for my name and regiment and I was decorated at the end of the campaign. So you see, Parquin, I am indebted to Schipska. It is true that I cut down or ran through more than one Cossack when I was at the prince's side, but I do not know if he was aware of it.'

'You are as modest as you are brave, Henry, and you do indeed deserve to wear the cross of the *Légion d'honneur*. But you have not told me as others have, that on 15 February when the Cossacks took us by surprise you, by your bravery, saved Lieutenant Dupont after he had received a wound which cost him an eye.' This wound prevented the lieutenant from controlling his horse and he would inevitably have shared my fate if Henry had not remained by the lieutenant and led him safely out of the confusion.

'That is true,' said Henry, 'but I am happy to have been able to help Lieutenant Dupont for he was well liked in the regiment. He is now in charge of a foundry in Dinant in Belgium. When he left the regiment he insisted that I accept 600 francs from him. I could not refuse for I was sure that a refusal on my part would have greatly upset him.'

'But Henry,' I said, 'was the regiment at the battle of Friedland?'

'You may well ask! Does anything take place without the 20th being there? We were not, however, engaged during the whole day. A few men and horses were killed by cannon fire, but these were our only losses. Late in the evening we pursued the enemy and the next day, the 15th [*of June*], we broke through his rearguard and the regiment clashed with the Bashkirs, the Cupids of the Russian army.

'Their arrows presented no danger to us, although they were poisoned. Only one chasseur was wounded, and he did not die. The Prussian hussars who wear a death's-head on their shakos,[1] but who are none the braver for it, wanted to avenge the Bashkirs' defeat. Not only were they unable to penetrate our line, although they outnumbered us, but the regiment moreover routed them completely and pursued them along the road to Königsberg.

'The corps under Marshal Soult entered this town on 16 June and found there 20,000 Prussians and Russians and also vast stores of every description, such as 16,000 English muskets which had not yet been brought ashore.

'On the 16th we also learned by an order of the day of the brilliant victory which we had won on the 14th over the whole of the Russian army and the remnants of the Prussian army. Fifty to sixty thousand men, including twenty-five generals, killed, wounded, or captured; eighty cannon and seventy standards lost; such was the extent of the defeat of the Coalition powers. We and the rest of Prince Murat's cavalry took up excellent quarters on the island of Nogat in Prussia. General Lasalle, who commanded our division, had his headquarters at Elbing. The general, who is as fond of good food as he is of the battlefield, devised a highly amusing way of issuing invitations for dinner to any of the officers of the division who happened to come into Elbing.

'One hour before dinner the general's servant would hang an unfolded napkin over the balcony of the general's quarters. This napkin would remain on the balcony until the twenty places at the general's table had all been taken. The officers from the division, when they saw this sign displayed, could go up to pay their call on the general in the certainty of being asked to dine with him. If, however, the napkin was not hung out, there was no point in going up as every place would have been taken.

'It was General Lasalle who gave a very amusing reply to the Emperor when His Majesty was reviewing the whole body of cavalry, a total of not less than 57,000 men, on 5 July. In the course of the review the Emperor had been very generous in giving promotions

[1] The Black Hussars commanded by General de l'Estocq.

and decorations to the men of Lasalle's division. The general himself had been made a *comte de l'Empire*, had received a substantial monetary award and had also been made a grand officer of the *Légion d'honneur*. The general thanked the Emperor, yet still did not seem fully satisfied.

' "What is it then?" asked the Emperor. "You do not seem altogether happy."

' "Your kindness makes me very happy, Sire, but I am not completely satisfied for I had hoped that Your Majesty would consider me for the command of the best regiment in the world. In short, I had hoped to fill the place of General Dahlmann, the Colonel of your *Guides*, who was killed at Eylau."

'The Emperor replied: "When General Lasalle no longer drinks, no longer swears and no longer smokes, not only will I put him at the head of a cavalry regiment of my Guard, but I will also make him one of my chamberlains."

'The general, anxious not to appear beaten, bowed and said to the Emperor: "Sire, since I have all the attributes of a sailor, I ought to ask Your Majesty for the command of a frigate."

' "Oh no!" replied the Emperor with a laugh, "that would not be my wish. You shall command the twenty cavalry regiments in the absence of Prince Murat who is returning to his duchy [*Berg*]."

'It was while he was holding this illustrious appointment that General Lasalle was mortally wounded at Wagram.

'During this same review the Emperor made many awards to the regiment. Colonel Castex was made an officer of the *Légion d'honneur*, a *baron de l'Empire* and was granted 4,000 francs. The two squadron commanders were made officers of the *Légion d'honneur* and *chevaliers de l'Empire* and each was granted 2,000 francs. The captain of the *compagnie d'élite* was promoted to major.

'When this officer was presented to the Emperor, he was asked how long he had been a captain.

' "Fifteen years, Sire."

' "This officer has been too long overlooked," said the Emperor, and he immediately promoted the officer.

'When Captain Péquignot was presented, the Emperor also asked him how long he had held his rank.

' "Fourteen years, Sire."

'This answer seemed to surprise the Emperor who promoted him to the rank of squadron commander and appointed him to be a captain in the Guard mounted grenadiers. Captain Kirmann, in response to the same question from the Emperor, said that he had served for thirteen years as a captain. The Emperor promoted him to the rank of squadron commander and appointed him to be a captain in the Guard chasseurs. Finally, when Captain Lion, who had but seven years seniority as a captain, was presented the Emperor said: "Too young."

'The colonel, however, intervened to say: "Perhaps Your Majesty would permit me to point out that Captain Lion merely seems young after the other officers whom you have just promoted."

'The Emperor, who had already started to move on, stopped when he heard this fair comment and, noticing a large scar on Captain Lion's face, he asked the captain where he had received the blow which had left its mark.

' "At Ulm, Sire."

'The captain was immediately appointed to be a squadron commander with the 14th Chasseurs. The remarkable thing about this answer which brought promotion to Captain Lion was that although it was literally true, it was not true in the sense in which the Emperor understood it. The Emperor had assumed that the wound had been received in the battle of Ulm, whereas it resulted in fact from a duel which Captain Lion had fought while the regiment was encamped at Ulm. The Emperor, who never made awards to duellists, would certainly not have promoted Captain Lion if he had known this fact. Not surprisingly, the captain did not volunteer any further explanation.

'I hasten to say,' added Henry, 'that Captain Lion, who subsequently enjoyed a brilliant career in the army, fully deserved this promotion. Finally, the Emperor decided that the vacancies caused by these promotions would be filled from within the regiment. He also conferred some twelve crosses of the *Légion d'honneur* upon the regiment.

'Afterwards we remained in our camp on the island of Nogat until the winter.

'And that, my dear Parquin, is all I have to tell you about what has happened to the regiment since you left us.'

Such was Henry's account, exactly as he gave it to me, for I can recall it perfectly even now.

The regiment left Silesia at the beginning of April 1808 and moved to the Baltic coast where we were billeted around Danzig. The headquarters and the *compagnie d'élite* were billeted in a small town called Lauenburg and we stayed there for six months. It was during this period that Sergeant-Major Pierre of the 3rd Squadron had a most unfortunate experience. He had drawn three months' pay for his troop from the regimental paymaster and, having lingered in the company of the N.C.O.s of the *compagnie d'élite*, he decided to set off late at night instead of waiting until the next morning as we advised him. He therefore started out in the dark, carrying his bag of money in a peasant's cart. He had only four leagues to go before reaching his troop's billets. However, sleep overtook him and as one of the floorboards of the cart was missing the bag containing the pay fell out on to the road.

As soon as he became aware of his misfortune he retraced his steps, but his search was in vain. When we heard the news from headquarters I had the happy inspiration of suggesting to my comrades, to whom I was due to give three months' pay that very day, that they should contribute something to offset Pierre's loss. The N.C.O.s willingly agreed and I asked them to draw up a list of donations. They started it by generously offering their three months' pay.

The scheme obtained the approval of the officers and they expressed a wish to contribute. Consequently, the loss was made good twice over within twenty-four hours.

Colonel Castex was delighted at our action and thanked us by an order of the day in which he expressed his satisfaction and pleasure in commanding a regiment where such a fine spirit of comradeship existed. The worthy sergeant-major, who had been so wretched on the day when he lost his troop's pay, was thus not held to blame for the mishap and he was both deeply grateful and overjoyed as a result of the way in which the officers and N.C.O.s had so generously come to his help.

The small town of Lauenburg is about fourteen leagues from Danzig and the quartermasters had to make the journey there every four days to draw white bread, soup and issue bread. Towards the end of December 1808, I was returning after drawing supplies and, as usual, the duty orderlies and I were wrapped in our cloaks as we lay on the straw in the carts. Night was falling and we were still two leagues from Lauenburg when our cart suddenly halted and cries of horror made us all leap down from the carts.

Holding our sabres ready we started running over the snow-covered road to the head of the convoy where the cries came from. The alarm had been caused by a pack of wolves which lived in the forest through which we were passing. Driven by hunger, they had attacked with extraordinary ferocity the horses and the leading carts containing the bread. The peasants who were in charge of these carts had taken refuge beneath them. The other chasseurs and I killed several of the wolves, but we realized that it would not be possible to hold out for long so we decided to escape as rapidly as we could, taking with us the two carts which had not yet been attacked. Having thus shared the spoils between ourselves and the wolves, we reached Lauenburg where I reported the incident to my captain. He, as was only right, ordered that the inhabitants of the town should replace the bread which the wild animals of their forest had stolen from us.

The next morning I rode out with several other N.C.O.s to inspect the place where we had been so violently attacked by the voracious wolves. We found that there was not the slightest trace of any bread and there were hardly any bones of the horses left. What seemed quite extraordinary to us was that the wolves which we had killed still lay untouched on the road, which would seem to prove the truth of the saying that wolves do not devour each other.

On 1 January 1809 we left Prussia, but before our departure we learned through an order issued by the Emperor that out of the reparations exacted from Prussia he had set aside one hundred million francs to be distributed among the army as follows: any N.C.O. or man who had fought at Jena was entitled to 15 francs: if he had also fought at Eylau he was entitled to 30 francs; if he had also fought at Friedland he was entitled to 45 francs. Moreover, any man who had been wounded in either the Prussian or the Polish campaigns was to receive the maximum award.

I was included in this last category and I received 45 francs. The Quartermaster General of the army, Villemanzy, was responsible for the distribution of the money. The officers, of course, received a bounty whenever they embarked upon a campaign.

Eventually we reached the quarters which had been allocated to us near Frankfurt-on-Main. The headquarters and the *compagnie d'élite* were billeted in the beautiful village of Bockenheim where the inhabitants are mostly Jews. It was here that my good friend Henry, no doubt thinking that soon we would recross the Rhine and be once more in France, said to me one day: 'Parquin, do you think *le Petit Caporal* is not going to lose his temper any more? Will there be no more campaigns for us?' Pointing to the space on his left shoulder for an epaulette, he added: 'Will we never obtain that?'

Then, putting his hand over my heart where the cross of the *Légion d'honneur* is worn and on my shoulder where the epaulette is worn, he asked: 'And will you never win this—and this?'

Alas! My brave and noble friend little knew that he would die gloriously in the campaign for which he so longed. That campaign would bring him the epaulette which he so desired, but he would wear it for only three months.

V

We were billeted at Bockenheim until 1 March and we greatly enjoyed our stay there thanks to the nearness of Frankfurt which was only half a league distant.

One day I went to Hanau, a small town four leagues away, where the headquarters of General Oudinot who commanded the combined grenadiers was situated. My father had sent me a letter from one of the general's friends, a Monsieur Grélé who was a lawyer in Paris, and had asked me to deliver it to the general.

The general received me in a most friendly manner and after enquiring how long I had served in the army, he told me as I left that I would shortly hear further from him and, indeed, a week later Colonel Castex sent for me and asked me if I would like to be made a sergeant in the 5th Troop. However, when I replied that I did not want to leave the *compagnie d'élite*, the question was not pursued. One month later when Sergeant Jouglas became sergeant-major with the 2nd Troop, I was made a sergeant in my own troop. This was on 2 February 1809.

I little anticipated the pleasant experience which befell me at the time of my departure from Bockenheim. I had been billeted for two and a half months with a rich Jew who was the rabbi of the local synagogue. He was a widower and his only daughter, Mademoiselle Sarah was a tall, dark beauty. She was twenty years old and looked after a school for young girls of her faith. I had lived on very good terms with my hosts; I had always been polite and considerate, especially with Mademoiselle Sarah, but our relations had stopped at that. The proximity of Frankfurt, where I spent most of my time very pleasantly, had probably caused me to neglect my hostess. I had therefore left my billet at five o'clock on the morning of our departure without feeling any regrets. I certainly did not think that anyone else might regret my going. I joined the other quartermasters and we were about to set out for Frankfurt when I looked in my sabretache and discovered that I had forgotten the notebook which I used for matters relating to the troop. The regimental sergeant-major granted my request to return to my billet.

When I reached it I found the main door open; my orderly who had left after me had forgotten to close it. I therefore hurried upstairs without knocking and made my way to my room which was on the first floor overlooking the street. When I entered I was astonished to see the lovely Sarah weeping by my bed! She was wearing a morning gown and her beautiful black hair hung in disorder over her shoulders. In her hands she held my notebook which she was covering in tears.

At this unexpected sight I was at first struck speechless, but I quickly recovered and approached her, saying as gently as possible: 'Why are you weeping, Sarah?'

'I am weeping for you, ungrateful wretch!' And more tears came flowing fast. This explanation left me in no doubt, so I did my best to console the delightful girl. I told her that now I was aware of her love, I too was heart-broken to be leaving. . . .

Our happy moments together flew by; the neighing of my horse which my orderly was holding in the street and the stamping of its feet on the cobblestones reminded me of my duty. I had to leave the tender-hearted Sarah who gave me my notebook with a plea that I should tear out and give to her the first page on which I had written my name.

Thereupon I wrote her name beside mine together with the date which, I assured her would be the happiest day of my life, and in this page I wrapped a locket containing some of my hair. I have always taken the precaution of having such a locket with me when serving abroad and this time its effect was magical.

'You make me so happy by giving me this souvenir, Charles,' she said, 'but we must say farewell, for if my father found me in your room he would have me locked up for the rest of my days.'

I tore myself from the arms of the tender Jewess and, deeply moved after this unexpected encounter, I left the house. As I galloped away, the cool morning air brought me to myself.

More than thirty years later I was passing through Frankfurt after visiting Switzerland and I stopped there to see one of my acquaintances, Monsieur de Saint-Georges, who had formerly been a partner in the banking house of Bethmann and Company. After dining with him and his family, I went with him into the portrait gallery to smoke some excellent Spanish cigars. I told him of my passing encounter with the beautiful Jewess of the nearby village of Bockenheim and I added:

'This morning was rather cold, but it was fine enough for a ride, so I thought I would go to Bockenheim to see Sarah and to find out what had become of her. I even started out, but halfway there it occurred to me that in all probability Sarah, if she was still alive, would be about fifty, married and surrounded by a flock of children.

That is what will have replaced the beautiful, graceful young girl, I thought, and I shall find only a faded portrait instead of that delightful moment which has remained so long in my memory. It is better to preserve a happy recollection than to destroy an illusion. And I returned to Frankfurt.'

Monsieur de Saint-Georges, who had listened carefully, said: 'Colonel, a German would have gone on. His determination would have taken him in spite of himself to meet Sarah, even after thirty years of separation.'

'But I suspect,' I commented, 'that the impeturbability which so clearly distinguishes the German from the Frenchman would not have given him the time in the circumstances to gather the rose which I plucked so rapidly in Bockenheim. Thus, if I may say so, a German would not have had cause to return to Sarah today.'

As we passed through Bavaria during the month of March 1809 the regiment halted for a few weeks at Bayreuth and in the surrounding villages. As I was the quartermaster of the *compagnie d'élite* at the time, I was billeted with the regimental headquarters in the town itself. Our captain had ordered an inspection for the troop on the first Sunday following our arrival. In order to purchase a number of items which were needed by my orderly for our uniforms I went into the haberdashery shop which was across the square from my lodgings. I was pleasantly surprised to find an attractive young woman in charge of the shop. More engrossed in studying her charming appearance than making my purchases, I stood there for a few moments before I recalled the purpose of my visit and it was only when she asked me a second time that I realized that I had not in fact entered her shop in order to look at a pretty woman.

Early next morning I returned to the shop to make some more purchases. A man who was in the shop and who seemed to be twice as old as the young woman was good enough to inform me of her name when he said to her in German: 'Louise, pass me the box of gentlemen's gloves.'

This request was made when one of my friends, who had come with me, asked for gloves. Thus, on my second visit I had learned the name of the lady who had so caught my attention and I wasted no time in using the information I had gained. On the third day I carefully observed the shop from my window until I saw the man leave. I immediately went across to the shop and entered on the pretext of buying a few small articles. There were a number of customers there and all I could do was to let the young woman see a letter which I held in my hand as I saluted on leaving. When I had left the shop I thought that my attempt had failed, but as I was going through the main entrance to my lodgings I felt someone tug the back of my jacket. It was the young assistant from the shop. She did not give me time to ask her what she wanted, but asked quickly: 'Where is the letter?'

'Here it is,' I said for I still had it in my hand.

The letter, which Gasner, one of the quartermasters, had translated into German for me, read as follows:

'My charming Louise, I desperately long to see you alone so that I may prove to you how your charms have captivated me. If you could find the means of meeting me alone, you would make me the happiest of men. Yours respectfully, Charles Parquin.'

A quarter of an hour later the same messenger brought me an answer which was as brief and to the point as my original note.

'Tomorrow at seven o'clock my husband is going out to play in an amateur concert. He will be there until nine o'clock. Be in the lane at a quarter to seven. The shop will be closed. There will be someone to guide you.'

Needless to say, I was at the appointed place on time. No sooner had I reached the darkened lane than I felt someone take my hand. It was the young assistant and she led me along the lane, across a yard full of casks and into a corridor. There my guide opened a door on the right and led me into a room lit only by a fire burning in the grate. She told me to wait there quietly and went out, closing the door behind her. I examined the contents of the dimly lit room and the first object which caught my eye was a bed.

'Good!' I thought as I sat down on it. A minute later the key to the room turned in the lock and the rustle of a satin robe indicated that the mistress of the house had arrived.

'Is that you, Louise?'

'Yes, Charles,' she answered.

Then, in true German style, she fell into my arms. It must be obvious that I was immediately made welcome and the story, so to speak, started at the final chapter.

An hour passed in this delightful tête-à-tête and our meetings continued in this manner for the next three weeks on the evenings when her husband went to play the bassoon at various concerts.

Louise apologized for not being able to give me a meal, but this would have meant lighting a lamp and such an action would have been most unwise in the circumstances.

She could offer only some excellent Alicante wine and biscuits, and in the comfortable darkness we both partook of these most pleasant refreshments.

The regiment left Bayreuth after being there a month. To take my leave of Louise I went to the shop itself for I made daily purchases there for the troop. Her husband had become so used to seeing me there that he offered me a farewell glass of wine. As I was leaving the shop Louise bade me goodbye in his presence, but it was in a more restrained manner than would otherwise have been called for by our relationship. I had, however, spent an hour with her the previous evening and then she had shown me by her passion and her sobs how sad she was to lose me—or at least, this was the impression that she gave.

Our regiment moved to Augsburg in Bavaria and we were given billets near to the town. On 10 April 1809 Prince Charles addressed the following letter to Marshal Davout:

'To the General commanding the French army in Bavaria:

'Consequent upon a warning given by the Emperor of Austria to the Emperor Napoleon, I have to inform the General commanding the French army in Bavaria that I have been ordered to advance with the troops under my command and to consider as enemies all those who oppose me.

'Dated this ninth day of April, 1809, at my Headquarters.'

Marshal Davout published this letter for the army to read and warned us that he was grouping his forces to march against the enemy who, in his arrogance, had dared to violate the territory of our allies.

In Paris, the Emperor had learned by telegraph on the 12th of the Austrian move and on the 17th he arrived at Donauworth in Bavaria. From this town he addressed the following proclamation to the army:

'Soldiers! The territory of the Confederation of the Rhine has been violated. The Austrian general believes that we will flee at the mere sight of his forces. I have come to join you with the speed of lightning. Soldiers! I was among you when the Austrian ruler came to my tent to beg for mercy and to pledge his eternal friendship.

'Victors in three wars, you have each time generously spared the Emperor of Austria; three times he has broken his word. Our past successes are a sure guarantee of the success that will be ours. Let us therefore march forward! Let our very appearance convince the enemy that he is already defeated!'

This proclamation was enthusiastically greeted by the whole army. We were part of the vanguard of combined grenadier units under General Oudinot, and General Colbert commanded our brigade which was made up of the 7th and the 20th Chasseurs and the 9th Hussars. It was popularly known as the *Brigade infernale*.

From the 10th until the 19th the army manoeuvred between Munich and Augsburg, but on the 19th we had a hard-fought engagement. Four thousand Austrians were captured or dispersed at Pfaffenhofen. The 7th Chasseurs distinguished themselves by a brilliant charge and took a great number of prisoners. The brigade pursued the enemy as far as Ratisbon [*Regensburg*], engaging him repeatedly. We reached there in the morning of the 23rd, the same day that the Emperor was wounded in the heel after he had approached within grape-shot range of the town. The news spread immediately throughout the army, causing a great sensation. Staff officers were despatched in all directions from the Emperor's headquarters to reassure the army. General Lauriston, one of the Emperor's aides-de-camp, whose son had recently joined the regiment as a lieutenant, came in person to tell us that the Emperor's wound was not serious.

The following day Marshal Davout won the battle of Eckmühl and for this he was made a prince. The King of Bavaria had just re-entered his capital which had been defiled by the presence of the Austrians who were now in complete disorder everywhere.

Before leaving Ratisbon, the Emperor thanked the army in these terms:

'Soldiers! You have lived up to my expectations; your bravery has more than compensated for your lack of numbers. In a few days you have triumphed in the battles of Thann, Abensberg and Eckmühl, and in your encounters with the enemy at Landshut and Ratisbon. The enemy, swayed by treacherous rulers, seemed not to have remembered what sort of army you are. You have shown him that you are more terrible than ever. But a short while ago did he cross the Inn and invade the territory of our allies; but a short while ago did he threaten to carry the war into the heart of our homeland. Today he is defeated, shattered and fleeing in disorder! My vanguard has already crossed the Inn; within a month we shall be in Vienna.'

General Colbert's brigade had led the way across the Inn and on 30 April General Oudinot requested the Emperor's permission to appoint as acting officers six N.C.O.s from each regiment of the vanguard so that they would be available to fill the various posts that would inevitably become vacant during the campaign.

On 6 May at ten in the morning the regiment, which was leading Colbert's brigade that day, caught up with the enemy rearguard at the village of Amstetten. The enemy was withdrawing towards Saint-Pölten in the general direction of Vienna.

There followed a sharp engagement in which Lieutenant Lacour was shot in the arm and several chasseurs lost their horses because of the fire from the enemy infantry which occupied a wood to the left of the road. At eleven o'clock an officer bearing a white flag appeared and was conducted to General Colbert. The Austrian general was seeking an hour's truce, and this was granted to him.

The regiment had been in the saddle since daybreak; both men and horses were in need of a halt. Colonel Castex immediately gave orders for the horses to be unbridled and to be given the feed of oats which every chasseur always carried in a small sack on his mount when in the field.

Not far from the spot where we had halted there was a swiftly-flowing stream of which we made good use. We did not waste a moment of our halt. The chasseurs, since they had no wine, drank the small quantity of brandy which they always carried with them in the field. A crust of bread, flavoured with garlic, constituted their modest lunch, but they ate this cheerfully for they were certain that at noon battle would be joined with the enemy.

Five minutes before the hour had passed, the trumpeters sounded for the regiment to mount and the colonel ordered the men to roll their cloaks and wear them in bandoleer fashion; this was the signal to the regiment that we were about to charge. We were drawn up in battle order; volunteers had gone forward to act as skirmishers and we were beginning to move forward when Colonel Castex said to me as he rode past my troop: 'Sergeant Parquin, I have your 2nd lieutenant's commission in my sabretache.'

He had just that moment received the answer to the request for six more officers for the regiment which had recently been made by General Oudinot and I was one of those who had been commissioned.

'Long live the Emperor!' I cried.

Then, turning to the others in my troop who were congratulating me, I said: 'Now that I am an officer I have to have two horses. If I cannot take one from the uhlans myself, I am counting on you to obtain one for me.'

'Rest assured, sir,' replied my worthy companions, 'we shall see that you have some horses for your stable.'

They kept their word, for the men from my troop captured twenty-two uhlans or hussars and after the charge they sought me everywhere so that I might choose whichever horse I fancied. But I had been wounded and was in the field hospital; moreover, I had myself taken two excellent horses from the enemy.

But to return to the moment when the regiment was about to charge, for I have jumped ahead of events.

We had just formed separate troops and had advanced a thousand yards down the road to Saint-Pölten when we perceived the enemy drawn up in two lines of battle on the plain. The first was formed by six squadrons of lancers and the second by the same number of squadrons of hussars. An hour later we learned that the lancers had all been recruited in that part of Poland which belonged to Austria. We soon recognized that they were Poles by their courage and by the way they handled their lances. They were, however, overcome in the pitched battle which they fought against the 20th and the 7th Chasseurs, although they were supported by Barko's Hussars who were rightly regarded as one of the best Austrian cavalry regiments. The uhlans and the hussars were cut down and put to flight; the pursuit lasted at least two hours. We cut down and captured about 300 of the enemy cavalry and General Oudinot, who recognized the true value of a victory on the battlefield, did not hesitate to say that he preferred this achievement by his vanguard to the capture of 10,000 militiamen.

At this point I should mention the rather unusual incident which involved one of my comrades. During the hour's halt when, as has been seen, the regiment took the opportunity to feed the horses, one of these animals wandered loose near the colonel's bivouac in the middle of the regiment and almost crippled him when it lashed out. Recognizing by its colour that it was from the 2nd Squadron, the colonel ordered 2nd Lieutenant Grignon who was nearby at that moment and who belonged to that squadron, to have the horse caught and returned to its rider.

I do not know what happened to prevent the colonel's order from being carried out before the animal, which was greatly enjoying its freedom, came through the bivouac a second time. The colonel, annoyed to see that his order had not been obeyed, had Lieutenant Grignon put under arrest. Arrest at that time meant that an officer was deprived of his sabre and it was clear that the regiment was going to charge for the trumpeters had just sounded for the regiment to mount and the skirmishers had already engaged the enemy.

A downcast Grignon approached the colonel and begged to have back his sabre which the regimental sergeant-major had taken. He said that he had but recently joined the regiment from the *Vélites*[1] and

[1] Special units raised by Napoleon in 1805. In them young volunteers were given an intensive educational course before being commissioned.

this was the first time that he had had the chance to cross swords with the enemy.

Colonel Castex refused and informed the officer: 'I have taken your sabre away for the day to punish you.'

'But not to prevent me from engaging the enemy,' said Grignon, spurring his horse forward. With his pistol he shot dead one of Meerweldt's lancers. He seized the dead man's lance and thus armed he continued to charge the enemy. In the evening the colonel, who had learned of Lieutenant Grignon's dashing action, congratulated him and told the regimental sergant-major to give back the sabre.

It saddens me to record that Lieutenant Grignon, with whom I became very friendly, died when serving as a captain in the regiment during the disastrous Russian campaign.

When I recall 6 May 1809, a day forever glorious in the annals of the 20th Chasseurs, I should not forget to mention the part played by the 7th Chasseurs. These two regiments from the same brigade were on the most friendly of terms with each other and supported each other wholeheartedly on the battlefield. When the uhlans were joined by Barko's Hussars they turned about and returned to the attack. This was a critical moment for the 20th who were engaged on all sides and whose only line of retreat was across a small bridge. However, Colonel Castex and the officers, taking no heed for their own safety, charged headlong against the enemy, thus giving the brave 7th time to arrive and the 20th time to rally.

In the midst of this mêlée Colonel Castex exhorted his men with words which still ring in my ears:

'Rally round me men, or you will lose the fruits of the finest charge ever made.'

Just then one of Barko's Hussars rudely interrupted him with a violent blow from his sabre which cut the colonel's cartridge-pouch in two. As soon as he felt the blow the colonel wheeled around to defend himself, asking: 'Who dared to do that?'

But the hussar who had dared to do that was no more, for even as he had struck the colonel he had been shot down by the colonel's trumpeter who was acting as his orderly. It was at this moment also that Major Bertin and another officer, Maréchal, who only an hour before had been promoted, were both mortally wounded. Two other officers, Boissard and Maille, were both seriously wounded by lance-thrusts. In short, the regiment was deprived of ten officers, including two killed, out of the thirty present. None too soon, Hulot, a young and fearless major of the 7th Chasseurs, arrived with his men. The troops commanded by Salmon and Paravay followed him across the bridge and charged headlong against the enemy, battering to the ground, cutting down and running through anyone in the path of their terrible charge. Then the 20th returned to the attack and the rout of the enemy was complete.

Major Hulot, who later became a brigadier-general and an honorary major-general, was the brother-in-law of General Moreau. He served on the staff of the Prince de Neufchâtel minus an eye and an arm during the Russian campaign.

As the enemy fled I advanced in a straight line with a few men from the *compagnie d'élite* towards a bend in the road so as to cut off the uhlans as they retreated, but one of Barko's Hussars whom I had overtaken rode up to me and fired his pistol at point-blank range. The bullet ploughed through the flesh of my left arm, pierced my jacket over the left breast, went through the forage cap which was inside my jacket and came out on the right side of my jacket. Realizing that I was wounded and losing a great deal of blood, I turned around and retired to the rear. I had gone scarcely fifty yards in this direction when I met Colonel Castex who asked me where I was going.

I replied that I was going to the field hospital for treatment and I showed him my wound and my sabre which was stained with enemy blood.

'As you see, sir, I have done my duty.'

'Yes indeed,' he commented, 'I have been watching you, Parquin.'

I then made my way to the field hospital which was on the main road a league to the rear. There I found the black horse with the short tail and short ears which had belonged to an officer of Barko's Hussars.

It was my property as I had shot and killed that officer. I had given the horse to a chasseur whose own horse had been injured. Another horse now belonged to me. It had formerly been the property of an uhlan whom I had wounded. I had given it to Saron, a boy trumpeter who was only twelve years old, and I had told him to lead it to the rear as he was not strong enough to exchange blows with an enemy as powerful as the one against whom we were fighting.

When I arrived at the field hospital the surgeon, seeing the quantity of blood that I had lost and that my jacket was pierced on both sides, feared that the bullet had gone right through my body. He was so anxious to verify this that he tore four buttons off my jacket in his haste to undo it. It was then that I was able to congratulate myself on being wounded in the arm only; the bullet which could have killed me had passed in front of my chest.

In this same encounter young Lauriston, who had been with the regiment but a few days, clashed with an uhlan captain whom he unhorsed. Having taken refuge beneath his horse, the uhlan raised his hands and cried: 'I surrender! I am your prisoner! Do not hurt me!'

Lauriston ordered the captain to emerge from beneath the horse and sent his prisoner to his father who, as an aide-de-camp of the Emperor, was at headquarters. When the prisoner arrived there, certain flatterers transformed the captain into a colonel whom the former page had engaged in single combat in the presence of the whole regiment. This is how misrepresentation of facts enters the history books, for this distorted account was reported to the Emperor and was published in full in army orders. These facts, which I record solely in the interests of truth, in no way diminish Lauriston's merit for he gave frequent proof of his courage during his service with the regiment. At the battle of Wagram he had two horses killed under him and he distinguished himself by his outstanding ability as a staff officer during the Russian campaign. One day in 1814 I happened to visit his father, General Lauriston, and I could not take my eyes from a painting which depicted his son on horseback engaged in single combat with the uhlan colonel.

'Captain Parquin, you are a member of the 20th Chasseurs; would you say that it is a faithful representation of the battle?'

I do not possess the art of flattery so I replied: 'Indeed sir, the uniforms are most accurately done.'

In this way I extricated myself from the embarrassing position in which the question had put me, without distorting the truth at all.

But to return to the hospital where I found many chasseurs and several officers who had been wounded. Among the officers there was a 2nd lieutenant who had just been appointed to the regiment from the *Vélites* of the Imperial Guard. This was 2nd Lieutenant Maille. I said to him: 'My friend, if we remain on the road, as things are at present, we shall be badly quartered and liable to unfriendly treatment. If you will strike out to the left or to the right with me we will probably find a more comfortable place.'

He agreed, so we went a few leagues to the rear and took the road to Linz which ran to the left of Amstetten. We arrived at the little town of Steyr where, in return for our offer of protection, the priest took in Maille, while I lodged with the burgomaster. With us were two chasseurs who had only slight wounds. We were able to rest in our new quarters and we were treated by the local surgeon who happened to be the burgomaster. After a fortnight we were well on the road to recovery, but for it to be complete we still needed another few weeks. When the burgomaster informed us of the battle of Essling he made it seem like an Austrian victory. I immediately asked my companion if he wished to rejoin the regiment, adding that at such a time when the army had suffered a setback, it was every officer's duty to rally to his regiment.

'But neither you nor I have recovered, Parquin,' he observed.

'We shall recover on the way. Our return will encourage the others.'

'Possibly; but riding a horse is out of the question for me. I would suffer too much from the lance wound in my stomach.'

'Do not let that hold you back; there is always the priest's carriage. I will ask the mayor to requisition it and you will be able to travel in comfort until you are able to ride a horse again.'

'Let us wait one more week.'

'Agreed. We will leave on 1 June.'

On that date we set out, my friend Maille in the priest's carriage, and I on horseback. I was able to stand the journey by carrying my arm in a sling.

The same day we reached the main road to Vienna and we passed over the ground where we had been wounded and where several of our comrades had been buried. This was the place where the brigade had covered itself with glory. On 3 June we entered Vienna. We were told that the brigade had been operating since 12 May with the cavalry under Major-General Montbrun which formed the vanguard of the army corps under General Lauriston. These forces were to link up at Neustadt with the Viceroy [*Prince Eugène*] who was driving the Archduke John and his army back into Hungary.

We found quarters in Vienna and it was there that I met an infantry officer of the Imperial Guard whose family lived at Joigny and knew my father well. Out of courtesy I invited him to dinner. Monsieur P. was serving in General Michel's division. This division had that very morning been reviewed at Schönbrunn on its arrival from France and its general had awaited the Emperor's comments with considerable trepidation since the division had arrived a day late.

'The reason for the delay is worth relating, Parquin,' said Monsieur P.

'I should like to hear it,' I said.

'Well, Parquin, you can imagine that a division of foot grenadiers drawn from the Young and the Old Guards is a unit which the Emperor can expect to be punctual. When General Michel left the

Ecole Militaire in Paris he had orders to join the Emperor on 1 June. The stages of his route had been carefully worked out and the general believed that no power on earth, short of an order from the Emperor himself, could hold him up for even a day, because once across the Rhine, the division was to press on without delay.

'However, when the division arrived in Stuttgart the general and his officers went to call on the King of Wurtemberg who welcomed them warmly and complimented the general on the smart appearance of his officers. Then, to General Michel's great astonishment, the king announced that he intended to review the division the next day. The general begged to be excused this honour; he explained that the days allowed for the march were finely calculated; that he had to arrive at Schönbrunn on 1 June and that the Emperor had given a specific order to this effect.

' "I shall review your men, General," said the king, "or else you will have no supplies, no quarters and no transport for your baggage-train."

'When the general protested, the king added:

' "I believe that I am the master here. You should therefore pay heed to what I have just told you."

'The general could well have said to the king: "Sire, with my division I could take my supplies wherever I choose; I could even take possession of your kingdom."

'Instead, the general merely said: "Your Majesty presents the case in such a way that it is impossible to refuse. At what time, Sire, will you review my division?"

' "At noon," replied the king and then he dismissed us.

'That same day General Michel despatched a messenger to inform the Chief of Staff of what had happened. The next day we were reviewed by the King of Wurtemberg. His Majesty was seated in an open carriage, but none the less revealed an enormous paunch. This provoked roars of laughter from the soldiers who, moreover, were quite taken aback by this novel manner of reviewing troops. In the evening the officers were invited to dine at the palace. The king courteously complimented us on the fine bearing of our division, saying that he had that day seen the bravest troops in the world.

'The following day we left Stuttgart, but the incident caused us to arrive a day late at Schönbrunn. The Emperor, who had been fore-warned, observed to the Prince de Neufchâtel in the presence of General Michel:

' "If that man (meaning the king) were thirty years younger and could shed two hundred pounds of fat in a day, I would make him my chief of staff for I cannot but admire his spirit." '

When Monsieur P. had finished his story he left me to return to his quarters. I bade him farewell as the next day I was taking the road to Neustadt with my friend Maille in order to travel to Hungary.

On 5 June we arrived at Oedenburg [*Sopron*], a small town in Hungary. Maille had borne the journey well. Unfortunately, I had not, for in the intense heat my wound had worsened and my arm had swollen considerably. When I had found quarters I sent for the doctor who, after examining my arm, expressed his surprise that I had undertaken a journey before the wound had closed. He added that gangrene might develop in the wound if I continued my journey, especially on horseback in such hot weather. I quickly came to a decision. I allowed Maille to continue alone and I set about making a full recovery. The doctor told me that I would be perfectly fit again within three weeks and I did not hesitate to spend that time in this town where the doctor treating me seemed an excellent man.

I had been in Oedenburg two days when I received a visit which took me quite by surprise. The burgomaster and two town councillors came to see me and when I asked the purpose of their visit, the burgomaster explained the position thus:

'Sir, the town of Oedenburg was occupied for the first time towards the end of May by the corps under General Lauriston. When he moved on, the general left no officer to be in charge of the town and to maintain order while troops are passing through. As a result, there are stragglers arriving daily and they are very demanding and behave badly towards the citizens with whom they are billeted. Since there are no French authorities here to maintain order, we have come to ask you, sir, if you will take command of the town until your wound has healed. The doctor treating you is a member of the town council and he has said that it will be at least three weeks before you recover completely. We should be deeply grateful, sir, if you would agree to our request.'

'Gentlemen, I will accept the offer which you have just made in the interests of both my fellow countrymen and of the citizens of this town. However, nothing will make me stay longer than my recovery requires.'

The very next day I had a sentry at my door and a detachment of four men under a corporal of the civic guard reported to me for their orders. I thus assumed the post of town commander of Oedenburg. I had been in this post for two days when a group of officers arrived on foot. They were members of the Viceroy's bodyguard and they were on their way to rejoin him. I allocated them the officers' quarters to which they were entitled, but I had the greatest difficulty in obtaining these quarters from the citizens who were convinced that these gentlemen were only private soldiers although their uniforms were bedecked with silver.

On 10 June a messenger from the Chief of Staff arrived, bearing despatches for General Marmont who was in Laybach [*Ljubljana*] in Illyria. I had no means of ensuring the delivery of these despatches for the road to Illyria and the road to Italy were cut by the irregular forces under General Chasteler[1] who had been detached with his cavalry from the Archduke John's army to harass the Viceroy's army in the rear. I was, however, anxious to ensure that these despatches reached General Marmont whose movements would certainly be important. The Chief of Staff's messenger was aware of the dangers and would not go further despite my urgings. He was due to stop at Oedenburg and, refusing to go on, he handed me the packet from the Chief of Staff. It was ten o'clock in the evening. I immediately summoned the town council and put my plan to them.

'Gentlemen, I have some despatches which must be carried to Laybach in Illyria for General Marmont. I want you to find me an intelligent man who speaks French; it should not be difficult to find such a man among your citizens. You will provide him with a good post-chaise and a servant. You will give him a passport showing him to be a Hungarian nobleman who is going to Illyria to take the waters for his health. If he is stopped by General Chasteler's guerrillas he will show his passport and they will certainly let him pass as the guerrillas do not search or otherwise trouble their fellow countrymen. If he does not meet any guerrillas, but meets French troops instead, then he will show them the despatches which he has to deliver to General Marmont and his mission will be accomplished.

'What do we need, gentlemen? Four things; an intelligent Hungarian, a post-chaise, a passport and money. Here are the despatches against which the burgomaster will give me a receipt. I would add, gentlemen, that if things are not done as I have instructed, then the Emperor will be informed of your bad faith and your citizens may expect to have to pay an exceptionally heavy penalty.'

The council conferred there and then and agreed to all the points

[1] General Chasteler (1763–1825) was Belgian by birth. He had fought in the service of Austria against the Turks in 1789 before being active against the French in the Tyrol. He ultimately became the governor of Venice.

of my plan. Before the week was out the messenger had returned, bearing a receipt from General Marmont whom he had found with his corps some distance beyond Laybach. The messenger also handed me a packet for the Chief of Staff and I likewise sent this on by means of a Hungarian messenger.

On 15 June a messenger from the Emperor's personal staff arrived with a letter addressed: 'To the Town Commander of Oedenburg in Hungary.' It was written entirely in Napoleon's hand and was quite illegible. General Lemarois, the senior aide-de-camp, had however copied it out quite legibly on the other side of the sheet. This was what the letter said:

'Commander, General Chasteler with a force of Austrian cavalry has come down on the rear of the Army of Italy to wage guerrilla warfare. The Polish Light Horse Regiment of my Guard[1] will arrive to garrison the town of Oedenburg. You will cooperate with its colonel to ensure that the road from your town to Komorn is not cut and you will remain alert to any enemy movement.

'Schönbrunn. 15 June 1809. Napoleon.'

The next day when the regiment arrived, fodder, supplies and billets were ready for it. I immediately went to call on General Krasinski, the colonel of the regiment, and I informed him of the contents of the Emperor's letter which he asked me to leave with him. As the letter concerned his regiment's movements he wished to retain it.

On 14 June, the anniversary of Marengo and Friedland, Prince Eugène won the battle of Raab over the Archduke John and the Archduke Palatine who had joined his brother at Komorn with six thousand Hungarians, conscripted in a new levy. The result of the battle was the complete rout of the archdukes who lost many men killed, several cannon, a number of standards and five to six thousand men who were taken prisoner. On the 16th several wounded men from the 20th Chasseurs arrived at Oedenburg. They included Corporal André from the *compagnie d'élite* and I hastened to ask him for news of the regiment.

'We suffered heavily,' he told me, 'especially the *compagnie d'élite*. Captain Capitant and 2nd Lieutenant Henry died of their wounds.'

These last words brought tears to my eyes. 'Poor Henry!' I cried. 'Did he die instantly?'

'I saw him fall from his horse, struck by a ball which shattered his

[1] Formed in 1807, this was the first of the three lancer regiments in the Guard. Like the 3rd Regiment it was recruited from among Poles.

thigh. He was taken to the field hospital and in the evening the troop was told that shortly after enduring an operation with great courage, he had died.

'Captain Capitant,' added André, 'was doubly unfortunate, for his death came about as a result of others trying to save him. It was seven in the evening and firing had ceased along the line. In fact, I think it was the last round fired by the enemy which struck the captain. He had just dismounted and had asked someone to hold his horse so that he could go a little distance away from the others in order to relieve nature.

'He was standing there with his legs apart facing the enemy when those who were still mounted suddenly saw a cannon-ball flying over the plain straight at him.

'Immediately they called out: "Beware, Captain, there is a cannon-ball coming straight at you!"

'At this warning the captain instinctively brought his legs together. As he did so his right leg was shattered. Without this fatal warning it is probable that the ball would have passed between his legs. A few moments later he was dead.'

I was truly sad to hear of the captain's death, but of course it was the news of Henry's death that most upset me.

On 20 June I received from the Prince de Neufchâtel's headquarters a number of proclamations which were to be posted throughout the town. The aim of these proclamations was to alienate the Hungarians from the cause of Imperial Austria. But in 1809 the Hungarians were deeply attached to the Emperor of Austria and their loyalty only increased as a result of his recent misfortunes. I remember that the Emperor Napoleon addressed them in terms which should have been capable of stirring them:

'Hungarians! I seek nothing from you. You have a national tongue; now become a nation! Assemble on the plains of Racos to elect a leader as once your fathers did. I will accept your choice.'

The Hungarians, as I have said, remained unshakably attached to their ruler. All the proclamations in Latin and German which were posted in the morning were torn down that night.

I had been three weeks in Oedenburg and my wound was healing splendidly. I wrote the following letter to the Prince de Neufchâtel:

'Sir, When the troops under General Lauriston went through Oedenburg in Hungary, no town commander was appointed. As I was passing through this town to rejoin my regiment, a wound which I had received on 6 May and which I thought had healed, opened and forced me to break my journey. The burgomaster and two members of the town council came and asked me to assume command of the town. I accepted their offer for, not being fit for active service with my regiment because of my wound, I felt that I could still be useful to the army in the post which had been offered me. Now that I have recovered and my duty requires me to rejoin my regiment, I have the honour to request that your Serene Highness send an officer to relieve me as commander of this town which, because of its importance, should be closely supervised. I have the honour, etc. 24 June 1809.'

On 28 June a staff officer holding the rank of major arrived with orders from the Prince de Neufchâtel to take over the command of the town of Oedenburg. He had been instructed to acquire all possible information about the town from Lieutenant Parquin and to authorize the latter to rejoin his regiment if his wound had fully healed.

I left the town the next day, taking with me, I think, the respect of its citizens. I decided not to go by way of Raab, but to take the most direct route to Vienna and I rejoined my regiment at the bridge over the Danube. I was happy to meet my comrades again and they gave me a very warm welcome. But it was heartbreaking for me not to find my friend Henry there. I was given more details about his death. Sergeant Nicoloux, who had attended to his removal to the hospital, told me that when the amputation had been carried out, he tried to encourage Henry about the outcome, saying:

'Now, sir, in a few months you will be in Les Invalides, marking out manoeuvres in the gravel with your stick.'

'I told him stories to take his mind off what had happened,' added Nicoloux, 'but I was most afraid that after such a serious amputation fever would set in and carry off poor Lieutenant Henry. I was dreadfully concerned, but I hid my fears. Suddenly the lieutenant asked me to give him his sabretache. I did so and I saw him take out a small travelling mirror. Then, after glancing at it, he shook my hand and said: "Farewell, Sergeant. Thank you for caring for me. Remember me kindly to my friends, both present and absent. (I counted myself among these for Henry and I were very close to each other.) Tell them I die happy for I have seen the face of death without flinching." A minute later this brave man died. His death caused much grief throughout the whole regiment.'

On 5 July we camped in a village three leagues from the plain of Wagram. That evening as we all lay sleeping on straw in an abandoned peasant hut, I awoke at midnight and I saw Lieutenant Raux still busily writing.

'What are you doing there at this time of night?' I asked.

'I am writing to my parents and to a young girl whom I love, who loves me and who is my fiancée. I am writing to tell her that in tomorrow's battle I shall be killed.'

'You are imagining things,' I said. 'You ought rather to believe that the opposite will happen.'

Thereupon I went back to sleep. At five o'clock I awoke for the trumpet was already sounding in the village. Soon afterwards I was in the saddle.

On 6 July the dawn, as it broke on the horizon, revealed a forest of bayonets which shone from all points of the plain as they reflected the sun's light in a thousand different directions. From afar could be heard the beat of drums. Everything indicated that it would be a fine, warm day. Our brigade had returned to its position as vanguard of the combined grenadiers in Oudinot's division. From eight in the morning we manoeuvred in the face of the enemy's fire. Then at midday the thirty-three squadrons of Colbert's brigade, to which we belonged, trotted forward in column to occupy the centre of the army behind the hundred cannon of the Guard commanded by General Lauriston.

We were still exposed to the enemy artillery fire which was answering ours from a strong position. The Guard gunners had taken off their coats to work in greater freedom.

Lieutenant Lauriston commanded a troop to the right of mine. Every half-hour his father would come over to see him. He had left him barely a minute when a cannon-ball went through Lauriston's horse. The ball went in behind the rider's left calf and emerged behind his right calf. Lauriston fell beneath his horse and when I saw him lying there I thought for a moment that his left leg had been blown off. I immediately ordered some chasseurs to dismount and extricate Lauriston. Then I asked him: 'Is your left leg causing much pain?'

He answered: 'My dear Parquin, it is quite numb; I have no idea whether it is broken.'

Finally the chasseurs managed to pull him from beneath his horse and our anxiety disappeared when we saw Lauriston jump to his feet.

'There, no harm has been done. It missed me.'

'Well my friend,' I said, shaking hands with him, 'I congratulate you. You have been very lucky.'

He went away on foot to obtain one of his father's horses as none of the regiment's led horses had been able to cross the Danube. The order had been given to allow combatants only over the bridges and our servants had remained behind.

Half an hour had gone by when I saw the general coming back, probably to see his son again. I immediately sent a corporal to meet him and to reassure him that nothing had happened to his son.

We had been an hour in this perilous but honourable position—for we were supporting the hundred cannon of the Guard in case the enemy cavalry should charge them—when at last the fire of our artillery silenced the Austrian guns. Then the brigade started moving forward in the same direction and in the same order as that in which it had arrived. Farther forward, cannon-balls were falling among us and some fell near the Emperor, past whom we were advancing. Before reaching our position, which was in front of the combined grenadiers, we crossed a broad stream which winds across the plain of Wagram and by two o'clock we were drawn up in line of battle. The enemy squares, six deep and supported by Prince Hohenzollern's artillery, occupied the plain ahead of us. Lauriston had hastily rejoined us, riding one of his father's horses. He had not had time to replace with his own regulation saddle the gold horse-cloth and fine saddle which were on his new mount.

General Oudinot galloped past his brigade and called out to Colonel Labiffe, whom he knew: 'Make ready, Labiffe, you are going to charge!'

At that very moment General Colbert gave the order for the brigade to charge and the 7th and the 20th Chasseurs and the 9th Hussars rushed fearlessly forward against the enemy squares on the plain. Led by the general himself, the 7th charged resolutely, but at one hundred paces a terrible volley from the square facing it caused the most fearful confusion in the ranks of this regiment.

General Colbert was hit in the head by a bullet and several officers and fifty or sixty chasseurs were killed or wounded. The 7th had to turn back. Seeing this, Colonel Castex, instead of charging the square in front of him as he had been ordered to do, chose to lead the regiment, which was advancing at the trot, against the square which had just repelled the 7th Chasseurs with its fire. He therefore ordered the squadrons to incline to the right and charge.

The square could not resist this new charge and was broken. To the left the 9th Hussars had overcome its square. Thus the brigade had taken two out of its three objectives in the face of artillery fire from the enemy who, seeing his squares broken, opened fire with grapeshot on both us and the enemy infantry whom we had captured. Lieutenant Lauriston had no sooner rejoined us than an enemy shot again struck down the horse which he was riding. This caused the general to observe later that evening: 'You might at least have taken the worst hack from my stable instead of my best horse if you were going to get it killed.'

My horse had received a bayonet thrust in the left shoulder while we were breaking the square and as I was making my way back with my lame animal I came across the same Lieutenant Raux who the previous night had forecast his own death. He was going to the field hospital with a slight wound in the thigh.

'There!' I said. 'You can now see there was no need to let your foreboding worry you.'

'You are right,' he said. 'I have escaped lightly. I was wrong to write home as I did last night.'

He had scarcely uttered these words when a flying piece of grapeshot shattered his head, killing him outright. I informed Colonel Castex of what had happened to Lieutenant Raux and also told him of the lieutenant's forebodings. The letter which he had written the previous day was recovered from the post orderly and the regiment's *conseil d'administration*[1] wrote to the family to say that this officer had been wounded and that he had died of his wounds a week later.

At half past three the battle of Wagram had finished for our brigade, whereas Massena's corps on the left was still engaged at midnight. The regiment bivouacked in the area where it had captured the two infantry squares of the Prince of Hohenzollern to make a total of 2,000 prisoners.

The battle of Wagram, in which Prince Charles put up the most strenuous resistance, brought the army 20,000 prisoners, various standards and thirty cannon. It can be seen that the brigade's action contributed greatly to the final result of the battle.

In this battle the army lost one of its most intrepid leaders, General Lasalle. On the morning of the battle he too had forecast his death. The horse which he rode in battle had been carelessly taken at four in the morning to be watered at a stream beyond the forward picquets and had been captured together with the orderly by an enemy patrol. This was the first unpleasant occurrence of the day for the general. A little later when he was looking in his saddle holster for a small bottle of excellent French brandy which his servant never failed to put there, he was disappointed to find only pieces of glass. The bottle had been broken.

[1] This council was composed of the senior members of a regiment under the presidency of the colonel. It dealt with the internal affairs of the unit.

'What a wretched day!' said General Lasalle. 'It is the sort of day on which I shall get killed.'

Two hours later he was mortally wounded in a brilliant charge made against the enemy squares at the head of the many squadrons which had so often followed him to victory.

Major Daumesnil and Major Corbineau who were chasseurs in the Imperial Guard each lost a leg. It is well known how the Emperor rewarded these two brave officers. He appointed Daumesnil to be the general in command of Vincennes and it was there that Daumesnil, at the time of our misfortunes in 1814, covered himself with glory by his retort to the enemy who had taken Paris and who called upon him to surrender: 'You may tell the Allies that when they give me back my leg, then I shall give up the keys of the fortress. Until then they would do well to keep out of the range of my cannon if they do not wish to feel their effect.'

It was this same Daumesnil who, as a trooper in the *Guides* under General Bonaparte, had risked his life to save that of his general at Acre. He was standing a short distance behind the Commander-in-Chief and Berthier, holding their horses and his own, when a shell landed four paces from the group. At the sight of the danger to which the general was exposed, Daumesnil did not hesitate; he rushed forward and with his own body covered the man who was to become his Emperor. Fortunately the shell had gone deep in the sand and it did not explode. Seeing that there was no more danger, Daumesnil returned to the horses. 'What a soldier!' was General Bonaparte's short comment, but coming from him this was the equivalent of any number of compliments.

General Corbineau waited until the Emperor had returned to Paris before asking for his reward. When the receivership of taxes for Rouen fell vacant in 1810, he appeared at a levee held by the Emperor and requested the post. It is well known that this post is one of the most important in France and a very substantial bond has to be deposited by the holder.

'And where will the bond come from?' asked the Emperor.

'My leg, Sire.'

'And from me probably,' said Napoleon with a smile.

The general received the post. Such rewards were merited by the devotion of these officers and the granting of them gave pleasure to the whole of France.

The Emperor wanted to choose personally a major-general for his Guard from among the colonels in the army. Marshal Bessières presented him with a certain number of candidates, the last name being that of Colonel Lion. The Emperor glanced through the list and stopped at the final name.

'I must have a lion in that regiment,' he said, and the Colonel of the 14th Chasseurs was made a major-general in the Guard Chasseurs.

It was in the battle of Wagram that the Polish Light Horse Guard Regiment, which had come to Oedenburg when I was there, had a bloody encounter with an enemy regiment of lancers. With their sabres and their carbines the Light Horse overwhelmed their opponents and then seized their lances, for the lance was the favourite weapon of the Poles, to complete the rout. Still armed with these lances they successfully attacked that day the regiment of La Tour's Dragoons, which was the Austrian equivalent of one of our regiments of mounted carabiniers. When that evening Marshal Bessières gave the Emperor an account of the glorious exploits of the Light Horse, the Emperor said: 'Let them henceforward be armed with lances since they are able to use them so well.'

The day after the battle of Wagram the army learned that the Emperor had made Major-Generals Macdonald, Oudinot and Marmont, Marshals of the Empire. In his camp-fire gossip the French soldier, with his usual perception in these matters, saw the appointments thus:

> Macdonald is France's choice,
> Oudinot is the army's choice,
> Marmont is friendship's choice.

VI

From 7 July until 10 July the brigade, now without its general who had returned to Vienna because of a head wound, operated under the command of Colonel Gautrin of the 9th Hussars.

On the 10th we were incorporated in General Montbrun's division which moved to Znaym [*Znojmo*] where we found that the enemy had concentrated and drawn up his army. We thought that a battle was inevitable. The two corps under Massena and Oudinot had advanced as far as the outskirts of the town; fighting had started and the guns were roaring when an officer under a white flag appeared at one of the outposts with a request for safe conduct for the Prince of Liechtenstein who wished to see the Emperor Napoleon and ask for a truce. The armistice was concluded on 13 July and was to last for a month with a fortnight's notice of termination on either side. This meant that the army, and the brigade in particular, had excellent quarters in Moravia until the peace was signed. I was sent with twenty-five men to a beautiful village which had two or three hundred houses and in which there was a vast palace belonging to Prince Esterhazy.[1]

I had drawn up my men in the square in front of the church so that the sergeant whom I had sent on ahead could allocate the billets. I was surprised to see that I was to lodge with the priest and not at the palace.

'Well, sir,' said the sergeant, 'I thought you would be better in a house where you would have a host than in the palace, for the Prince is absent and there would only be his steward to receive you.'

A certain vanity at the thought of being able to give Prince Esterhazy's palace as my address in my correspondence caused me to choose the palace as my quarters even though it was empty. I therefore rode up to the palace and gave notice of my intention to stay there. The steward gave me most comfortable rooms and when he came to ask me if I had any orders he assured me that they would be carried out in every respect. In addition, he informed me that the cellar was well stocked. Indeed, he seemed to want me to incur expenses rather than avoid them. To have some company I invited my sergeant to come up to the palace to dine with me every day.

I was not long in my isolation. A few days later General Piré, his

[1] Prince Nicholas Esterhazy (1765–1833) is remembered now, not so much for his wealth, but for being the employer of the composer Haydn.

aides-de-camp, the headquarters and the *compagnie d'élite* of the 16th Chasseurs arrived in the village. General Castex had agreed that they could share the area allocated for our billets and that General Piré himself could move into the palace, provided that they did not displace the officer and twenty-five chasseurs who were already settled in. I hastened to offer my room to the general and he accepted it on condition that I would take the next best room available and that I would agree to dine at his table. This I did willingly. The general's aides-de-camp were Lieutenant Castelbajac and my old friend Guindey who in 1806 had become a lieutenant in the 10th Hussars.

Everyone enjoyed the most comfortable conditions. The Prince's steward was a sight worth seeing; far from being annoyed he was beside himself with joy. Rubbing his hands together, he said to me: 'This is capital! Now you will be able to live in a style worthy of Prince Esterhazy! With guests such as these, guests like General Piré who never travels without a good cook, it will be worth the effort of keeping the accounts, for I must admit sir, that as far as you were concerned, I would have been ashamed to have presented the Prince on his return with an account for expenses which did not exceed ten florins a day for you and your men.'

'Is your master so rich then?'

'What! Have you never heard of the wealth of Prince Esterhazy?'

'No, I have not, although his name is familiar to me; prior to the Revolution the 3rd Hussars bore the name of Esterhazy.'[1]

'Well, my master is, I believe, the richest prince in Europe. Apart from his vast fortune in diamonds which is handed down from generation to generation, his estates, which are largely in Hungary, are so extensive that there are up to ten thousand sheep grazing on his lands.'

Twenty years after the period of which I am talking, Madame Parquin and I received a visit from Prince Esterhazy at Wolsberg. He had just bought the château and the island of Maiman which were situated on Lake Constance a few leagues from Wolsberg. The Prince was a well-preserved old man who was still quite capable of riding a horse well and who was as charming as possible to the beautiful woman with him. It would have been difficult to meet a more elegant man; he was one of those great noblemen of the *ancien régime* of whom Monsieur de Talleyrand was one of the last representatives in France. A well-informed acquaintance in Constance told me that the Prince's fortune had been taken over by a family council which was

[1] The Esterhazy Hussars were raised in Strasbourg in 1734.

administering his estates. I was not at all surprised that such a misfortune should have overtaken him—if only because of his choice of such a lavish steward in Moravia. But to return to our stay in Moravia in 1809 which lasted three very pleasant months.

The general was an excellent soldier who lived well and who enjoyed the company of young people. Among his men the tale was told of how as a hussar captain in the Prussian campaign he had gained entry under cover of darkness to an enemy-held fortified city—Graudenz, I think—with a body of soldiers who nearly all spoke German. He had exacted a considerable sum of money in taxes and had returned to his regiment at daybreak, leaving behind an astonished enemy army which had never seen the like of his audacity.

At ten o'clock lunch was served and at five o'clock there would be dinner, followed by coffee and liqueurs. There was an excellent billiard table for passing the time, apart from dice and cards which were constantly in use on the gaming-table.

On 15 August the shooting season opened and heaven knows how much of our time this pursuit took. The general was a very good shot. We never returned without bringing back vast quantities of game to the great joy of the steward who was exceedingly proud of anything which was a new proof of his master's wealth and a new excuse for expense. In this area shooting is the exclusive right of the local nobleman and the owner of a field is liable to the severest punishment if he kills game on his land with anything other than a stick. The general, his aides and I would never go shooting without having behind us one of the Prince's huntsmen who would carry loaded double-barrelled guns which he would hand to us when we had fired.

One morning when we were tired of killing hares, partridges and foxes, Castelbajac and Guindey struck a bet as to who would shoot down the most swallows. After a quarter of an hour neither of these two gentlemen had killed a thing. They were squabbling with each other about their mutual incompetence when Guindey, to prove his accuracy, suggested to Castelbajac that he would fire at one hundred paces at a part of the body which shall be nameless, using shot. He also promised that after he had fired he would put himself in the same position to receive his opponent's attempt. One had to be very young, as indeed these gentlemen were, for such a challenge to be issued and accepted. Nevertheless, they had taken up positions at the agreed distance and were about to start the wager when I fortunately intervened.

'My dear Guindey,' I said, 'I do not want to prevent you from exercising your skill at your own expense, but I must ask you to return immediately the pair of trousers which I have lent you and which you are wearing, for I do not care to see them perforated in this new game which you have invented for yourself.'

This request, which I made with a most serious expression on my face, put an end to the challenge which would undoubtedly have left a painful mark on one or other of them.

On 15 September General Colbert, who had recovered from his wound, drew up his brigade, which was thirty squadrons strong, on a plain near the road to Brunn to be reviewed by the Emperor who arrived on the stroke of noon. It was a fine day at the end of summer. The brigade was in three lines formed by the 9th Hussars, the 7th Chasseurs and the 20th Chasseurs. The Emperor went along the ranks and seemed to be quite pleased. He made several promotions and awarded a few decorations. The number of these was never more than twelve for each regiment in each campaign. The Colonel was made a commander of the *Légion d'honneur* and a few days later his promotion to the rank of brigadier-general was announced. The two majors in the regiment requested, and obtained, their release from the army. Monsieur Curély and Monsieur de Vérigny, two captains from the 6th and the 7th Hussars were appointed to be majors in the regiment. They were excellent officers, as will be seen later in these memoirs.

Lieutenants Lacour and Lauriston were made captains. Among the officers decorated was my friend Maille. He was an excellent officer, but not at all military-looking; he seemed more like a retiring but worthy civil servant. This impression, moreover, was an accurate indication of his future career; thirty years later I met him again and this time he was the very popular mayor of the small town of Doullens.[1] When the Colonel presented Maille and told how Maille had been wounded in the charge against the uhlans, the Emperor, perceiving nothing very martial in Maille's appearance, said:

'Wounded? That is not enough! Did he wound any of the enemy? That is the point!'

'Sire, this officer has done his duty,' answered the Colonel, and Maille was decorated. The Colonel also nominated the regimental paymaster for a decoration.

Either because his name, Jeanjean, did not conjure up visions of a man of action, or because of some other reason, the Emperor merely rubbed his thumb and first finger together and said: 'Paymasters have their own rewards.'

[1] It was at Doullens that Parquin died while in prison in 1845.

The Colonel, however, pointed out that the officer in question had served the regiment well for four years—and this was true. To settle the matter one way or the other, the Emperor asked: 'Can he take command of a troop?'

The Colonel affirmed that he could, although in fact it was most improbable that he could—and Jeanjean was decorated. The review concluded with all the squadrons galloping past to cries of 'Long live the Emperor!' Afterwards the Emperor told the Colonel that the regiment would wear cloth overalls after 1 October. Until then we had worn twill overalls in the field.

Following the signing of the peace in October the regiment started its return to France at the beginning of November. At the same time, Major Cavroi of the Guard Chasseurs was appointed as colonel of the regiment. The regiment returned to Bavaria and halted in the region of Bayreuth. Towards the end of January 1810, the news of the Emperor's divorce became known throughout the army. I must say that as far as I could judge by what I saw in the regiment at least, this action was not viewed with favour in the army where the Empress Josephine enjoyed great popularity. The fact was that nothing was more true than the comment of the Emperor himself: 'Josephine, you win over hearts for me, whereas I win the battles.' Well-informed people realized that the divorce was a political and dynastic act. The soldiers, however, when they saw someone as good, as gracious and as charitable as Josephine cast aside, considered that here was an act of base ingratitude. The name of Josephine often returned to their lips at the time of our defeats. When they spoke of the Emperor, they could often be heard to say: 'He ought not to have left Josephine; she brought luck to him, and to us as well.'

On about 10 February 1810 the regiment left Bavaria to return to France and by 1 March we were at Strasbourg. General Castex, who had married and settled there, came with General Colbert to review the regiment at Kehl. The officers of the regiment gave a dinner for the generals at the Hôtel de la Maison-Rouge in Strasbourg. It was at this time that I became acquainted with Monsieur Bro and Monsieur de Brack who were aides-de-camp to General Colbert. The second of these two officers was known in the army as 'Mademoiselle de Brack'; not that there was anything unmanly about him. On the contrary, he was known to be a very good soldier and an excellent officer. However, his youth, his extremely white skin, his blond hair, the absence of any moustache and his elegant figure were responsible for this name.

When we returned to France across the bridge at Strasbourg in

1810 it had been almost four years since we had left across the Rhine at Mayence. During these four years I had taken part in the Prussian campaign of 1806, the Eylau campaign of 1807 (when I had been wounded and taken prisoner), and the campaign of 1809 when I had been shot in the right arm. I might add that, to use the Emperor's expression, if I had been wounded, this had not happened without my wounding quite a few of the enemy. The only reward for my seven years of service, however, was a second lieutenant's modest epaulette. Yet this was a time for self-sacrifice. Ambition was satisfied by the very act of fighting so that our country would triumph over its enemies, so that France would deserve her title of *La Grande Nation*. The Emperor rewarded us for our sleepless nights, our exhaustion and our wounds with these words: 'Soldiers, I am pleased with you; you have surpassed my expectations.'

In 1810 I had just turned twenty-three; I was both proud and happy; I was an officer in the French Army!

In the first week of March General Colbert's brigade was divided into detachments, made up of fifty men and one officer, to cover the route from Strasbourg to Compiègne. These were to act as escorts to the new Empress, Marie-Louise. I and my detachment were at Sarrebourg. Our orders were to escort the coaches which were to travel at a trot on the open road and to go through the towns and the villages at a walking pace so that the people could approach and see the Empress. His Excellency the Prince de Neufchâtel, who as the Emperor's proxy had solemnly married the daughter of the Holy Roman Emperors on 11 March in Vienna, was responsible for the safe passage of the coaches. General Lauriston, who was one of the Emperor's aides-de-camp, travelled in the Prince's coach. The sixth coach was that of the Empress, on whose left sat the Emperor's sister, the Queen of Naples.

General Colbert was acting as equerry to the Empress; there was also one of the Emperor's chamberlains in attendance. He should have ridden close to the righthand door of the coach in which the Empress was travelling, but he often fell behind and seemed to be suffering from the strain of the journey. Because of this I received an orange which Marie-Louise passed out of the window. It was probably intended for him, but I took it from the hand of the Empress; not seeing the chamberlain, she left the fruit in my hand.

The general had invited the officers of the brigade to have one of their own horses ready for him at the point where each detachment took over the escort duty. At Strasbourg my servant brought him the horse which had belonged to the Barko's Hussars officer and which had become my property after the clash with the uhlans. This horse, with its short ears and short tail, was far from being young or handsome. It was, however, most pleasant to ride for it moved with a very regular shortened hunting gallop to which it seemed to have long grown accustomed. When he arrived at Blamont, which marked the end of the stage, the general came to tell me that my horse had allowed him to relax for the first time during a tiring journey and he asked me to let him keep my horse for another stage. I agreed to the general's request for I was anxious to oblige him.

I had just had the opportunity of seeing Marie-Louise closely and she seemed to me to be a very beautiful woman. She had a most graceful figure, a very fresh complexion, beautiful teeth and a particularly pretty hand—which is always the sign of a pretty foot.

At the stop at Blamont, after the inevitable formal speech by the mayor, a naïve-looking villager wearing a three-cornered hat approached the coach and, having removed his hat, said to the Empress:

'Madame, make our great Emperor truly happy, and be sure to give him many children.' Then he finished his short speech by crying: 'Long live the Empress Marie-Louise and the Emperor Napoleon!'

At the simple words of this Lorrainese peasant Marie-Louise could not hold back a smile and, turning the the Queen of Naples, she said: 'This Frenchman seems to me to be very impatient. He will have to wait until I am married, at least.'

That evening the procession continued on its way. Whenever it halted for the night the Empress never failed to receive a letter from her illustrious husband.

The general returned with many thanks the horse which I had lent him. A few days later I received from Lunéville a letter in which he instructed me to send him this same horse and to indicate the price I was asking. I hastened to do as I was requested and I said I was asking fifteen louis. I was pleased to let the horse go since I was entitled to fodder for one horse only when in France. A week later I received from the general not fifteen louis but thirty, which was the price at which he had sold the horse to the Prince de Neufchâtel who wanted it for hunting at Grosbois. Furthermore, the general wrote that he had never in his life ridden an animal with such a pleasant gait.

The regiment reassembled and remained at Nancy for twenty days before setting out on 1 May 1810 for Nantes. On 1 July came an order to despatch six hundred mounted men to Spain under the command of Major de Vérigny who came himself to see me one morning. He wished to know if I would go with him to act as his adjutant since the officer who held this position had fallen ill. I was very flattered by this honour, but I pointed out to the major that, being the most junior officer in the regiment, I could accept this post only if given a definite order. Indeed, I could not accept it until my appointment had been officially promulgated in an order of the day to the regiment and to the detachment which was leaving for Spain. When the position had been officially confirmed I purchased an excellent charger from Major Curély, who was remaining in Nantes, and on 5 July I set out for Spain.

We arrived at Irun on 5 August; by the 15th we were at Vitoria, where we became part of the 9th Corps which was commanded by the Comte d'Erlon. The general inspected our squadrons and then grouped us around him in a circle and complimented us, saying that he already knew our regiment for it had served under him in Moreau's campaigns. He added that he hoped we would uphold in Spain the good reputation which he had seen us make for ourselves beyond the Rhine. The six hundred men of the 20th Chasseurs provided four full-strength squadrons and together with a similar number of men and horses from the 7th and the 13th Chasseurs formed the brigade commanded by General Fournier-Sarlovèze. The 9th Corps remained for one month in Navarra and then set out for Salamanca where it arrived on 15 September. The brigade was quartered in Salamanca, Toro and Zamora and in the areas around these towns. The *gros major* of the regiment arrived to take command of the detachment; he had just left the regimental depot which for five years had been at Bonn.

At Salamanca my duties as adjutant obtained for me excellent quarters in the house of a beautiful Spanish noblewoman, Doña Rosa de la N . . . whose husband, a colonel in the Spanish army, had died two years previously. Like any widow who still retains a touch of vanity she had instructed her maid to say she was twenty-five and this was the answer I received when I sought this detail from the maid. But this little lie, if indeed it was one, was not at all necessary for, whatever her age, Doña Rosa was one of the most enchanting women I have ever seen in my life. She was quite small, but her movements were marked by a supple gracefulness. When she started to dance to the sound of the castanets and the tambourine which she played herself, she was thoroughly Spanish; when she sang to her own piano accompaniment she seemed quite Italian. She had no children and lived alone with her servants in a house where comfort and even luxury were clearly in evidence.

Mine were very good winter quarters; I could have had none better. Every evening I would spend an hour or two by the fire with my hostess. I had to avoid politics in our conversation as Doña Rosa, who was as proud as any Spaniard could be, would not tolerate contradiction. In the end I persuaded her to agree to banish politics from our conversation. This was a considerable achievement, but had I not a far more pleasant subject to touch upon with this charming woman. . . .

The town of Salamanca is fifteen leagues from the Portuguese border which Marshal Massena had crossed in the spring of 1810 on the Emperor's orders. The whole country was in rebellion. The roads were cut and that winter the rivers had all burst their banks. On the morning of 11 February 1811, Major de Vérigny sent for me. He instructed me to arrange for one officer and fifty chasseurs to be ready and mounted by noon; he himself would command the detachment. The men were to take only their weapons for they were to return the same day from their mission in the area around Salamanca. They set out exactly at noon.

The strictest secrecy had been maintained about this mission. These were the circumstances which had led up to it.

A French merchant, Monsieur Magnan, had wanted to return from Ciudad-Rodrigo to Salamanca and had taken advantage of the departure of a detachment of infantry for Salamanca to start out with his young wife. He had already completed the first stage and two-thirds of the second when, urged on by his wife who was anxious to finish the journey, and also thinking that he was out of danger, he whipped up the mules pulling his carriage. He had not gone a league when, at a bend in the road at a spot where it ran through a forest, the carriage was attacked by a band of brigands with pistols in their hands. Any resistance would have been useless.

Monsieur Magnan, his pretty young wife, his servant, his mules and his carriage were led half a league into the forest. The bandits robbed the prisoners of all their possessions and were preparing to put the men to death and to make the unfortunate woman submit to an even worse fate when the leader of the band, prompted by the thought of obtaining a substantial ransom, offered Monsieur Magnan his life and his wife's honour for 10,000 francs in gold. This sum was to be paid by one of Monsieur Magnan's friends in Salamanca. The offer was joyfully accepted and the merchant wrote a note to one of his associates, telling him to pay the bearer the sum demanded. At eight in the morning one of the bandits left with the note, but without any weapons. If he had not returned by three in the afternoon the prisoners' fate would be sealed.

Monsieur Magnan had some funds deposited with his associate and he was sure that the latter would hand over the 10,000 francs, but in the meantime he, his wife and his servant had to endure an agonizing wait. The carriage which the brigands had seized contained food and the captives were given a share of it.

Armed with his letter of credit the messenger arrived at the house of the person who was to pay him. This was a Frenchman who, like Magnan, followed the army with the purpose of selling supplies to it. The undated letter was so brief that his suspicions were aroused. He questioned the Spaniard who, not being able to speak French, said nothing but *dinero* as he rubbed his forefinger and thumb together. The merchant sent for his neighbour, Major de Vérigny, and informed him of his difficulty. The major immediately had the Spaniard arrested and ordered him to speak the truth or he would be hanged without delay. Some of his men prepared to carry out the major's threat. Thereupon, the bandit confessed everything; he revealed the danger which threatened the captives if help did not reach them by three o'clock. He offered to lead the French to the spot in the forest where poor Magnan, his wife and his servant were awaiting their fate. He said he would take a back-road which would enable them to surprise the bandits.

'If you keep your word and guide us there successfully,' said the major, 'I promise you your life, your freedom and a large reward.'

When the detachment set out at noon the Spaniard was riding an army horse held by a chasseur on either side. They had orders to kill him if he made the slightest move to escape. They had been riding for some time when the bandit signalled to the chasseurs to halt a Spaniard whom they met along the way. He was a scout belonging to the band of brigands and he was immediately seized. This man told the major that if they were to surprise the band they would have to take a path which he alone knew and he offered to lead the chasseurs along it. The major agreed, but warned the two guides that in the event of an ambush they would be instantly put to death.

The detachment went deeper into the forest and after moving in absolute silence for about ten minutes they suddenly came upon the band. They were not a moment too soon! The leader had become concerned and pointing to the time by Magnan's own watch which he had seized, he had said: 'It is now three o'clock. If, within the quarter of an hour which I generously allow you, my messenger has not returned with the 10,000 francs in gold, you and your servant may commend your souls to God. . . . As for your charming wife, who is all the more charming for her tears, her fate, although different from yours, is decided!'

Providence willed that this crime should not take place. Before the fatal hour came, Major de Vérigny and his men arrived and opened fire on the brigands without giving them time to reach for their weapons. Many of them were wounded or killed; the remainder flung themselves on their knees and, wringing their hands, begged for mercy.

Monsieur de Vérigny quickly undid the ropes with which the prisoners had been bound, gallantly starting with the lady, who was more dead than alive. All that had been taken from the travellers was returned to them and this allowed Magnan to give five gold *onces*[1] to each of the two thieves who had guided the expedition to such a happy conclusion. The major set both of them free with a warning to live more honestly in the future. The party started back for Salamanca. The dead, among whom was the leader of the band, were left where they lay. The rest of the band, who included nine wounded men, were bound and placed in carts which were requisitioned on the way back.

When they arrived in Salamanca the prisoners were handed over to the Spanish authorities who wasted no time in sending them to grace the various gallows beyond the town where it was customary to hang, albeit much against their will, all highwaymen caught in the act.

This incident, which was so skilfully and so successfully handled by Major de Vérigny, brought him considerable fame. I was assured that he was most pleasantly rewarded by the very real gratitude of the pretty young woman whom he had saved from the hands of such unscrupulous bandits.

Monsieur de Vérigny, who was only twenty-eight years old, was an outstanding officer. He was five feet four tall and had the most handsome features, his martial appearance being enhanced by a superb moustache. His elegant looks were matched by a highly original and amusing wit. In short, he was a most attractive person. I would like to mention one of his actions which did him great credit and illustrated so well his genuine consideration for others. When the *Légion*

[1] Gold coins worth approximately 85 francs.

d'honneur was founded he was a captain in the 6th Hussars and he was made a *chevalier*. Some months later he arrived home on leave at the same time as his elder brother, Monsieur de La Chasse de Vérigny who was a captain in the Engineers. Immediately the hussar captain removed his decoration and placed it in a drawer of his writing-desk, informing his family that for as long as he had the joy of being with his brother he would not wear a decoration which made him different from that brother. He was true to his word in spite of the earnest entreaties of his brother who was more proud than jealous of his younger brother's decoration. I saw both of these brothers in the Army of Portugal and they were a fine example of brotherhood.

My duties as adjutant gave rise to an unpleasant incident with a lieutenant of the 20th Chasseurs who was probably jealous of the fact that I had been preferred to him. Whenever I was on duty with him he always assumed an attitude of careless indifference. One day I warned him that he should arrive at the beginning of the roll-call and not, as was his habit, at the end. He took no notice of my warning and when he did not arrive on time to take his troop on a foraging expedition, I reported the fact to the major. As a result, Monsieur Hymonet received four days restrictions. When the four days had expired he came to find me and upbraided me in such a way that a duel was inevitable. He chose sabres, but we had no sooner taken guard than, parrying, I shattered the blade of his sabre. I could not riposte against an opponent who had been disarmed, so I said: 'I shall expect you in the same place in an hour's time.'

'Yes,' he replied, 'I shall be here and this time with weapons which will not break.'

I went to breakfast with my second and at ten o'clock I was once more face to face with my opponent. Lieutenant Hymonet had brought foils which had no *points d'arrêt*. They did not, however, bring him luck for my counter went home and he cried out: 'I have been hit!'

We rushed forward to help him. The result of this wound was that he was confined to his bed for a month and this caused him to observe that he would have done better to be on time for duty than to challenge me to a duel. He was not a particularly unpleasant man; he was simply an example of a swashbuckling type whom one met in the army. He was always ready for a fight. Having had little education and being endowed with a cantankerous and quarrelsome nature, he daily provoked incidents such as this one for example. A few months after our duel an officer of the regiment was in the mess talking quite modestly about the part he had played in a clash with a band of guerrillas. Hymonet, without the slightest provocation, abruptly asked him: 'Since when have you been so bold?'

'Since you have ceased being so,' replied the other to the satisfaction of everyone else present.

Another time at Zamora he went past my window with another officer. I supposed, quite rightly, that he was carrying weapons hidden under his cloak.

'Where are you going so early in the morning, Hymonet?' I asked.

'I am on my way to see off a depraved old blackguard.' (This was the way he used to speak.)

'Who?'

'Fage.'

This was an officer of the 13th who was a very brave and skilful swordsman.

'But, my dear fellow,' I said, 'you should be careful. That particular old blackguard is too good for you.'

'Good or bad, I take them all on.' This he said with no more emotion than a barber talking about his customers. Hardly an hour had gone by before Lieutenant Hymonet came back past my window with his arm in a sling; he had just been wounded in the wrist.

He was always unlucky in duels and his fellow-officers had dubbed him 'easy'—which was short for 'easy to kill'. In fact, he was very brave, but his idea of using a sabre was to swing it wildly in all directions. He never learned that a straight line is the shortest one and with his open style he never failed to be hit first. This is no way discouraged him; he would try different weapons, but misfortune would still follow him.

He used to predict to his colleagues that he would soon be a captain because his sister, the beautiful proprietress of the Café Feydau was, in his words, making strenuous efforts on his behalf. Indeed, she must have made some very strenuous efforts for he was in fact promoted and it was as a captain that he died in his final duel. This was how it happened. In 1823 during the war in Spain, Monsieur Delpech, a captain in his regiment, was mentioned in despatches for his part in an action against the enemy. This was too much for Captain Hymonet. He asserted that he should have been the one to be mentioned. This claim, which was completely unfounded according to the officers who were present at the action and who were in a position to judge, gave rise to a duel. The choice of weapons belonged to his opponent and he decided on pistols. The two men faced each other at twenty paces and this time the duel was fatal for Hymonet. The first shot fired by his opponent knocked him down. Unable to use his weapon to fire back, he dropped it and clasping his left side where the bullet had hit him, he cried: 'It is all over! This is the end! Farewell, all my bad habits!' These were his last words.

One morning during the winter of 1811 as I was walking in the arcade around the town square I met one of my friends, Monsieur V. . . . I had last seen him at Augsburg at the beginning of the 1809 campaign when he had just passed out of the Ecole Polytechnique[1] as a lieutenant in the Artillery. Now, two years later, I met him again and he was wearing the uniform of an aide-de-camp with a captain's epaulette and the cross of the *Légion d'honneur*.

'Tell me my dear V . . .,' I said, 'how is it that you have abandoned the Artillery when once you were so proud to belong to it?'

He told me that his decision to change resulted from a debt of gratitude, but as his story was rather a long one he invited me to go into Mariquitta's café to have a cup of chocolate while he told his story.

My friend was almost as fond of the pastries which Mariquitta sold as he was of the beautiful woman herself and I was quite happy to accompany him. This was his story:

'You no doubt remember, my dear Parquin, the splendid part played by Claparède's division in the battle of Ebersberg.[2] That day seven thousand Frenchmen sustained the onslaught of thirty-seven thousand Austrians and took six thousand prisoners, thirty cannon and three hundred waggons. The brigade which formed the vanguard included the battalion of Corsican riflemen who were known throughout the army as *les Cousins de l'Empereur*. They rushed the bridge over the Traun which was four hundred yards long and, needless to say, those brave Corsicans suffered terrible losses.

'The day after the battle the Emperor inspected the division and made a number of awards to the men. General Claparède presented me and said I was the officer whose six guns sited on the heights above the bridge had taken a heavy toll of the enemy and had successfully protected the division when it crossed the bridge. The Emperor was pleased to promote me to the rank of captain, but as you can imagine, Parquin, this was not the object of my ambitions at that stage, for in

[1] The Ecole Polytechnique was founded in 1794 to provide engineers for public works. In 1804 Napoleon instituted a military regime within the school which from that time also had to provide officers for the technical arms.

[2] Massena defeated the Austrians at Ebersberg in 1809.

such a victorious campaign promotion would inevitably have come my way. Therefore, as I followed the general during the inspection I begged him to ask the Emperor to award me a decoration.

'The general was kind enough to ask the Emperor, saying: "Sire, this is an officer whom you have just promoted to the rank of captain. However, he is not altogether happy about this as he would have preferred to receive the *croix d'honneur*."

'The Emperor turned on me sharply and, looking me up and down with his eagle eye, he said: "Young man, you want this decoration and you do not even have a beard yet!"

' "True, Sire," I said calmly, "but it was not a beard that commanded my battery yesterday."

'The Emperor was pleased with an answer which made him smile. He decorated me on the spot and allowed me to retain the rank of captain which he had conferred on me a few minutes previously. At the end of the campaign the general asked me if I would serve as his aide-de-camp. Out of gratitude to him I agreed and I came to Spain when General Claparède was appointed to command a division in the 9th Corps.'

I complimented Captain V . . . on his coolness and presence of mind and I swore that I would follow his example if the opportunity arose, as indeed it did at a later date.

Captain V . . . had just said farewell to Mariquitta, with whom he seemed on the best of terms, and we were about to go out of the café when I pointed out to my friend two infantrymen who were having a heated discussion in the arcade. Curiosity prompted us to open a window and we heard the following words:

'What!' the one was saying to the other who was searching in his pack, 'is there nothing left in the fund already? I thought there was still some money left.'

'You know quite well that we got only one *once* for the last piece we exchanged at the goldsmith's and we spent that on the way here from Coimbra in Portugal,' replied the other.

'Well, there's no shortage of goldsmiths here in Salamanca,' said the first soldier. 'Look, there's one here in the arcade. Let's try him with a piece of the Saviour.'

Thereupon the one with the pack unwrapped a gold statue of Christ which was about six inches high and from which the right arm had already been removed.

The two infantrymen then went into the goldsmith's shop to make some money by selling, as they put it, a piece of the Saviour. No doubt they would have to settle in another world the account for the sacrilege committed in this one. Soon afterwards my friend and I parted. He was leaving the next day to join the Army of Portugal.

I had been staying at the house of Doña Rosa de la N . . . for more than six months and I had not wasted my time there for I had eventually become the acknowledged favourite of this piquant Spanish noblewoman. The first week she had refused to see me and our only contact had been when I had sent my card to her. Soon afterwards I sent a note to her and I employed bribery to learn from the maid who brought me chocolate every morning that her mistress watched from behind the curtains of her room when I mounted to leave the house or dismounted on my return. This encouraging sign made me so bold as to ask if she would allow me to spend one hour each day in her company. This favour was granted me. Later on, as one can imagine, I did not stop there. I made further requests and in short, I was happy, very happy indeed.

Then I was ordered to organize a detachment of some two hundred men drawn equally from the 7th, 13th and 20th Chasseurs for an expedition into the Kingdom of Leon under the command of Major de Vérigny whom I was to accompany. Our first mission was a drive against the guerrillas who had been active everywhere for some time.

The drive was to last ten days and then we were to return to Salamanca. The second drive was to last the same time, after which we were to rest in the town of Toro. The third was to take us to Zamora. When I told Doña Rosa that I was to leave the next day, she kindly asked me to stay with her for supper. The meal reflected the circumstances and was not a happy one. When, however, I assured Doña Rosa that I would see her again in ten day's time, her natural gaiety gradually reasserted itself. Nevertheless, she would not dance or sing for me despite my earnest entreaties.

The next morning at six o'clock I was in the saddle and I made my way to the square where I found everyone present and correct. We set out at walking pace towards Toro. As I rode alongside Major de Vérigny, he said to me: 'Parquin, when we stop halfway, you will go on ahead with one officer and fifty men to act as the detachment's vanguard. You will find out from the alcalde [*magistrate*] of each village if any guerrilla bands have been seen in the locality. As you move on from each village you will leave a report of any information you have obtained with the alcalde. When we have gone seven or eight leagues we shall stop at the next village to which we come and spend the night there. We shall bivouac to avoid any chance of a surprise attack. You will establish a picquet with your men in the main square and post mounted sentries around the village. You will order a meal for the officers at the best hostelry in the village and this is to be paid for by the alcalde. Double rations of food for the men and fodder for the horses will be supplied by the village. You will make it clear that the N.C.O.s and men are strictly forbidden to demand anything from the villagers; their rations will be enough for them.

'General Fournier has ordered me to carry out a series of sweeps throughout the province of Leon and to employ the tactics of the guerrillas themselves. I have complete freedom of action; I can go in whichever direction seems best to me and I can move by night rather than by day if it means surprising the enemy. In our present role speed is of the utmost importance; there will be only two trumpet calls, one to mount and the other to dismount.'

We rode for nine days without encountering any guerrillas. It was not that there were none in the region, but the local population warned them of our arrival and as their function was not to engage forces against which they were almost certain to be defeated, they did not allow us to catch up with them. However, on the tenth day as we were returning to Salamanca I suddenly came upon the band led by El Pastor[1] at the ford across the Tormes three leagues above the town. Half his men were already on the other bank and the remainder could not stand up to a powerful charge by our chasseurs. We killed several of them, others were drowned in the river, and the ten who were taken prisoner bore the number of our regiment, as our expression was, where our sabres had marked them. Easy though this victory was, Major de Vérigny was delighted not to return to Salamanca without some results and our entry into the town was almost triumphal.

Before he dismissed me, the major gave me orders for our departure in two day's time. Then he went to report to the general and I hastened to Doña Rosa's house. When I arrived at the door I looked up at the window, but I was not rewarded for the curtains were not moving and I supposed that she had gone out. I soon learned otherwise; she was in her rooms and when I went to see her, her faithful maid told me that her mistress wished to be alone. I thought she was being unduly capricious, but I did not insist and I went into the town to while away the time before going to dine with the major. It was late when I returned to the house and when I was alone in my room

[1] El Pastor had been a shepherd in his youth. He was one of the most daring of the guerrilla leaders, operating mostly in the Ronda area.

I tried to enter Doña Rosa's room by means of a door which only I used, but the key had been removed. At first, I did not think that this had been done deliberately, so I went to bed, thinking that I would discovered the reason for Doña Rosa's strange conduct the following day.

As soon as I saw the maid in the morning I gave her a note for her mistress. Shortly afterwards I received an invitation to lunch with the lady of the house. I hastened to her room. There I greeted her with more reserve than might have been expected in a relationship such as ours and I tried to make it clear by my expression that I expected an explanation of her coldness towards me. During the entire meal she spoke only of quite unimportant matters, without making the slightest reference to my absence. I became increasingly irritated and yet I contained my impatience. When the servants had left and we were finally alone, I asked her openly: 'Madame, would you be good enough to explain your extraordinary attitude towards me? I am more than anxious to make amends if I have offended you in any way.'

'What!' she said, 'do you think I could have received you when you were still covered with the blood of my fellow-countrymen?'

'But I am innocent of your charge. If we should fall into the hands of the guerrillas, we are put to death, but the fellow-countrymen to whom you refer were taken prisoner by me and I took no reprisals against them. Everyone saw them when they were brought back to the town.'

She seemed to soften a little when she heard what I had to say, but I was so tactless as to add: 'But my lovely Doña Rosa, you are so patriotic!'

At these words she seized a small dagger which she always carried with her and, holding its point against my chest, she said with such ferocity that the words still ring in my ears: 'Of course I am patriotic! Charles, I am very fond of you, much too fond of you, for my duty should not allow me such feelings. But if I could free my country from the presence of foreign troops merely by plunging this blade in your heart, you would die at my hands.'

Then she hastened to add: 'But you may rest assured that my own death would follow immediately.'

'Madame, I much prefer you with your castanets and your tambourine. You should stop this tragic act; it is so unladylike.'

I had no sooner said this than she became so hysterical that I had to call her maid. Then, fortunately, she started to weep floods of tears and this calmed her greatly. The doctor who came did not want to bleed her as she had just eaten. He had her put to bed and prescribed a sedative. My mind was in such a turmoil that I went out to take some fresh air. I returned early and asked how Doña Rosa was. I was told that she was much better and that she had got up from bed in the evening.

I read a little until the time when I normally visited her room. Once again I was disappointed; her door was locked! Without lingering, I withdrew to my room for I took this as a sign that I had been formally and irrevocably dismissed. The next day as I left her house I sent a letter thanking her for the hospitality which I had received from her and stating that I would no longer require my quarters. In the courtyard I automatically looked up as I had done in happier times and glanced towards Doña Rosa's window. I was surprised to see her, although it was barely light, behind the curtains which she had pulled back slightly. I smiled regretfully in her direction and then galloped off, never to see her again.

VII

Once again the detachment set out, this time in the direction of Valladolid. We were still employing guerrilla tactics ourselves, but the enemy was always aware of our movements. However, one day, before we reached Nava del Rey we had an encounter with a band led by Lampessinado.[1] We put them to flight and took some prisoners. These were shot for previously we had come across several of our infantrymen who had been hanged by the roadside. In Spain the French infantryman was generally over-confident and for this he often paid dearly. One day I reprimanded a small group of soldiers who had fallen behind their companions and even behind the cavalry acting as rearguard. I asked them what they would do if a band of guerrillas found them where they were, cut off from the main body. In all seriousness they answered: 'Well, sir, we would form a square.' There were three of them!

One day the detachment halted at a village which suited us perfectly. There was ample fodder and the inn was a good one. To wait on us there was a Figaro-like character who impressed us as being very intelligent; so much so, that Major de Vérigny formed a liking for him and after supper several times offered him some mulled wine. This he drank as he smoked the cigars which he made so expertly himself. He played the tambourine, danced and sang Spanish songs which were not very complimentary towards us, but which were even less so towards the wife of the former king, Charles IV. We took him to be the innkeeper's son. He stayed with us until midnight and when he disappeared, we thought he had gone to bed. As for us, we stayed awake all night drinking mulled wine as we were leaving at daybreak. This, moreover, was our custom during these ten-day expeditions.

As we moved out of the village at five in the morning, I was surprised to see a shepherd, who was surrounded by his flock, beckoning to me. I left my place at the head of my men and galloped over to him. When I reached him he pulled a letter from his smock and handed it to me. I was astonished to read on the back of the folded letter the following address:

[1] Juan Martin Diaz (1775–1823). Known as El Empecinado, he became a general. After leaving the army in 1814 he entered politics and was hanged when absolute monarchy was restored.

'To the Adjutant of the French military force.

'For the attention of Major de Vérigny.'

Thinking that the letter might have some bearing on our mission, I opened it. These were the contents:

'Major,

'I El Pastor, the leader of the band with which you had a sharp encounter at the ford across the Tormes, wished to discover what sort of man you were, since you spared those of my men whom you captured. These, incidentally, have already escaped from the prisons of Salamanca and have rejoined me. I disguised myself and came to the inn where you spent yesterday, knowing that I could trust the innkeeper. Not only did I wish to discover what sort of man you were, but also to find out how watchful your picquets were and what sort of life you led. I compliment you on your precautions; they are too good to allow you to be taken by surprise. I assure you that otherwise, the Figaro who was waiting on you yesterday and who was none other than myself, would have returned with his band to take you by surprise in the middle of the night. As for your way of life and your idea of pleasure, I congratulate you wholeheartedly; you have the same devil-may-care attitude towards living as you have towards fighting. Since I do not care to measure my strength against men whom I admire, I shall move on to another region in search of opponents other than you.

'I wish you good health and good luck,

'Your humble servant,

'El Pastor.'

After giving a franc to the shepherd, I continued on my way and when I rejoined the major I handed the letter to him. I told him that I had read it as I thought it might concern our mission. Monsieur de Vérigny approved of my action. We could not but admire the boldness of the Spanish rebel leader and at the same time we paid tribute to the loyalty of the innkeeper who had made himself liable to a heavy fine for not warning us. The major told me to mention the matter to no one for General Fournier would not fail to exact a considerable sum from the innkeeper if he were to learn the facts. I recall the following saying of the French soldier, who did not hesitate to write it in large letters on the walls:

'This war in Spain means death for the men; ruin for the officers; a fortune for the generals!'

We made our planned halt at Valladolid and two days later we resumed our mission. In the middle of the day I was leading my men and from my seat in the saddle I could see over the wall of a burnt-out house. I was astonished to see a bright object glittering in the sun. I ordered my trumpeter to investigate the object. When he came back, he shouted to me:

'Sir, they are brigands' horses and they are saddled and carrying weapons.'

I immediately detached twenty-five men to surround the tumble-down cottage and to search it. We found two horses just as the trumpeter had described them. They were attached to a post and were eating some barley which had been spread out on a cloak for them. The pistols in the holsters were French. Lances were hanging from the saddles. It was clear, therefore, that the riders were not far away. It occurred to me to ride to the top of a nearby hill and from there I observed two men running towards the forest. I despatched some men after them and when the riders closed with them the breathless men stopped and were captured. When the major arrived with the main column I handed the prisoners over to him.

When they were interrogated they revealed that they were members of a band led by an unfrocked priest. Their leader was a pitiless man who regularly attacked the road between Valladolid and Salamanca. Prisoners taken by him were hanged from gallows which he

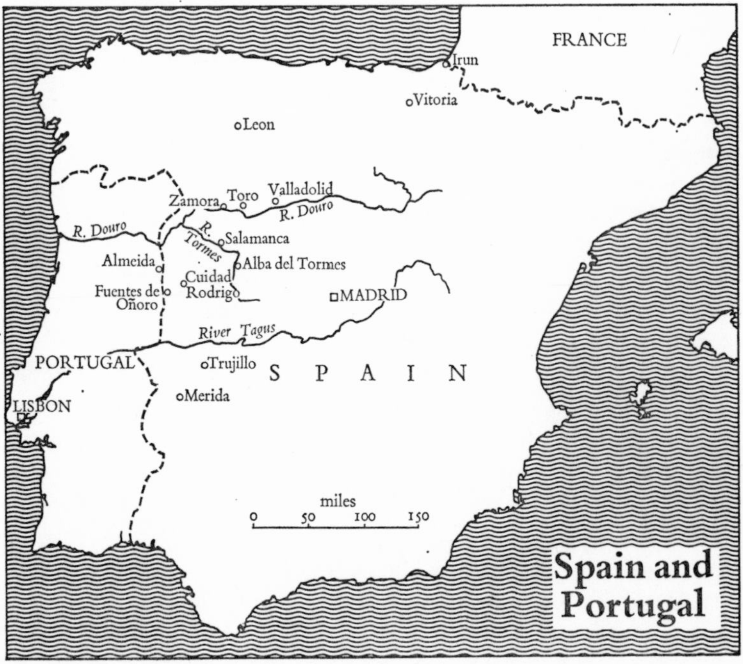

Spain and Portugal

erected for the purpose by the roadside. His cruelty was such that he even went so far as to disembowel any woman who fell into his hands. An unfortunate *cantinière*[1] had suffered this fate when she had been captured by his band a few days before we passed through Valladolid. If we had been returning to that town no doubt the sight of our two prisoners would have so enraged the troops there that their death would have been certain. The major, however, decided to take them to Zamora as the brigade had moved to this town. It seemed they would escape with their lives, but the order to search them was given. One of them, who looked like an officer and who had a recent sabre-cut on his face, was found to have a wallet containing a despatch written in French on blue paper for the garrison at Valladolid. This wallet belonged to a French officer whose body we had found lying on the road. The trial was not long. The major gave orders for them to be placed in front of one of the walls of the derelict house. A squad took aim and they were executed after they had crossed themselves and said:

'Every Spaniard is ready to die for God and his country.'

After this act of retaliation we continued on our way. The day before we arrived at Zamora an officer and twenty-five men joined us in the town of Toro. The officer, who was from the 7th Chasseurs, had brought a letter from General Fournier for Major de Vérigny. It ordered him to strike out towards the left to a ferry over the Douro, to arrive there before daybreak and to seize a band of smugglers. These were due to cross the river by the ferry with mules carrying colonial and other goods which they were smuggling across the border from Portugal into Spain.

The order was carried out as laid down. The location was so accurately indicated and our measures so efficiently executed that none of the men and none of the goods escaped us.

The smugglers, the mules and the goods were all taken to Zamora, except for a few of the mule drivers who were cleverer than the rest and who escaped. Major de Vérigny took advantage of the incident to distribute the mules of those who had escaped to the officers of his force. This was our only prize in a month of campaigning. Apart from these mules the whole convoy was handed over to General Fournier who disposed of it as he himself saw fit. We were not in a position to call him to account in this matter.

[1] *Cantinières* were engaged by the regiment's *conseil d'administration* in order to supply extra comforts to the men. There was one per battalion and she was usually the wife or widow of a non-combatant such as a musician.

We had been a fortnight in Zamora when one Sunday Major de Vérigny and I, who were dining with General Fournier, witnessed an extraordinary scene. To explain it properly, I have to go back to its origins.

The town of Toro, seven leagues from Zamora, was commanded by General Poinsot. He was noted for his bravery; when he had fought under Dupont at Baylen,[1] he had refused to surrender and had successfully reached Madrid with two squadrons of cuirassiers and a battalion of Guard marines.

One day, General Fournier visited him and found him sick in bed. He enquired after General Poinsot's health and then he noticed two piles of Spanish gold coins on the mantelpiece. In each pile there were twenty coins. Without any further ado, he pocketed one of the piles and said to his fellow general:

'As it is improbable that your paymasters in France send you coins like these, and as I am the general commanding the cavalry in this area, it is right that I should share them with you. I must go now. I wish you a good night and a speedy recovery.'

Thereupon, General Fournier, who had his horse and escort at the door, mounted and galloped back to Zamora.

General Poinsot was quite taken aback, but he swore that as soon as he had recovered he would go to Zamora to have the matter out with his colleague and to take back what belonged to him. He arrived on the morning of the Sunday of which I have spoken. I do not know what passed between the two generals, but, as I have already said, we were dining at General Fournier's house that evening. Suddenly General Poinsot entered the dining-room without being announced and said to General Fournier:

'It would seem that you want to have me killed by the guerrillas on the road back to Toro since you have given orders to your brigade not to provide me with an escort.'

General Fournier seemed to find the whole matter amusing and this infuriated his colleague, who addressed him thus:

'General Fournier, I am aware that you are able to snuff out a candle at fifteen paces with a pistol-shot. My ability is with the sword and I could hit you exactly on the spot where the fourth button of your uniform would be. That is my way of snuffing out insolent fellows like you.'

Then he left, saying: 'Until tomorrow!'

[1] In 1808 General Dupont, who had been sent to subdue the south of Spain was forced to retreat and his men were trapped in the pass at Baylen.

When he had gone, General Fournier merely ridiculed General Poinsot and asked Major de Vérigny to act as his second and to call upon the other general that evening to arrange a time for the duel.

The next day the major succeeded in preventing the duel for it would have been a very bad example for the army. He also settled the matter of the gold coins. In exchange for the ones he had taken General Fournier handed over an old grey horse which was reputed to have belonged to Marie-Antoinette and for which General Poinsot would certainly not have paid twenty gold coins, the equivalent of 1,700 francs, if he had had any choice in the matter.

On 1 May 1811 the brigade crossed the Douro and reached Ciudad-Rodrigo where we were incorporated in General Montbrun's division. The general was the most handsome warrior that I have ever seen. He was famous throughout the whole army for his bravery and for the rather forceful but fairly original comment which he made when he was encamped at Znaym in 1809. Captain Lindsai, his aide-de-camp, galloped up to him, shouting: 'Good news, General! I have just come from Vienna where peace has been made.'

'What damned use is that to me when I would rather have a good fight!' was the general's reply.

Two days later while out reconnoitring, we came across a unit of the British army. The major was anxious to meet some English officers, so he said to me: 'Parquin, here is a bottle of excellent French brandy. Gallop close to the English line and wave your white handkerchief. When they come to ask you what you want, tell them you have come to offer them a drink. If they accept, I and the other officers will join you.'

I immediately put the bottle in my sabretache and galloped forward, waving my handkerchief. When I was a little distance from the English line, an officer of the 10th [*Light*] Dragoons[1] galloped forward to me and when he had reached me, he asked what I wanted.

'I have come to ask you and your fellow-officers to share this bottle of brandy with me and my colleagues before we make contact with each other in a different manner.'

He accepted my offer and signalled to the other officers to come forward. I did the same to the major who arrived with some ten officers. The same number of English officers rode out to us. The The bottle was passed around and soon emptied. We all agreed that it was excellent, especially the English officers who thanked us for our friendly gesture which they seemed to appreciate greatly.

[1] Later 10th Hussars.

We started to talk amongst ourselves. They asked us how long we had been in Spain.

'But a short while,' I answered. 'This time two years ago we were at grips with the Austrians and now we have just arrived from France to make your acquaintance, gentlemen.'

'You are most welcome,' they all said.

One of them, with some pride, added: 'We have already met some of the best cavalry in the French army. We had an encounter with Napoleon's *Guides* and we took their leader, General Lefebvre-Desnoëttes, at Benavente [*29 December 1808*].'

'The general's rashness in attacking twenty of your squadrons with only four squadrons of *Guides*, together with an error of direction which prevented him from finding the ford across the river, were the causes of his reverse,' answered the major. 'We shall probably have the opportunity to take revenge for them in the coming campaign.'

An English officer asked us if there was anyone among us from the town of Moulins who would be kind enough to send on a letter for one of his friends who was a prisoner in that town. Dulimbert, the adjutant of the 13th Chasseurs, whose father was the Prefect at Moulins, was glad to offer to do so and the letter was brought to him under a white flag the next day.

It appeared that our meeting had lasted longer than the English general wished, for two or three shells fired from their lines fell near our group and forced us to break up our conversation, though not before we had drunk some of the rum which the English officers offered us in return for our hospitality.

The next morning General Fournier sent for me and ordered me to take command of a detachment consisting of a trumpeter, fifty chasseurs, a lieutenant and a 2nd lieutenant. We were to go to a village two leagues from Almeida to obtain as much information as possible about the movements of the English. He added: 'Parquin, this mission which I am giving you must be carried out intelligently.'

'I shall see that it is, sir,' I said to the general.

Ten o'clock was striking when I entered the village. I went through it at a gallop. Then I posted mounted look-outs beyond it in the direction of the Portuguese border and I ordered half of my men to dismount, to unbridle their horses and to feed and water them. Afterwards they replaced the other men who likewise attended to their mounts. Supplies including bread, wine and brandy were organized by the alcalde and brought out to the men at their posts.

Our unexpected arrival in the village had surprised the town-crier who was reading out a proclamation calling on the villagers to support Don Julian,[1] a notorious guerrilla leader, and to replace the losses in men and horses which he had just sustained. This was the last appeal which the alcalde was making for him and there would be no further requests for contributions after that day.

Followed by my trumpeter I went to see the alcalde from whom I learned that a strong English patrol had come at two o'clock in the night but it had required nothing of the inhabitants. After obtaining this information, I took out the proclamation which I had in my sabretache and I instructed the alcalde to hand over to me the sum of money he had collected for Don Julian's guerrilla band. The poor man fell at my feet; he expected to be hanged. I managed to make him understand that I would be satisfied with the money, but I wanted it intact without any of it missing. He rose to his feet and led me to his office. From behind some books on a shelf he took a box containing gold and silver and a variety of coins down to the smallest peseta. It came to a total of 6,000 francs, a sum which I would never have expected to find there. I put my trumpeter in charge of the money and I took my leave of the alcalde who seemed very relieved to be let off at this price.

When I returned to my detachment I divided the money into two sums of 3,000 francs each. The one was for my men; out of the other, I kept 1,500 francs for myself and gave 1,500 francs to the two officers under my command. Then I made a short speech.

'Men,' I said, 'the money which I have shared out would have been in the guerrillas' hands if we had delayed our entry here by only a few minutes; here is the proclamation by which the alcalde was asking for the money. The money, therefore, belongs to us. I ask only one thing of you, and that is, not to mention the matter outside yourselves.'

They all promised to reveal nothing and we returned to the brigade headquarters where I reported the details of our reconnaissance of the English movements to the general. The next morning the brigade mounted and set out. General Fournier and the 13th Chasseurs spent the day and the night in the village we had visited, but my regiment passed through it and camped a league farther on. Two hours later a messenger brought me an order to report immediately to General Fournier. When I arrived at the village I saw with some concern that

[1] One of the most influential and dynamic of the Spanish leaders, Don Julian was given overall command of the guerrilla bands in Estramadura.

he had taken up quarters in the alcalde's house. Nevertheless, I resolved not to be intimidated by the situation.

My fears were well founded. The general had made a demand for money too and the alcalde had told him that he had come too late, for an officer who had come the previous day had taken the 6,000 francs which he had in his possession. When I reported to the general he adopted a harsh tone and ordered me to hand over the sum which had been given to me the previous day.

'I am very sorry, sir,' I said, 'but I have only a quarter of it myself. The rest was given out to the officers and men of the detachment. But permit me sir, to point out that the government owes me more than a year's pay and it is not thanks to the government that I am able to have three good horses available, or to have good maps of all the provinces of Spain, or to be always ready to move whenever you have a difficult operation to be carried out. These assets have earned me your commendation as an intelligent officer on more than one occasion. Are you going to tell me, sir, that I should not from time to time use such an opportunity to restore my finances when official payment is so much in arrears?'

I made as if to take the 1,500 francs from my belt and I was telling the general that I would recover the rest from the officers and men, when he told me that such a step would not be necessary.

'The fair way in which you shared the 6,000 francs with your men,' he added, 'causes me to draw a veil over the whole affair. But, the next time, do not attempt the same thing without informing me.'

I thanked the general and assured him that I understood the position. Then I returned to the regiment. I should add in fairness, that General Fournier was very lenient towards officers concerned in this sort of compulsory levy.

The next day, 5 May, as we were mounting early in the morning, I noticed that Major de Vérigny had had his beard trimmed. His gauntlets and his shirt were clean, his boots highly polished and his spurs gleaming. He was riding his best horse, a fine Turkish mare and its harness was covered with cowrie shells. His colpack was crowned with its plume and its bag fluttered in the wind. His moustache had been waxed and turned up. In short, he was immaculately turned out. I complimented him on his appearance.

'My dear Parquin, this is how one should look when one is meeting the enemy,' he said. 'One is never too well dressed when the cannon roars.'

The brigade set out and joined up with General Montbrun's cavalry division. The British army had assembled to give battle on the Portuguese border in a rather critical position with a river behind it and passes made dangerous by overflowing torrents. Our army under Massena had formed up in front of the enemy in about equal strength. Everyone was eager to come to grips with the English. If Massena had set his mind on winning the battle [*Fuentes de Oñoro*], the enemy would in all probability have been defeated and heaven knows what influence such a victory would have had on the course of events in the Peninsula.

Neither the fine work on the right by the Claparède division, which thus bade a noble farewell to the Army of Portugal since it was leaving the next day for Andalusia, nor the forceful charge by the four *compagnies d'élite* of the 6th, 11th, 15th, and 25th Dragoons, which was so bravely led by Colonel Ornano through the English lines, could bring Marshal Massena out of his tent where he had retired with General Loison. Unfortunately for the army Marshal Ney, *le Brave des braves*, was no longer there for he had handed over his command a week previously. A difference with the Prince d'Essling [*Massena*] had deprived the army of his talents and his sword. The previous day Massena had received from France the information that he had been replaced as commander by Marshal Marmont who was expected to arrive at any moment.

This battle, which all the morning had gone in our favour, ceased immediately once Wellington effected his retreat. Our brigade was the last unit to engage the enemy. General Fournier had his horse killed under him as he charged an enemy line which was completely broken. The regiment's senior instructor, Captain Lasalle, Lieutenants Labassée and Hymonet, as well as several chasseurs, were unhorsed by the enemy artillery and infantry fire and a bullet fired at point-blank range smashed into my face and knocked out six of my teeth. I had to retire to the field hospital for treatment.

One of Major de Vérigny's outstanding qualities was his ability to talk to the ordinary soldier and make him respond at the most critical moment. Our squadrons were in the main target for the English artillery, but the major, whom I was accompanying, rode slowly among the men, talking to them quietly as was his usual custom at moments of danger.

'Parquin,' he said, pointing to a chasseur who was under fire for the first time and whose pale face betrayed the apprehension he felt, 'Parquin, I can see by this fellow's face that he is going to make good use of his sabre when we charge.'

The chasseur, who immediately recovered his determination at these words, brandished his sabre and declared: 'You may count on that, sir.'

He kept his word, for a minute later he was one of the first to penetrate the English ranks and there he was killed. It was in this charge that a bullet fired at point-blank range hit me in the face and knocked out six of my teeth. When the major learned that I had been wounded he was kind enough to send a message enquiring how I was.

I took a pencil and wrote a note for him saying that my wound would not be serious, but to take six of my teeth seemed excessive on the part of the English.

On 12 May the Duc de Raguse [*Marmont*] arrived to take over as the marshal commanding the army; everyone was glad of his arrival.

For 15 francs I had bought a bottle of eau-de-Cologne in Ciudad-Rodrigo and with this I made a solution in which I soaked a piece of lint which I then applied to my face morning and night. In this way I ensured my recovery from my wound. For a week I could drink only soup which my servant poured into my mouth through a funnel, but I was soon well again because gashes on the face usually heal more quickly than wounds elsewhere on the body.

I was living with a wealthy Spaniard in a village not far from Salamanca which was occupied by a detachment from our army. After the initial pain, my wound no longer hurt me much, but it condemned me to complete silence. I could not say a word. My host, who was a most worthy man, would come every morning to enquire after my health and to hold forth on the disastrous effects of a war, about which no doubt I felt strongly since I had been wounded in it.

'But,' he added, 'whatever evils the French have brought with them to Spain, whatever evils they have in store for us, they will never do us enough harm to equal the good they have done by destroying the Inquisition!'

I took my pencil and wrote: 'And by giving you institutions which you would never have had without our presence.'

He nodded in agreement and added: 'Let us hope that we are wise enough to retain them!'

Everyone knows what happened when events forced us to leave that unhappy country and when Ferdinand VII replaced Joseph Bonaparte on the throne.

Our quarters were moved in to the outskirts of Salamanca. I had scarcely recovered when the general learned that Don Julian was about to make an attack on the road to Zamora and he ordered me to take fifty chasseurs and to destroy him and his band. I surprised them in the village where they had stopped for the night. When he saw that his men had been killed, wounded or captured, Don Julian leapt on his unsaddled horse and took flight, leaving behind all his documents and baggage. My chasseurs were richly rewarded that night.

The general congratulated me and a few days later selected me to carry an important despatch to General Kellermann at Valladolid. He authorized me to take twenty-five chasseurs as an escort. I suggested to him that as the distance was not even fifteen leagues I could undertake the mission with only my servant if I left in the evening. It was decided that I should do this and I set off. At eleven o'clock I arrived at a lonely inn about halfway between Salamanca and Valladolid. There I intended to take fresh horses before going on. Great was my astonishment, however, when I rode into the courtyard and saw that it was full of men, horses and mules. I thought at first they were a band of smugglers, but I soon learned otherwise when I saw the carbines and pistols which were levelled at us. I had stumbled across a band of guerrillas led by Lieutenant d'Aguillard [*José de Aguilar*]. Resistance was useless, but I maintained a firm and resolute attitude.

When I had been disarmed and taken before the leader, I said to him: 'My life is in your hands because of my own carelessness. You should, however, be grateful for this carelessness; if I had had an escort, you would have been taken by surprise and you would be in my hands. Do not forget moreover, that if you harm a single hair of our heads, tomorrow ten of your comrades who are prisoners at Salamanca will be shot.'

I fell silent and casually took the cigar that Lieutenant d'Aguillard was smoking from his mouth—this is a great honour among Spaniards. I put it in my mouth and without revealing my feelings sat down calmly to wait for our fate to be decided.

Complete silence followed. Then the leader of the band translated my words for the others. After a short while he got up and said: '*Hombre demonio*, our decision is not influenced by the fate of our comrades. They would know how to die like good Spaniards for God and their country. But we shall not free our country from its oppressors by killing you. We admire you for your attitude. You are spared! Take back your weapons and let us be friends for a few moments while you partake of all the hospitality that a guerrilla chief can extend to you.'

He held out his hand to me and I took it gratefully before sitting down beside him. My servant, whose firmness had not wavered, also shared the modest meal which we were offered and then we remounted. We took the road to Valladolid where we arrived at daybreak. I must admit that during the further year I spent in Spain I always made a point of helping any Spaniard we took and I think I earned the gratitude of a considerable number of them.

At the beginning of June we were quartered around Merida after Marshal Marmont had raised the siege of Badajoz. Montbrun's division, of which the brigade was part, occupied Medellin, which was eight leagues from Merida. This town was famous for the victory won on 28 March 1809 by Marshal Victor over General Cuesta's army. The *gros major*, who was commanding the regiment, sent for me and told me that he had just nominated me to fill a vacancy for a staff officer at the headquarters of the Duc de Raguse. I accepted gratefully and the next day I left for Merida. Little did I foresee the unpleasant incidents in which I would be involved at the headquarters.

Two days later I received a letter from an officer in the regiment named Duclos. He asked me to cash for him a warrant for 259 francs which represented expenses incurred by him in the course of a mission which he had just completed. The certifying documents were attached to his letter. I therefore called on the army paymaster general. He was absent and the divisional paymaster, who happened to be his brother, was performing his duties. When I went to the pay office at midday I was told by a clerk: 'The paymaster is taking a siesta; he cannot see you.'

At six o'clock I returned to the office and this time I was told that the paymaster was dining. Annoyed by this answer which meant that I would have to return the next day, I exclaimed: 'Good heavens! If the paymaster spends the rest of his time taking his walk, when will I ever be able to find him? Is there not anyone here who can act for him?'

These ironical words of mine were overhead by the paymaster. Still holding his napkin, he came out of the dining-room into the office and examined my documents in an offhand manner. He asked me if I was Monsieur Duclos. I told him I was not, but offered him the letter in which my friend authorized me to collect the money for him. Thereupon the paymaster unceremoniously dismissed me, saying that he could not accept such a delegation of authority to me.

I was going down the stairs in some temper when a well-meaning clerk caught me up and explained: 'The paymaster is being unnecessarily difficult. He was rude and over-officious to you merely because you disturbed his dinner. If you care to go and see Monsieur

Marchand, the commissary general, and explain the matter to him, I am sure he will clear up any difficulties.'

I thanked the clerk and went to the commissary general's house. He was dining, but was glad to interrupt his meal to see an officer who needed his help. He inspected the documents which I had and was good enough to endorse Monsieur Duclos's warrant with a note saying: 'To be paid to Monsieur Parquin, an officer of the same regiment who is authorized to receive payment on behalf of Monsieur Duclos.'

It was too late to go back to the paymaster's office, so I put off my visit until the next day. I was resolved, however, not to go on this occasion at a time when the paymaster, who seemed so fond of his rest, might be taking a siesta or dining.

The next morning Monsieur Malet was in his office. He had no sooner read what the commissary general had written than he handed the paper back to me and said: 'Monsieur Marchand does not know what he is doing and neither do you. I shall not pay you.'

'I see you have made up your mind in this matter. But you might, sir, refuse more politely. I trust that you will give me satisfaction for the uncouth manner in which you have treated me.'

'My rank places me above an officer such as you,' he replied disdainfully. 'Get out of my office before I have the sentry throw you out.'

'You may be sure,' I said to the divisional paymaster as I left immediately, 'I shall not forget your conduct.'

When I reached my quarters I was ordered to take an officer and fifty men from the 70th Infantry Regiment and to march to Almaras to ascertain whether the bridge which the marshal had ordered to be built across the Tagus had been completed. Our march lasted a week and during it there were no untoward incidents. We were in the middle of a barren plain near Trujillo on our way back when suddenly a cloud of dust rose in the distance. The infantry officer said to me: 'You see that cloud of dust over to the right. In five minutes time we shall be in action against the guerrillas.'

He ordered his men to load their muskets and to fix bayonets and we marched on. The guerrillas were soon upon us, but when my infantry officer gave the timely command: 'Halt, Aim, Fire!' the Spaniards wheeled away like a flight of pigeons, though not without firing a hail of bullets at us and one of these hit the officer in the thigh. I ordered the men to halt and to level their bayonets for the few moments it took me to bind the wounded man's thigh with my handkerchief. When they saw us halt the guerrillas returned, calling out: 'Soldiers, hand over the cavalry officer who is probably carrying despatches. We wish you no harm. We are your friends!'

This was said in French and I supposed that there was a deserter among them. The guerrillas charged again and when they were ten yards away I gave the order to fire and the bandits were dispersed. One of them had fallen and was taken prisoner. I should have had him shot on the spot. But I recounted the story of my adventure with Lieutenant d'Aguillard to the infantry officer and his men, and I asked the officer if he would allow me to deal with the wretched prisoner.

'My friend,' he replied, 'he is your prisoner rather than mine. Do what you wish with him, for although they wounded me, it was your blood that they were after. They shouted enough about you.'

Then I took a piece of paper and wrote: 'Charles Parquin, an officer of the 20th Chasseurs who, as a prisoner of Lieutenant d'Aguillard and his men near Salamanca, owed his life and that of his servant to their generosity, hereby shows his gratitude to them today, 10 August 1811, in Estremadura, near Trujillo, by setting free a Spaniard belonging to the Medico guerrilla band.'

I gave the paper to the man together with a gold coin and had him released, with a warning to him not to cross our path again. The poor devil, who was more dead than alive, kissed my feet and made off after crossing himself.

Once back in Merida I reported on my mission and then hastened to my rooms to change my clothes before visiting the delightful owner of the house in which I was living; in other words, I was living in a house owned by a pretty woman. To my great astonishment my servant informed me that Malet, the divisional paymaster, had become a frequent visitor to the house since my departure; every evening he was spending two hours with my hostess and even at that moment he was with her.

'Here,' I thought, 'is a fine opportunity to have my revenge on that insolent fellow.'

When I had changed I went upstairs to my hostess who, as soon as she saw me, offered me her hand to kiss. It was clear that the paymaster, who was standing with his hat in his hand, was preparing to leave and I was going to lose the moment of satisfaction to which I was looking forward. I therefore turned sharply on him and addressed him thus:

'Sir, how do you behave in other people's houses when you are so rude in your own?'

'Sir, I am not in your house. This house belongs to this good lady here.'

'Possibly, but that does not prevent me from telling you that you are an impertinent fellow wherever I meet you.'

At these words the paymaster left. I followed him and summoned my servant and my orderly who were in my rooms and who appeared at once.

'Throw out this person coming downstairs,' I shouted, 'and do not ever let him come here again!'

The paymaster, who was quite strong tried to resist, but my men threw him out. By treating him in this way, I wanted to force him to fight. I was sure that he would make a complaint about me, so I went immediately to the office of General Lamartinière, the Chief of Staff. The paymaster was there already and his torn jabot was proof that my orders had been only too well carried out. General Lamartinière was absent; he was dining with the marshal. However, Captain Fabvier, an aide-de-camp to the Duc de Raguse, was there and he was listening to the paymaster's story.

'What is your complaint, sir?' I said, interrupting him. 'A week ago you had me thrown out; today I have had the same thing done to you. But there is still one difference between us: you have refused to give me satisfaction, whereas I am ready to give you satisfaction. I am at your disposal.'

'You seem well and truly involved here,' said Captain Fabvier to the paymaster.

'Very well, sir,' Monsieur Malet said to me. 'You will hear from me shortly.'

I returned to my quarters to await word from the paymaster and an hour later I received the following note:

'Sir, your behaviour towards me has been unworthy of an officer and I am forced to demand satisfaction from you. I shall expect you on the far side of the bridge at five o'clock tomorrow morning when I shall chastise you with my sword.

'Malet, 15 August 1811.'

I wrote back acknowledging his note and then went to bed. I told my servant to wake me the following morning at exactly four o'clock so that I would be able to dress properly. This he did, and after dressing I left the house and went outside into the square. There I met a grenadier captain of the 70th Infantry Regiment named Bellegarde who had once been a drum-major.

'Kindly do me the favour of lending me your sword. If you have a second like it, would you be good enough to lend me that one also. This,' I said, showing him the letter from the paymaster, 'is why I need these weapons.'

'With pleasure, my friend,' he answered, 'but only on condition that I accompany my weapons. I am never parted from them.'

'That goes without saying; I am glad to have you as my second.'

When we arrived at the appointed place the paymaster was already there. He was wearing a cornflower-blue, silver-embroidered jacket, white cashmere trousers and close-fitting riding boots. I had put on a dress-coat, nankeen trousers and light shoes. Within two minutes he had chosen his sword and taken off his coat. Then he remarked ironically: 'You are somewhat slow, sir.'

I needed more time than he, for I had to take off a flannel waistcoat which I was wearing.

'You will lose nothing for having waited,' I said, taking guard.

I realized immediately that I was facing a man who was very skilful with the sword; but, having turned aside his attempted disengagement I slipped my blade over his and hit his braces. The buckle took the force of the thrust, but blood spurted out.

'You are wounded, Paymaster,' said my second.

'It is nothing,' he replied very calmly.

We began to cross swords again, but he had become more cautious. He no longer attacked me and now it was my turn to advance forcefully on him. By attacking him with a rapid succession of blows I obliged him to adopt a different stance and I was able to drive him back on to ground which had been ploughed. On this surface he was handicapped by his heavy riding-boots. A vigorous thrust entered his right side and he fell.

I hastened towards him to help him, but Bellegarde, my second, when he saw him fall, cried out: 'Ah! Paymaster, before you fall out, you might at least give me the keys to your chest!'

'Come and help me give my opponent the aid he deserves, instead of making jokes in bad taste,' I told Bellegarde.

The paymaster's two seconds hurried off and soon returned with two soldiers who put the wounded man on a litter and started carrying him to his house. Our little procession was met by General Ferray and his aide-de-camp Goudmetz who were out for a morning walk. They went off to inform the marshal. No sooner had I returned to my quarters than an orderly arrived with instructions for me to report to the headquarters. I put on my uniform and went immediately. As soon as the marshal saw me he said: 'So, sir, you have barely arrived at my headquarters and you have already attacked my paymaster general.'

My answer was to take from my sabretache the paymaster's letter which I had been careful to bring with me. I handed it to the marshal and said: 'My lord, this is my justification. Would you please read it.'

The marshal glanced through the letter and said: 'The paymaster has received what he deserves. Moreover, I remember that when he was serving under me in Illyria, he wounded two infantry officers with whom he quarrelled.'

Thereupon he dismissed me. Some time later I learned that the paymaster was recovering and was able to spend two hours a day on a couch in his room. I went to his office to present my friend's warrant once more. When the clerk went into the paymaster's room to ask if he was to pay me, I distinctly heard Monsieur Malet's answer, for there was only a glass door between us.

'Yes! Yes!' he said. 'Give it to the gentleman in gold.'

Thus I received three gold *onces* in payment of the warrant for 240 francs[1] which had caused me so much unpleasantness and the paymaster a painful wound. I sent on the money to my friend Duclos who thought I had forgotten the task he had asked me to undertake for him.

So as not to deprive two regiments of their *compagnies d'élite* as this would have seriously weakened the regiments, the marshal called for one officer and twenty-five men from each of the eight cavalry regiments in the army. This made a total of four officers[2] and two hundred men to act as escort to the Duc de Raguse. To his great joy Monsieur de Vérigny was offered the command of this escort and when he accepted he asked the marshal if he might have me as his adjutant. His request was approved and this greatly pleased me as it showed that the Duke harboured no resentment against me for having given a lesson to his paymaster general. The escort received double pay and double rations; the marshal paid for the extra out of his own pocket.

In September the army moved against the English who were besieging Ciudad-Rodrigo. Ten thousand men of the Army of the North and the whole of the Imperial Guard under General Dorsenne, who was known as *le beau Dorsenne*, joined us. But the British Army did not wait for us; it withdrew into Portugal, adopting its usual delaying tactics which were so unattractive, but which were to prove

[1] Parquin originally gives the sum as 259 francs.

[2] The correct figure would seem to be eight officers.

so disastrous to us. The officers in the brigade no longer drank glasses of rum and brandy with their English counterparts when they found themselves facing each other. Our chasseurs had a less civilized way of obtaining rum when they wanted it—something which happened quite frequently. It was not unusual to hear one of them call to his comrades: 'There is no brandy left. Who's going to catch a *goddam*?'[1] and the chasseurs would take turns to capture an English soldier with the little flask of rum he always carried. The chasseur also made a profit of three napoleons, the price paid for any captured horse.

The English officers were very brave and extremely good company, but they were sometimes very cutting in their remarks. They were always ready for a joke, and I remember one particularly amusing incident. Near Sabugal, Monsier Fage of the 13th Chasseurs was pursuing an English officer who, thanks to his superb horse, was able to remain ten yards ahead of his pursuer. Fage, despite all his efforts, could not close the gap. Without slowing his horse the Englishman turned round casually and coolly observed in a mocking tone:

'I presume that is a Norman horse you are riding, sir.'

Enraged by this sarcastic remark, Fage drew his pistol and aimed at the English officer, but the pistol misfired.

'I presume,' commented the Englishman quite calmly, 'that you get your weapons from the armaments works at Versailles.'

At this second remark, Fage was besides himself with rage, and he shouted: 'Wait for me, and we can find out which of us has the better blade to his sabre!'

But the Englishman did not respond to the challenge. I would add that this is not said in order to decry the bravery of these officers, for they found us very dangerous when we attacked with our sabres. We always thrust with the point of our sabres, whereas they always cut with their blade which was three inches wide. Consequently, out of every twenty blows aimed by them, nineteen missed. If, however, the edge of the blade found its mark only once, it was a terrible blow, and it was not unusual to see an arm cut clean from the body.

The army occupied quarters in the province of Leon, while the headquarters were in Valladolid. During our time there Major de Vérigny, who had now commanded the marshal's escort for several months, was made an officer of the *Légion d'honneur*. He had deserved this honour and when I congratulated him he said: 'I am particularly touched by your congratulations, my dear Parquin, in view of the

[1] A nickname derived from the oath, which had become common with the French at the beginning of the eighteenth century.

fact that you ought to be resentful, for I put your name forward to the marshal for the decoration, but his recommendation on your behalf was unsuccessful. You were on a list of twenty names and the Emperor who is never over-generous to armies which are far from him and who confirmed only a quarter of the recommendations, unfortunately did not select your name. If your name had been Tarquin instead of Parquin, it would probably have caught the Emperor's eye and you would have been decorated.'

As he pinned his gold cross on his chest, he added: 'I should have been delighted, my dear Parquin, to pin my own silver cross on your chest. But do not give up hope. I shall put your name forward again at the first possible opportunity, and I know the marshal thinks highly of you. Let us hope that the next time we shall be more successful.'

VIII

On 21 February 1812 I was overcome with grief at the loss of my commanding officer and friend, Major de Vérigny, who was murdered by a soldier from the garrison at Valladolid. That day he had invited me and some other officers of the escort, together with his nephew Monsieur Soufflot,[1] a young second lieutenant, to a dinner which he was giving for his friend Colonel Thureau of the 1st Hussars. The colonel was passing through Valladolid on his way back to France to join the expedition which was about to leave for Russia. The dinner had been a very merry affair and after it we all set out for our quarters. Monsieur de Vérigny was walking back to his with his nephew in the dark, for it was half past ten. When they were going through the arcade around the square they were quite roughly pushed aside by two gendarmes from the garrison who were returning to their barracks after staying late in a tavern.

Monsieur Soufflot told them to be more careful, but they answered with crude insults and one of them, carried away by the wine he had drunk, came back with his sabre drawn. Monsieur de Vérigny, who was wearing his forage-cap and not carrying his sabre, went to seize his nephew's sabre and said: 'I will settle this, Jules.'

His nephew handed him the sabre and cried: 'Do you dare to draw your sabre against a superior officer, you scum?'

At that moment the man wildly swung his sabre which grazed young Soufflot, but which sank deep into the unfortunate major who was not defending himself as he came forward with his sabre at his side. The major fell instantly and said: 'Hold me, Jules, for I am dying.'

In spite of all the measures taken by the senior surgeon, our beloved major could not be saved. The murderer, for whom the marshal instituted an extensive search, was arrested the next day and executed before we left Valladolid. The major was given full military honours when he was buried within the cathedral itself.

In the course of April 1812 the army proceeded a third time to the relief of Ciudad-Rodrigo which was once more besieged. Once more the British army withdrew. In the valley of the Mondego we caught up with the rear-guard which was formed by a Portuguese division. Major Denys [*Damrémont*], who had succeeded Monsieur de Vérigny,

[1] Jules Soufflot was born in 1793 and lived until 1893. Even in his final years he was able to confirm the accuracy of Parquin's account of his time in Spain.

suddenly fell upon these troops with the two hundred men of the escort. The weather favoured this attack against infantry for driving rain prevented them from firing. Their squares could not stand up to the charge. The disintegration of the first led to disorder in the others which wavered and broke when the troops who had formed them fled to the neighbouring woods.

In this charge I was the first to arrive in the middle of a square and with my sabre I wounded an officer who was carrying the standard of the Eurillas Regiment, a multicoloured pennon with the number 1808, which was probably the date of its founding. The officer hastened to offer me the standard he was carrying and begged me to spare him. The square was formed by what was reputed to be one of their best regiments. The four other standards of the division were inside it. Second Lieutenant Soufflot, Lieutenant Dubar of the 11th Dragoons and two other officers each came back with a standard.

Fifteen hundred prisoners and five standards were brought back to the marshal who thanked the escort and promised decorations for those who had taken them, but later the battle of Les Arapiles cancelled out the results of our charge. The army returned to Spain and camps were set up behind the Douro. In July the English again penetrated into Spain. On the 15th of this month at a place a few leagues from Salamanca, Marshal Marmont, accompanied by some officers of his staff, was making a reconnaissance near the enemy line when an English officer came out beyond his forward picquets and rode up and down within sight of our picquets.

'What does the fellow want?' asked the Duc de Raguse.

Since I was the adjutant of his escort I answered: 'No doubt, sir, he wishes to measure sabres with someone and were I not a member of your escort . . .'

'Do not let that hold you back; you have my permission.'

No sooner had he said these words than I galloped forward to meet the English officer. I parried his blow and countered with a vigorous thrust which unhorsed my opponent. I briskly hooked the reins of his horse with my sabre and led the animal back to the applause of the marshal, his aides-de-camp Richemont, Perregaux and Lanselot, and Major Denys.

I immediately returned the wounded man's saddlebag containing his personal belongings with an inquiry about his condition. I was glad to learn that although his wound was dangerous it would not prove fatal. I was thanked for my gesture and for the fact that nothing was missing from his bag and I was asked if I would sell back the horse for forty guineas, although I was warned it was not a thoroughbred. I sent back word that this might be so, but that I liked the idea of riding an English horse and I intended to keep it.

During the period from the 16th until the 23rd of July the army assembled on the plains between Salamanca and Alba de Tormes. The Imperial Guard had left in haste to take part in the Russian campaign. We had only two thousand horsemen; the English had twice this number. In the other arms the strengths were more or less equal. The French army called this historic day the battle of Les Arapiles [*Salamanca*] which were the names of two fairly high hills situated at about a cannon-shot from each other. They were in the middle of the plain where the two armies fought all day long. One was on the edge of the British army and the other was within our lines. The marshal and his staff dismounted and climbed it on foot.

At eleven o'clock on a fine summer morning the Duc de Raguse was standing on the hill observing the enemy army. His servant had just laid out the silver plate on the grass and His Excellency, his aides-de-camp and the Chief of Staff were going to take lunch when several shells, fired by guns which had been manhandled to the top of the other hill, put a sudden end to the lunch which was about to start. We hastened down the hillside to return to our horses. At the bottom of the hill I was sent to Foy's division with the order for it to advance.

When I was coming back I saw a number of horses belonging to my regiment and since I had been away from it so long, the natural desire to find out what had happened in my absence caused me to approach a group of men holding the led horses.

'What are you doing here?' I asked Narbonne, an officer of the 13th Chasseurs whom I found near the *cantinière*, holding a sausage in one hand and a bottle of brandy in the other.

'I am having my lunch as you can see. Will you join me?'

'Alas, no; I am in a hurry. Just hand me the bottle so that I may moisten my lips for it is warm today.'

I swallowed a mouthful and gave him back his bottle. I thanked him and said: 'You have no cause for concern here; the balls will not bother you here. Are you due to go into action with the brigade?'

'What, Parquin, do you expect me to fight against the English when they were so good to my father and me when we had to take refuge in England in '93? Never! I could not be so ungrateful.' Then he added firmly: 'If they want me to fight, well let them find some other country for me; the Austrians for example!'

I laughed heartily as I galloped away, for this Narbonne was a young man from Saint-Germain, the fashionable quarter of Paris, who, one day when galloping along the road to Malmaison, had covered the Emperor with dust as he was riding in his coach. The next day Narbonne received his commission as a second lieutenant and instructions to report to the army where he would not be able to go around raising dust. No one could ever make this officer do any duties and he was returned to the depot. From there he was sent home, where, I believe, he eventually went mad.

The marshal had just had his artillery sited on the hill also and had gone up the slope again with his staff. He told Major Denys to station the escort where he saw fit. The major put us into the line on the right of the 5th Hussars where for an hour we were subjected to the enemy's fire. We moved from this trying position to charge a regiment of heavy cavalry which was wearing red uniforms.[1] As we returned I saw a chasseur of the 20th who was being closely pursued by two English horsemen.

'Turn and face them!' I cried, going to his help. But he did not stop and one of the Englishmen, whose horse was obviously out of control, cannoned into me and we both went down. Then the second Englishman galloped up and shouted: 'You are my prisoner!'

With his sabre he gestured to me to walk ahead of him. The memory of my captivity in Russia flashed through my mind. I noticed that my would-be captor had not drawn his pistol; if he had done so, I would have been forced to obey him. Instead, I parried the blows which he aimed at me with his sabre for I had quickly risen from beneath my horse which made off towards the escort. I endeavoured to strike the legs of his horse so as to unhorse him. When my horse returned without me the other members of the escort became alarmed and two of them came to look for me and to bring me my horse. As soon as they saw me they rode towards us at full speed and the Englishman, when he saw them, retired immediately.

In this unequal fight I had received a blow on my wrist. My gauntlet had deadened the blow which had been aimed at my head; otherwise, I would certainly have had my wrist cut through. In the heat of battle I had not felt the blow, although I had lost much blood. I noticed it only when I tried to put my hand on the saddle to remount. It was impossible for me to pull myself up with my right hand, despite the assistance of the two chasseurs. I had to mount from the right

[1] Oman in his *History of the Peninsular War* (Vol. V) suggests that these were scattered parties from Le Marchant's brigade.

and to leave that dangerous place without taking the time to pick up my colpack, which I thus lost. I was quite happy to escape so lightly.

A chasseur was waiting to tell us that the escort had gone at the gallop to the hill where the Commander-in-Chief had just been seriously wounded. We were to make our way to the field hospital which had been set up at Alba de Tormes. To reach it we had to ride a league, half of which was through woods. We left at the gallop for it was indeed time to move elsewhere as large numbers of enemy cavalry were threatening our left flank. I lost so much blood as I rode with my sabre hanging by its knot from my wrist that I would surely have fallen from my horse if the chasseurs had not observed my state and helped me to dismount. The enemy was advancing and the musket-shots which were gradually drawing nearer indicated clearly enough that we were losing the battle. The chasseurs had nothing to give me to help me regain my strength. They cooled my face with some water from a stream which ran near the spot where we had halted, but still I lay motionless. Then I heard the one say to the other: 'It is a dreadful thing to have to abandon this brave officer to the enemy.'

I opened my eyes and when they saw this, they cried: 'Bear up, sir!' and carrying me rather than helping me, they put me on my horse. We started off again at a walking pace. It was six o'clock when I crossed the bridge over the Tormes into the town. The marshal had arrived there at four o'clock; his wound, although very serious, was not fatal. A shell had smashed his right arm and two ribs. General Clausel took over command of the army. At midnight Foy's division, which had been in reserve, formed squares and halted the enemy. If Marshal Marmont, who had waited seven days before giving battle, had waited a further day, he would have been joined by King Joseph and Marshal Soult who were coming to his aid with forty thousand men, a force which included ten thousand cavalry. Marshal Soult, however, would have had supreme command because of his seniority. Thus ambition caused the loss of a battle which, if it had been fought with the additional strength of the Army of Andalusia, would have meant the destruction of the whole British army.

The Duc de Raguse was replaced by General Souham and he left for France. I accompanied him. His wound was causing him great pain; he was not strong enough to stand the journey on horseback or in a carriage. His doctor had suggested transporting him on a stretcher carried by mules, with one harnessed in front and the other behind, but the uneven progress of these mules made the stretcher jolt and this caused the marshal unbearable suffering. As soon as the members of the escort learned these facts, they spontaneously offered to carry him in a litter on their shoulders to spare him any jolting.

Twenty-four men dismounted and twelve of them carried the front shafts of the stretcher while the other twelve carried the rear ones. These twenty-four men were relieved by their comrades when they became tired. In this way the journey was made less painful for the marshal. The party halted at Valldolid, Burgos and Vitoria. When it reached Bayonne the marshal found that his wife had come to meet him. He thanked the escort for its services and disbanded it so that its members could return to their respective regiments.

I had made the whole journey on horseback since my arm was in a sling. My wound had not by any means healed. I made my way to join the regimental depot at Nantes, but the squadrons to which I belonged and which were part of the army of Portugal had just been incorporated into the 13th Chasseurs. It was with deep regret that I left the regiment in which I had started my career and to which I was so attached. The 20th Chasseurs were involved in the Russian expedition and this had necessitated the measures which had been taken in regard to the squadrons serving in the Army of Portugal.

In the month of October 1812 I arrived at Niort and there I fell sick with rheumatic pains which resulted from my wounds in the Polish campaign of 1807, the Wagram campaign of 1809 and finally the wretched war in Spain. The bivouacs in which I had slept in Spain, where it is impossible to obtain straw that has not been finely chopped, had greatly contributed to the pains I felt. I sent a request for sick leave to the Minister of War and this was granted. I returned to my family home in Paris and spent the winter there.

The Emperor suddenly arrived in Paris on 19 December 1812. Preceding him had come his twenty-ninth bulletin; it was as accurate as those from Eylau and Essling, but how terribly different were its contents. On 6 March 1813 I went out of curiosity to see the review at the Tuileries. In the Carrousel courtyard I saw General Lefebvre-Desnoëttes who was Colonel of the Guard Chasseurs. I approached him and asked to be allowed to join his regiment.

'Young man,' he said to me after asking me various other questions, 'Do you know anyone who takes an interest in you and to whom I might speak about you?'

At that moment I caught sight of the Duc de Raguse; his arm was in a sling and he was alighting from his carriage prior to entering the inner courtyard of the Tuileries. I pointed him out to the general and said: 'There is the Duc de Raguse under whom I served in Spain; if you wished, you could ask him about me.'

After asking me my name, the general approached the marshal who, when he saw me and heard my name, called me and said in my presence: 'You should take this officer into your regiment, General; you would be making a good acquisition.'

A few days later I received my commission as a *lieutenant en second* (I had been made a lieutenant in the 13th Chasseurs on 17 February) in the Chasseur regiment of the Old Guard. On 15 March I was at the barracks at seven in the morning when all those present were ordered to assemble on the Champ-de-Mars to take part in the general inspection which the Emperor himself was to make. Not having received my uniform, I pointed out to the general that I was still wearing civilian clothes, but he told me to attend in morning dress. It was thus attired that I appeared in my appointed place. The Emperor was inspecting every column on foot. When he and his staff reached us, he seemed astonished to see me in civilian dress and commented upon the fact to the general. The latter explained that I had but recently arrived from Spain and had not yet received my uniform. The Emperor beckoned to me and asked: 'To which army did you belong in Spain?'

'To the Army of Portugal, Sire. I was wounded at the battle of Les Arapiles.'

'What was your regiment then?'

'The 20th Chasseurs.'

'So you were a member of the two [*four*] squadrons I sent to Spain in 1810?'

'Yes, Sire,' I replied, amazed that he should remember such a detail. I then resumed my place.

On Sunday, 6 April 1813, my troop was part of the two squadrons of the regiment which were present at one of the reviews which the Emperor frequently held in the courtyard of the Tuileries after his return from Russia. This time I was wearing the full-dress uniform of the regiment. I was anxious to speak to the Emperor and, as I feared there would be no opportunity since the Emperor did not spend much time with his *Guides* on these occasions and often galloped past them without stopping, I dismounted when our squadrons were at ease. I went and stationed myself to the left of an infantry regiment of the Young Guard which the Emperor was inspecting.

'Who are you?' he said when he reached me.

'An officer of the Old Guard, Sire. I stepped down a rank in order to obtain a post nearer to Your Majesty's person.'

'What would you have me do for you?'

'You could award me a decoration, Sire.'

'What have you done to deserve one?'

'I was born and bred in Paris, but at the age of sixteen I left my native city as a volunteer. I have taken part in eight campaigns. I was commissioned on the battlefield and have received ten wounds, although I would not exchange them for the number I have inflicted on the enemy. I captured an enemy standard in Portugal. On that occasion the Commander-in-Chief put forward my name for a decoration, but the distance between Portugal and Moscow is so great that I have not yet received the answer.'

'Well! I must bring it to you personally. Berthier, make a note that this officer is to receive the cross and make sure that the official confirmation is sent to him tomorrow. This brave officer must not be made to wait any longer.'

In this way I was decorated. I was so delighted that when I returned to my place with the regiment I gave the news to several other officers who had recently joined the Guard on their arrival from Spain where they had not been decorated. Lieutenant Goudmetz followed my example and approached the Emperor with a similar request.

'What have you done to deserve a decoration?'

'Sire, two of my brothers and I joined the 3rd Hussars as volunteers ten years ago. I believe our service in Your Majesty's cause deserves recognition.'

'So this is what you believe?' said the Emperor.

'Yes, Sire, all the more so since my two brothers have been killed and I am the only one left to serve our country.'

Clearly moved, the Emperor told the Prince de Neufchâtel that this officer was to receive the cross.

A third officer presented himself and he was asked what he had done to distinguish himself. The officer, Legout-Duplessis, said to the Emperor:

'Sire, as a sergeant in the 5th Dragoons at the battle of Talavera in Spain [*1809*], I captured the standard of the Walloon Guards after killing the officer who was bearing it and scattering the escort which was guarding it. I was mentioned in despatches for this exploit.'

'A very fine exploit indeed,' said the Emperor with a smile, 'but who can confirm the truth of your story?'

'Your aide-de-camp, General Corbineau, who is with you now,

Sire, was colonel of the regiment at the time and it was he who led the charge.'

General Corbineau nodded in agreement and Legout-Duplessis was decorated.

After the parade had marched past, the Emperor gave orders for the men to receive an extra issue of wine and food for which he himself paid and he invited the officers to dine with him that evening. Two hundred officers from all the regiments which had been present at the parade assembled on the Terrasse des Feuillants in the Tuileries gardens. It was here that banquets organized by the famous caterer Véry were held at that time. Four tables, each set for fifty guests were put out and Generals Lemarois, Lauriston, Lobau and Rapp each sat at the head of a table. As aides-de-camp of the Emperor, they were representing him on this ceremonial occasion and acting as hosts on his behalf.

As can be imagined, the meal was a joyful affair and toasts were drunk to the Emperor, to the Empress and to the King of Rome. Many of those present had just been promoted or decorated and others with less service had the prospect of rewards to come. The opportunity of winning such rewards would not escape them for the next day we were leaving for Germany. For a number of those present, however, this was to be the last meal prepared by the famous Véry that they would ever enjoy.

The next day I received three thousand francs from the regimental quartermaster. This was the grant made to officers on their appointment to the Guard and it was intended to help them purchase their equipment and uniform, for these items were very costly.

On 10 April I left Paris with part of the regiment in order to join the Army of Germany which was under the personal command of the Emperor. As I passed through Epernay I had an amusing, and moreover most pleasant, experience which I put down to the stimulating nature of the wine in this area. It was a long-standing custom of officers of the Guard to gather at the Hôtel de l'Ecu whenever they were in Epernay. There they would dine together and drink the health of the Emperor in the best champagne.

At midday I made my way to my quarters which were in the house of a rich widow on the main street. I had just entered my room, still covered with dust after riding that morning, when a tall, beautiful girl came in with refreshments for me. She apologized for the fact that her mistress, to whom I had sent my card, was unable to receive me, but she had been obliged to go out a few moments previously to see her lawyer on urgent business. I thanked her for telling me this and gave no further thought to the mistress of the house as my mind was fully occupied with the extremely pretty girl who had brought me the refreshments.

'What is your name, Mademoiselle? You must surely be the prettiest young woman in this town.'

Without commenting on my observation, which made her blush and laugh at the same time, she answered promptly: 'My name is Adèle, sir; I am Madame's chambermaid. If I can be of service to you, sir, you have only to ask.'

'I will take you at your word, Mademoiselle, and take immediate advantage of your offer. Would you sew this ribbon on to my *croix d'honneur* in place of the old one which is faded?'

The young girl took the ribbon and hurried away to her room which was near mine. In a few minutes she was back with my cross. She was kind enough to attach it very skilfully to the braid of my dolman. Then she bent forward rapidly and put her lips to the image of the Emperor. Her enthusiastic kiss was so full of feeling that it made my heart pound beneath my decoration. I was quite moved by her gesture and said: 'Truly you are devoted to the Emperor.'

'Sir,' she said, 'were I a man, the Emperor would have no better servant than myself.'

'Indeed! You are tall, handsome and strong. You should become one of his servants. I assure you I would have the greatest pleasure in helping you to become one.'

She entered into the spirit of my jest and I won the friendship of Mademoiselle Adèle who willingly agreed to meet me in her room at eleven o'clock. That evening I went to the Hôtel de l'Ecu where I dined merrily with my fellow-officers. I returned to my quarters by eleven o'clock and without delay I slipped into the nearby room where Adèle awaited me. A few moments later we were the best of friends. However, just as our friendship was at its most pleasant, a sudden knock on the door startled us.

'What is it, Madame?' asked Adèle. 'Do you need me?'

'No, Adèle, but you are not alone in your room.'

Adèle, who was holding me tightly, for at this alarm I had started to leave her, replied with complete calmness: 'Possibly, Madame, but it is not Monsieur G . . . who is with me.'

No sooner had she said this name than we heard the good lady go away and to our relief the unexpected visit had ended.

'Would you explain to me the magic power of the name you have just mentioned?' I asked Adèle.

'Certainly, sir, for you do not belong to Epernay. The gentleman whom I mentioned is Madame's lover and every day I let him in to see her. Today he is in the country and that is why we were disturbed. Otherwise, the problem would not have arisen.'

Then after a short while, Adèle added: 'Do you not think Madame was most unfair to me? I am younger than she and do not carry on affairs; just because today for the first time a handsome young officer takes a liking to me, she expects me not to respond.'

I was too involved in the situation not to agree with Adèle. Before I finally took my leave of this charming young girl I gave her one of the lockets containing a piece of my hair which I always carried with me on my travels. She seemed very pleased with it.

I expressed my concern about any possible consequences of her mistress's discovery, but she said: 'Do not worry. In the first place, Madame is a kindly soul. Moreover, it is not in her interests to bear a grudge towards me when I am so useful to her. She will sulk for a few days, but I have already received compensation for that.'

I tenderly took my leave of this charming girl, assuring her that I would always have the happiest memories of her. I was about to mount my horse when, to my surprise, I noticed the lady of the house in the garden adjoining the courtyard. She seemed absorbed in gathering roses, but there was no doubt that it was some other reason which had brought her out so early in the morning. I had not had the honour of meeting her the previous day and I could not fail to greet her without being discourteous. I complimented her on her early rising and said that this was a sign of good health. The widow, who was very pretty, did indeed have an admirably fresh complexion. Hiding a smile, she inquired if I had slept well that night.

'I slept perfectly, Madame,' I answered. 'I was a little upset at first by the champagne which I had drunk freely with my friends, but afterwards a fascinating dream brought me a delightful night which I shall always remember.'

Thereupon I bowed deeply to Madame M . . . and inwardly complimented Monsieur G . . . on his good taste, for the lady was indeed most charming.

IX

On 1 May we crossed the Rhine at Strasbourg and on the 10th we arrived at Dresden. The regiment was billeted in the villages around the town. With us was Major-General Lion whom I had known for many years; he had served as a captain in the 20th Chasseurs. He made me most welcome and I was most grateful to him for appointing me to the 10th Troop of the regiment. This troop was commanded by his brother-in-law, Captain Klein de Kleinberg, who was one of the best cavalry officers I have ever known during my military career; he later became a general. On 12 May we witnessed the return of the King of Saxony to his capital which he had left at the approach of the allied armies. The Emperor, at the head of a division of his mounted and foot Guards, went to meet him a quarter of a league beyond the town. He had sent the Comte de Flahaut, one of his aides-de-camp, as far as Pirna to congratulate the King of Saxony on his return. On the 20th the battle of Bautzen took place; the next day the battle of Wurschen was won. But our lack of cavalry deprived us of the fruits of these pitched battles which were dominated by our artillery and infantry.

Between the 20th and the 30th of May I and my troop were part of the squadron of chasseurs (who were more frequently known as *guides* when in the field), which was directly under the Emperor's orders. In wartime the Emperor always had at his disposal four squadrons drawn from the different arms of the Old Guard cavalry; these he could throw against the enemy if the need arose. The squadron of chasseurs had a special task. A lieutenant, a sergeant, two corporals, twenty-two chasseurs and a trumpeter rode in front of and behind the Emperor. A corporal and four chasseurs galloped ahead of the Emperor and cleared a way for him. One of the chasseurs carried his despatch case and another his field-glass. If the Emperor stopped and dismounted, these chasseurs would immediately do likewise, fix their bayonets to their carbines and move about in a square with the Emperor in the centre of it. The officer commanding the escort troop followed him constantly. Only Murat and the Prince de Neufchâtel had precedence over this officer.

If the Emperor took quarters in a house, this officer occupied the room nearest to that of the Emperor. The chasseurs in the escort troop dismounted and stood holding their horses in front of the house occupied by the Emperor, who always had one of his own horses held in readiness there by two grooms. This troop was relieved every two hours so that the same arrangements held good whatever the time of day or night. The first person the Emperor saw on leaving his rooms was the officer in charge of the escort. It was a post of great honour and responsibility. This body of men was entirely devoted to the Emperor and was, moreover, well rewarded for its devotion. In each troop there were four chasseurs who received not only the cross of the *Légion d'honneur* and the cross of the *Couronne de Fer* with its income of 250 francs, but also dividends from the canal companies or the Mont de Milan which brought them between 500 and 800 francs. None of these fine men was lacking in gratitude towards his Emperor. I should like to quote one of the acts which illustrate the devotion and unselfish service of the chasseurs of the Guard.

At Leipzig on 18 October 1813 a chasseur from my troop, one of those who had been decorated and received a monetary award, had his horse killed in the battle. I thought he had returned to the regimental forward depot to obtain a new mount and this would have meant an absence of eight to ten days. I was therefore astonished to see him the next day in his correct place mounted upon a superb horse. When I commented on this, he replied earnestly: 'Sir, when you receive an award from our Emperor and King, you always keep a year's money in your belt to buy a horse on which you may be killed in His Majesty's service. If, in the campaign ahead, I have the misfortune to lose my horse again, then I shall return to the depot to obtain another. The horse I am now riding I bought yesterday with my own money from a dragoon officer who no longer needs it for he has had his leg amputated.'

'How much did it cost?'

'Twenty-five louis, sir.'

Napoleon, who was well aware of the devotion of his *guides*, often permitted them to make remarks which he would certainly not have tolerated from others. One day the horse of one of the escort galloping in front of him went down. The *guide* was struggling to his feet when the Emperor, as he passed, called him a clumsy fellow. The comment had scarcely been made than Napoleon, whose mind must have been on more important things than keeping a firm seat, rolled into the dust with his mount. While the Emperor, aided by his equerry, was mounting another horse, the chasseur, who had himself remounted, galloped up to resume his place in the vanguard. As he passed the Emperor the chasseur shouted loudly enough to be heard: 'It would seem that I am not the only clumsy one around here today.'

On 22 May at four in the morning the Guard cavalry, the *lanciers rouges*[1] under General Colbert and a division of Saxon cuirassiers pursued the Prussians and the Russians towards Silesia and took a great number of stragglers, carriages and waggons. But the Russian artillery caused great losses among the Saxons. Only one officer of the *Guides* was hit; this was when Lantivy was wounded in the hand by a shell fragment. The army suffered a heavy loss when General Bruyère was killed by a cannon-ball which shattered both his legs. During the fighting that day, the Emperor, on seeing a chasseur of the escort struck dead near him by a cannon-ball, said to the Grand Marshal[2] who came up to him: 'Duroc, Fortune is truly against us today.'

Two hours later Fortune was to strike Napoleon an even more cruel blow. Leaving the village of Reichenbach, he took the road to Gorlitz where he hoped to spend the night. He was riding rapidly along the sunken road from the village towards a nearby hill when a stray cannon-ball glanced off a tree, killing outright General Kirgener and disembowelling General Duroc. Both of them had gone off a little to the right of the road to water their horses at a pond. This was a disastrous blow. An officer of the *Gendarmerie d'élite*,[3] who had seen General Kirgener struck dead, brought the news to the Emperor. A minute later another officer brought the Emperor the sad news that the Grand Marshal had just been badly wounded. The Emperor's first reaction was to tell the officer that he was mistaken; that he must mean General Kirgener whose death had just been reported.

'Sire,' said the officer, 'the sad truth is that the same cannon-ball struck them both. General Kirgener's death was instantaneous and the Grand Marshal has just been carried in a desperate state to the local pastor's house.'

Just then Colonel Gourgaud, the senior staff officer, came to report to the Emperor that the movement of the Prince de la Moskowa [*Ney*] on Gorlitz had been successful. Without saying a word the Emperor retraced his path and went immediately to the Grand Marshal's bedside. A battalion of the Old Guard as well as the escort troop took up positions around the house.

[1] Formed in 1810, these were the second of the three lancer regiments in the Guard.

[2] The title given to the head of the Imperial household.

[3] Formed in 1804, this was a cavalry unit in the Old Guard.

When he left this fatal place the next day the Emperor granted the pastor an annuity of 1,200 francs and gave him a sum of money for the purchase of the house on the condition that he should erect and maintain on the spot where the Grand Marshal's bed had been, a stone with this inscription:

'Here General Duroc, Duc de Frioul and Grand Marshal of the Emperor Napoleon, after being struck by a cannon-ball, died in the arms of his Emperor and friend.'[1]

On 4 June, after the armistice of Pleswitz, we settled into quarters near Dresden. On 10 August the whole Guard was reviewed by the Emperor; present were some 50,000 men from the artillery, the infantry and the cavalry. As he went along the ten lines formed by his troops, Napoleon never failed to raise his hat to the cries of 'Long live the Emperor!' and to call out himself, 'Long live France!'

On 15 August we left Dresden and, preparing for action, we moved towards Bautzen. Austria had just resumed hostilities against us. The Allies threatened us with 500,000 men and we had but 300,000 men together with the Imperial Guard. But the Emperor was with us!

On the 23rd the Emperor defeated Blücher at Golberg and drove him back into Silesia; then with the Guard he countermarched towards Dresden where we arrived on the 26th at ten in the morning. We were none too soon for 200,000 Austrians were encamped near the town. That same day at four in the afternoon they attacked the outskirts of the town from all directions. In a valiant defence of the town several generals of the Guard were wounded, particularly General Gros, the commander of the 1st Regiment of *chasseurs à pied*, who was so well known for his bravery and for his ready answers to the Emperor.

One day on the Champ-de-Mars the Emperor, wishing to tease him, had said: 'Gros, the grenadiers handle their weapons better than the chasseurs.'

'Sire,' replied the general, 'I will wager six francs that my chasseurs perform drill better than your grenadiers.'

The pronounced Auvergnat accent with which these words were said made it obvious that, among other things, Gros had not been born in Paris.

During the battle of Dresden I was crossing a street in the suburb of Berg which my regiment was holding, when I was saluted by a corporal of the 3rd Troop who was wearing the decoration of the *Légion d'honneur*. I returned his salute without stopping, but he called

[1] The Allies were to prevent Napoleon's wishes from being carried out.

to me: 'Sir, I hope you will forgive me if I ask how you are since we are old acquaintances, but you probably do not recognize me now.'

'I have been in the Guard only five months and I do not know many people there. What is your name, please?'

'I am the trumpet-major from the 8th Hussars whom you wounded in 1806 when we fought a duel near Warsaw.'

'Ah! Now I remember. So you gave up your trumpet and your regiment to join the Guard?'

'Yes, sir.'

'I am delighted to see you again. How long have you been in the Guard?'

'Since the Russian campaign. I was promoted to corporal a year ago.'

'What is your captain's name?'

'Monsieur Achyntre.'

'I know him. I shall be glad to recommend you to him. And do not hesitate to speak to me whenever you meet me in future. I shall always be happy to share a drop of brandy with you.'

Alas! only once was he able to take advantage of this offer which I gladly made. When, on the evening after the battle of Dresden, I went to see Captain Achyntre, I was saddened to learn that the corporal whom I wished to recommend had been killed by a cannon-ball.

'I am truly sorry to have lost him,' said his captain. 'Poor Auguste was a first-class fellow and I would certainly have made him a sergeant in my troop.'

Then he added: 'After talking to you, Parquin, the poor corporal was telling his friends how you had beaten him when you were a quartermaster. He was saying that you were not the sort of quartermaster who could only write and keep the books, but that you could really handle a sabre.'

'Poor Auguste,' I said. 'He will never challenge anyone again. Now he is where we shall all go one day.'

The battle of Dresden, in which the rest of the army covered itself with glory, brought us only the most wretched driving rain and enemy cannon fire. Lieutenant Brice, the regimental paymaster, had a magnificent horse killed under him. The animal was worth at least 3,000 francs, but curiously enough the incident earned the lieutenant a sharp reprimand from General Lefebvre-Desnoëttes who objected to his accountant's presence on the battlefield where, said the general, he had no business to be; his post was within Dresden itself with his clerks and the regimental chest.

It was in this battle that General Moreau was struck dead at the side of the Emperor Alexander while riding with a group of Allied generals. At five o'clock the Saxon peasant, to whose dwelling Moreau had been taken with two shattered legs after being hit by a cannon-ball, brought a superb Great Dane to the Emperor. Around its neck the dog had a big brass collar on which was written: 'I belong to General Moreau.' The peasant came to report what had happened and to sell the dog for ten napoleons. The Emperor saw that he received this amount, but allowed him to keep the dog.

The manoeuvres employed in the battle of Dresden were compared by the Emperor with those of Jena and their result was that the Austrians lost 30,000 men, of whom 12,000 were taken prisoner, and 200 cannon. The Emperor spent that night on the battlefield and the following day returned to Dresden. We moved towards Pirna without halting, but having reached there, we again returned to Dresden. On 7 October we started out for Berlin, but once more we returned to Dresden. It was from there that we left on 10 October to move with the main body of the army to Leipzig.

On 13 October I was in command of the escort troop which was guarding the Emperor's bivouac a quarter of a league before the town. At four o'clock I witnessed the arrival of the King of Saxony and his family who had come from Dresden to Leipzig with their royal escort. As soon as he saw the dust raised by their approach, the Emperor walked some fifty paces down the road and would have walked right up to the King. But the King of Saxony had already alighted and with his hat in his hand he came straight to greet the Emperor. I can still picture the King; a tall, handsome old man with powdered wig and long queue. He was wearing a white uniform and the chains of the two watches he carried hung at his sides. He hastened to take off his gloves and to offer his hand to the Emperor, but the latter embraced him, calling him his brother. Together they went over to the coach in which the Queen of Saxony sat with her daughter, the Princess Augusta. I was very close to the Emperor, who moreover spoke quite loudly to the ladies through the open right-hand door of the coach. This was the dialogue I heard:

'Sire,' said the Queen, 'how are the Empress and the King of Rome?'

'They are both well; I received a letter yesterday.'

'Will you give battle tomorrow, Sire?'

'Yes, I think so.'

'And you will be victorious,' added Princess Augusta.

'Ah! how typically feminine to have no doubts at all! Nevertheless, we must hope you are right.'

The Emperor saluted his distinguished guests who returned to the town; he himself soon made his way there also.

On 16 October at nine in the morning, the action at Wachau, which occupied the first day of the battle of Leipzig, began. The cannonades from the enemy artillery were the signal for the start of a terrible bombardment by 200 guns, and cannon-balls rained down upon us. The Guard cavalry was placed in the centre of the army. I can still see General Drouot standing in front of us indefatigably directing the fire of some hundred cannon of the Guard.

The Emperor noticed that the extreme right of his line, commanded by General Oudinot and comprising 19,000 infantrymen of the Young Guard, was in danger. He despatched General Letort with a cavalry force of 800 men made up of 200 chasseurs, 200 lancers, 200 dragoons and 200 mounted grenadiers drawn from the Old Guard. The Duc de Reggio [*Oudinot*] had taken the precaution of breaking his line and had formed squares. I was in the column despatched by Napoleon. In troops we moved to the right flank. When we reached the threatened area, we moved into the gaps between the squares and immediately prepared to give battle. An Austrian cavalry charge against us failed completely; in fact, it brought us an outstanding success. Because of the nature of the position we had just occupied, all retreat by a regiment of La Tour's Dragoons was cut off and the only way back to the safety of their own lines was through our ranks.

Marshal Oudinot, whose difficulties had been solved by our arrival, emerged from a square and suddenly appearing among us called: 'Cavalrymen, about turn! Here comes the enemy!' and indeed, preceded by a cloud of dust, the La Tour Dragoons were riding down on us with their sabres ready. We met them with a wall of steel and 190 or 200 of them fell into our hands. In the confusion of the battle I saw Marshal Oudinot alone and in danger in the path of the charging enemy. He was trying to draw his sword but he could not get it out of its scabbard. I wasted not a moment in placing myself in front of the illustrious marshal who quickly drew his pistol. Thus I was fortunate enough to extricate him from the danger and to allow him to reach the centre of a square of his infantry safe and sound. That evening his son, who was a captain in my regiment, took me to his father's bivouac. The marshal embraced me, thanked me and made me share his modest supper which consisted of a cold chicken washed down with a bottle of wine and a bottle of brandy.

The following day the armies remained in a state of readiness facing each other. We spent the day on the plain near a windmill in which the Emperor's headquarters had been established. The regiment remained in reserve the whole day; the few losses we suffered were caused by enemy gunfire. I was to lose one of my friends, a lieutenant in the regiment whose name was Henneson. He was hit full in the chest by a cannon-ball. After shattering his stomach the ball lodged in his cape which he had slung diagonally over his back.

At nightfall the regiment bivouacked alongside a hedge which enclosed a meadow. As I was making my way to a part reserved for my troop I heard someone call my name; it was one of my friends who was a lieutenant and assistant adjutant of the 7th Voltigeurs[1] of the Young Guard. He invited me to share his modest supper.

'I shall be delighted to do so, my dear fellow, but allow me a few moments to fetch some brandy which I have been able to buy from the regimental *cantinière*.'

A quarter of an hour later I returned with a loaf of bread under my arm to rejoin my friend Servatius. When we were all present, someone took a mess-tin and in it prepared a vast quantity of stew made of pieces of hare flavoured with potatoes, onions and other vegetables. We all agreed that it was an excellent meal.

'Did you send someone into the market at Leipzig?' I asked Servatius with a smile.

'No, my friend, One of our quartermaster-sergeants shot the hare we are eating. The animal took it into its head to run across the battlefield—fortunately for our appetites—just in front of the company.'

'What splendid luck! But why have you not invited your sergeant to share the meal?'

'Well, that would be rather difficult, for one minute after shooting the hare and shouting to me that our supper tonight was taken care of, the sergeant himself fell, struck by a cannon-ball which sent him to have his supper elsewhere . . . I inherited the hare, and that is the story of our supper.'

'Well, my dear Servatius,' I said to him, offering my flask of brandy, 'let us drink to the memory of your sergeant.'

After we had done this, I took my leave of the gentlemen whose supper I had shared and returned to my bivouac. At two o'clock in the

[1] In 1804 Napoleon formed *compagnies d'élite* of able infantrymen who were too small for companies of grenadiers or carabiniers. The role of the voltigeur was to skirmish rather than to fight in the line and he sometimes fought with the cavalry, being transported into action on horseback behind the rider.

morning the regiment broke camp to return to Leipzig. The Emperor, who had slept at the Black Eagle Inn beyond the bridge over the Elster, came back at six o'clock with his escort to the palace of the King of Saxony to say farewell to the King who wept as Napoleon left. At seven o'clock the Emperor had recrossed the bridge when the sound of a terrible explosion made us all turn round. We saw thick smoke rising and we realized that some disaster had taken place. The Emperor immediately rode back the way he had come and we followed him towards Leipzig. Half an hour later we discovered that the bridge had been blown up and a part of the army had been left at the mercy of the enemy.

The army started its retreat towards Mayence with 150,000 Austrians behind it and with 50,000 Bavarians ahead of it. These latter troops had, after defecting to the enemy, proceeded as quickly as possible along the road to Hanau in order to block our route back to France. The army was still in good spirit and carried out the retreat in an orderly manner. Every day the rearguard commanded by the Duc de Trevisse [*Mortier*] was engaged in desperate actions. On 27 October the regiment was crossing the Fulda when a convoy of wounded arrived at the river. They were travelling in light carriages which had specially been constructed to carry four wounded men.

'What are you doing there?' I asked my friend Servatius whom I suddenly spotted among the wounded.

'My dear Parquin, I am with my Colonel (General Couloumy, who was to die on 29 October) and two other officers who, like me, are wounded.'

'How is your wound?'

'I am in considerable pain from a bullet in my leg. I had a field-dressing put on three days ago, but the wound has not yet been treated.'

'Can you manage to ride a horse for two hours?'

'I do not have one; my horses were not able to get across the bridge over the Elster.'

'I can let you have one.'

I immediately sent for my servant and within a few moments I had extricated my friend from his critical position, for the wounded had to be left on the other bank of the Fulda. I was able to arrange for the regimental medical officer to treat Servatius and four days later we safely reached Mayence where he went into hospital.

The Bavarians who were waiting for us at Hanau on the Kinzig had anticipated an easy victory. But it was the Guard they were fighting and the Emperor was with us!

On the morning of 30 October Marshal Macdonald was ordered to debouch from the forest, but it was midday before he succeeded for the enemy, supported by a strong force of artillery, resisted strenuously. The Bavarians had entrenched themselves behind the walls of a farm to the left of a road across the plain and they were defending the position fiercely.

The Emperor summoned General Cambronne.

'How many *chasseurs à pied* of the Old Guard have you?'

'Eighteen hundred, Sire.'

'You will personally lead them and capture that farm which is held by some ten thousand Bavarians. I give you two hours to accomplish the mission.'

Within an hour the Bavarians had been dislodged without firing a shot. A headlong bayonet charge had persuaded them not to wait for the 'bee-hives'—the name the enemy gave to the bearskins worn by the grenadiers and the chasseurs of the Old Guard. These superb soldiers spread terror wherever they went.

At three o'clock the artillery arrived. Emerging from the forest, General Drouot positioned his fifty cannon along its edge and opened fire. In fours the regiment rode out on to the highway running along the edge of the forest. I saw the whole file of four chasseurs in front of me mown down by a cannon-ball. I lifted my horse's head and, moving forward rapidly, I brought my legs hard down on its flanks; my horse obeyed and leaped over the obstacle which had so suddenly formed in front of me. Already six of our guns on the road had been surrounded and the gunners were defending themselves with side-arms when Captain Oudinot, the son of the marshal, charged with his troop of chasseurs and saved both men and guns.

The mounted grenadiers charged headlong against the Bavarian cavalry. Their assistant adjutant, my intrepid friend Guindey who had killed Prince Louis of Prussia at Saalfeld, was found dead on the battle-field that evening. His body was covered in sabre-cuts, but the half-dozen dead Bavarian cavalrymen around him showed that he had sold his life dearly. That same morning in the forest this brave officer had been present when the Emperor remarked to the officers standing around him:

'What do you think of these Bavarians? They were our allies yesterday and now they try to bar our way and prevent us from returning to France. They even go so far as to try when we are within sight of the church-steeples of Mayence.'

'They go too far, Sire,' Guindey had said. 'But have no fear;

these Bavarians will pay for their arrogant treachery today.'

Our victory proved the truth of these words, but poor Guindey himself was to pay for this success with his life. I had shaken hands with him just before he had set off in the charge from which he was not to return.

In the course of that morning I made the acquaintance of the son of the famous Marshal Moncey. We had come to see his friends Lauriston, who was a major in the 1st Regiment of the *gardes d'honneur*,[1] and Oudinot, who was a captain in the Guard chasseurs. Major Moncey had just left the infantry where he had served for some years to join the 7th Hussars. He had taken part in the Russian campaign as a captain in the Guard *chasseurs à pied*. At Smolensk, when the Emperor was giving out various awards and decorations to these famous soldiers, he had gathered together the officers and had said: 'I have just made a number of you happy, but there remains one cross of the *Légion d'honneur*; it shall go to the officer who is considered by the others to deserve it most. I shall endorse your choice, so speak out. Who is it to be?'

Everyone called out Moncey's name.

'My former page,' objected the Emperor. 'You are choosing him so as to flatter me. Someone else shall have it . . .'

'But Sire, did you not tell us to speak frankly? We assure you that we could not choose a bolder officer.'

'Well,' said the Emperor, to the great satisfaction of all the officers, 'in that case I will place the cross upon his breast in the name of you all.'

But to return to the battle of Hanau. By five o'clock complete victory was ours. Captain Schmidt, leading a squadron in which I found myself, forced two battalions of infantry to surrender at the gates of Hanau. In this action I received a bayonet wound across my face; afterwards I was promoted to the rank of captain in the Young Guard Chasseurs.

On 31 October we reached Frankfurt and on 2 November, Mayence. On that day I had the honour to command the escort troops in front of the imperial palace. When I was relieved, instead of returning to my own troop which was three leagues away in some of the surrounding villages, I arranged for the Guard supply officer to

[1] These were cavalry units created by Napoleon in 1813. The men came from wealthy families and equipped themselves at their own expense; they were commissioned after a year's service in the field. The four regiments, each under a major-general, were disbanded in 1814.

issue the bread, beer and brandy needed by my detachment. My sergeant was to take the men back and I gave him a note for the captain to inform him that I was staying two hours in Mayence to purchase some items of clothing.

I was hungry; I had not eaten since the previous day in Frankfurt. I made my way to the first hotel I could find; this was the Ville-de-Paris. But I found it completely invaded by soldiers from every regiment who were queuing up at the kitchen in order to cook their veal cutlets and mutton chops. This was the only meat available and, moreover, each man had to stand by the fire with sabre drawn until the meat was done so that it was not stolen half-cooked from him. I decided to make do with a crust of bread which my orderly was carrying for me, for there were the same crowds of soldiers in all the hotels and restaurants. I was therefore making my way towards the road leading out of the town to Paris with the intention of returning to my regiment when, from my mounted position I glimpsed in the dining-room of a private house a table fully laid for ten people. At the sight of this splendid discovery I was struck by an idea. I dismounted and gave my horse to my orderly. I went up five steps and banged the knocker on the door. A servant opened the door and asked in German: 'What do you want, sir?'

'I should like to speak to your master.'

'Ah, you wish to see Monseiur Hermann,' he said and led me into the dining-room. He left me there while he went to inform his master that I wished to speak to him.

A gentleman, whom I took to be the master of the house, entered and I said to him: 'Monsieur Hermann, could I prevail upon you to be so kind as to ask the lady of the house if I might share the meal for which the table has been set? I escorted the Emperor Napoleon across the bridge into Mayence two hours ago; I have not eaten for twenty-four hours because the crowds of hungry troops in the town make it impossible to obtain any food. I was passing your house just now and, seeing your table laid, I thought that the lady or the master of the house might have pity on my famished condition. If I am mistaken, sir, I will gladly trouble you no further.'

'Sir,' said Monseiur Hermann, 'my wife does not speak French,' and he indicated one of the ladies who had just come in with the guests. 'But I know how kind she is and I am sure she will be most happy to have you at her table among the friends whom we are entertaining.'

I thanked him and, having greeted the assembled company, I sat down beside Madame Hermann with whom I exchanged the few words of German I knew. The general conversation was in that language and I did not enter into it. I did, however, do great justice to the extremely good meal. I asked Monsieur Hermann if he would allow a servant to take a bottle of wine to my orderly. He immediately sent word for my orderly to come into the yard and to put the horses in the stable. My man went into the kitchen where, like his master upstairs, he had an excellent meal. In short, Monsieur Hermann was the perfect host. The cathedral clock was striking four when I took my leave of my hosts. I thanked them for their hospitality and when I gave Monsieur Hermann my card, I said:

'I hope that this card will enable you to remember the name of the officer of the Guard whom you treated so charitably. As for your name and that of your wife, they will long remain in my memory.'

As I left I gave the servant six francs. Then I took the road leading to the regiment's quarters where I arrived at seven o'clock.

X

While we were in our quarters we spent our time attending to our weapons and repairing our uniforms. After such a rapid and exhausting campaign this was very necessary. The arrival within the walls of Mayence of such a great number of troops and the overcrowding of the hospitals by so many sick and wounded gave rise to an outbreak of typhus which within a few days carried off many of the brave men the battlefield had spared.

Our village was a large one which, as its contribution to the war, had to supply all sorts of food and goods to the garrison at Mayence. On the day before we left I was sitting by the kitchen fire with my host, a man of some importance in the district. He was giving an animated account to one of his neighbours of what he had seen in Mayence where he had gone that morning with a load of hay. My orderly, who was present, spoke German and he translated the conversation for me.

It seemed that deaths resulting from the outbreak of typhus had been exceptionally numerous over the previous week and all the vehicles bringing supplies in from the country were being requisitioned as soon as they were unloaded. These vehicles were then being used to take the bodies which were filling the hospitals to the cemetery. This was going on well into the night. My host was saying that his produce had been found satisfactory and the supply officer at the army stores had accepted it, but afterwards his waggon, drawn by four good horses, had been requisitioned for transporting bodies to the cemetery. He had already made one journey from the hospital to the cemetery and was on his second one when, as he passed the road leading out of the town to his village, he gave a sharp blow with his whip to the lead horse and pulled it to the left towards the road out of town. Whipping up his team, he was soon beyond the town. Then, to rid himself of his load he had raised the floorboards of his waggon every five minutes in order to let one of the corpses drop out. When he had finally reached the village, only one of his original load remained. He added, however, that he had insisted on giving this one a decent burial in the village cemetery.

I could not help feeling that, although not all the local countryfolk were as grasping as traditional Norman peasants, this particular one was the equal of the meanest of them.

The Emperor spent five days at Mayence to reorganize the army and on 6 November he left for Paris. On the 9th he arrived at Saint-Cloud. On 1 December we resumed our move back to France. On 21 December I received my commission as a captain in the 2nd Regiment of the Guard Chasseurs. I was also ordered by General Lefebvre-Desnoëttes to proceed to Paris to take command of the 11th Troop; in this troop all the N.C.O.s were drawn from the Old Guard.

The first day of January 1814 saw me reunited with my family in Paris. That same month eleven years before, I had joined the army. My service in the field had brought me promotion to the rank of captain in the Imperial Guard and membership of the *Légion d'honneur*. No doubt my parents were proud of me for I was only twenty-six, but I must admit that not once did they tell me of their pride for they had never approved of my becoming a soldier.

I assumed command of the 11th Troop and on 6 February we were ordered to join the Old Guard in Champagne, although the 2nd Regiment, of which my troop formed part, was with the Army of the North at Antwerp. I still do not know why it was that my troop and a troop of Mamelukes should have had the privilege of fighting through the campaign in France side by side with the chasseurs of the Old Guard. The captain of the Mameluke troop who made the journey with me was far senior to me since he had been with the Mameluke Regiment from its formation at the time of the Consulate, but a regulation peculiar to the Guard laid down that foreigners, whether Egyptians, Poles, Italians or Dutch, would, regardless of their seniority, be subordinate to a French officer of equal rank. This captain had been living in retirement at Marseilles for fourteen years. He had rejoined the Mamelukes following the Emperor's decree issued after the invasion of France by the Allies on 2 January 1814.

Captain Ibrahim Bey had commanded the troop of Mamelukes which had come to France after the Egyptian campaign. One day after his arrival in Paris he had lost his way in the capital.

The oriental clothes which he was wearing had astonished the Parisians and a curious throng gathered around him. By chance he wandered into the area around the corn-market and there people jeered and whistled after him. Some even threw mud at him and shouted that he had no business to go around dressed as a Turk since it was not carnival time. Captain Ibrahim Bey, who understood neither the language nor the reason for the mocking, drew his pistols and in a flash shot dead two enormous market porters. He was preparing to continue the fight with his scimitar and his dagger when a civil patrol arrived and with some difficulty overcame him.

News of the incident reached the Tuileries. The First Consul summoned Ibrahim Bey who, when questioned, answered that he had merely acted as he did in his own country when the mob created a disturbance.

'You are not here to maintain order in that manner,' said the First Consul through his interpreter Roustan.[1] 'Tomorrow you will leave for Marseilles. There the climate is warm and you will be able to live on your pay of 6,000 francs which I will allow you to retain. But 2,000 francs will be deducted as a pension for the two women whom you have made widows. People are used to your dress in Marseilles, but I forbid you to use your arms or even to carry them.'

Only fourteen years later did Captain Ibrahim take them up again so as to use them against the enemy which was invading France.

On 6 February the body of 600 men left Paris under the command of Major Kirmann who was an old friend of mine. We met up with

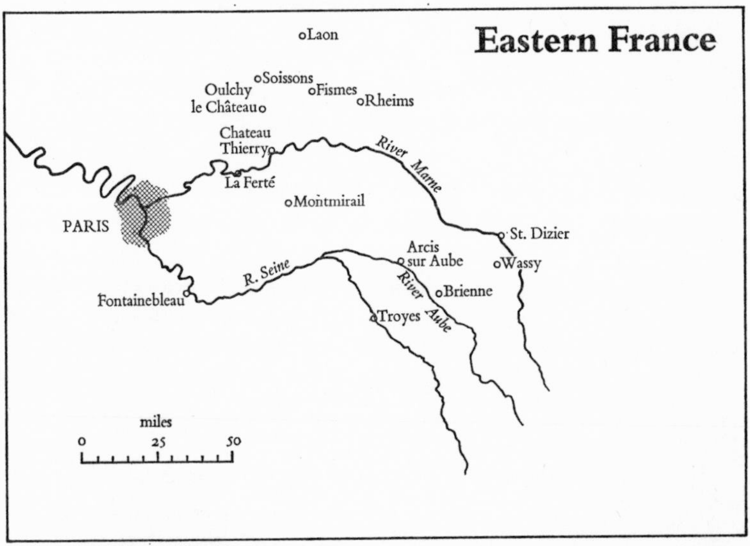

[1] Roustan (1780–1845), although a Mameluke, was a Georgian by birth. He began his career as valet to Napoleon in Egypt, but he refused to follow his master to Elba in 1814. He was imprisoned during the Hundred Days, but was rewarded with a lottery concession after the Restoration.

the army on the 10th, the day before the battle of Montmirail. The action on the 11th took place at noon on the plateau. My orders were to charge from the left with my troop against a Russian square which was simultaneously charged from the right by a squadron of Guard dragoons under General Letort. We were completely successful and our two formations came together in the middle of the square. The Russians had been so sure that their square would not be breached that they had taken off their packs and put them on the ground. We had to allow them time to pick them up again and to lay down their muskets in their place.

The farm at Les Greneaux was difficult to capture as it was protected by heavy artillery fire. The enemy troops were sheltered by the walls behind which they had taken up position and they were not driven out until two o'clock in the afternoon. The difficult task of driving them out was given by the Emperor to Marshal Ney. The marshal dismounted and with sword in hand went to the head of the six battalions of the Guard. Before leading them forward, however, he ordered the men to open the pans of their muskets and to throw away the percussion caps. The enemy was to be driven out at the point of the bayonet. He led the men forward in a charge and his boldness was fully rewarded. The Russians and the Prussians fled from the farm, leaving behind their guns, their limbers and even their cooking pots.

While Ney was thus ensuring victory, General Henrion was ordered to proceed with his regiment of *chasseurs à pied* against a redoubt containing enemy artillery. A brigade of infantry of the line had shortly before failed to take it, but the general formed up his men in an attacking column and they dashed forward, undaunted by the terrible fire from the enemy.

The Russian general, seeing the danger to his guns, threw a mass of cavalry against the flank of the column. Immediately General Henrion ordered the column to halt and to form a square.

When the enemy cavalry was only ten yards away it was met with a hail of fire and forced to turn back, leaving a great number of dead behind. The general ordered the column to reform and without reloading, he and the men charged the redoubt. This they carried, in spite of the desperate resistance of the Russian gunners who were run through as they tried to defend their guns. The Emperor, who had closely followed the attack, galloped up to the captured redoubt and called for General Henrion. He shook the general by the hand and appointed him a commander of the *Légion d'honneur* on the spot, adding: 'General, I fully approved of your little halt during your charge.'

The victory was complete and Yorck and Sacken retreated, or rather fled, towards Château-Thierry. We caught up with them on the 14th when they were still a league from the town. One of my former commanding officers in the 20th Chasseurs, Colonel Curély, who was commanding the 10th Hussars was promoted to the rank of brigadier-general as the result of two brilliant charges which he made at the head of his regiment and which were witnessed by the Emperor himself.

The enemy, who the day after the battle of Montmirail, no longer possessed any artillery, supplies or transport and who had abandoned his wounded to the mercy of the victors, hastened to reach Château-Thierry and to put the Marne between himself and us.

The Emperor, satisfied at having utterly shattered these two divisions, moved with his Guard against the army under Schwarzenberg, which was advancing along the Seine. On the 17th he caught up with it on the plains near Nangis. The dragoons who had come from Spain under General Treillard inflicted a heavy defeat upon the Austrians. This would have delivered the whole of their army into our hands if Marshal Victor had seized the bridge at Montereau as he had been ordered to do. On 2 March Blücher with the main body of the Prussian army and a Russian army corps crossed the Marne at Château-Thierry. To protect his rear he blew up an arch of the bridge and we were forced to halt for twenty-four hours. During this time we were able to take the rest which we so badly needed. The Emperor set up his headquarters in the postmaster's house which was in the suburb we were occupying. The next day, 3 March, the engineers had arrived and at ten o'clock the Emperor moved to a bivouac by the banks of the Marne so as to be present at the work on the bridge. He asked General Bertrand, his Grand Marshal whom he had ordered to supervise the work, how long the task would take.

'Four hours,' answered the general.

'I will give you six,' said Napoleon.

Four o'clock was striking in Château-Thierry when the bridge was reopened.

That morning General Colbert had ordered me to be ready with 100 men of the Old Guard for a mission which the Emperor himself would give me! At four o'clock I was at the bridge with my men. When I reported to the Emperor he said to me: 'Captain, you will pursue the enemy and bring back some prisoners for me.'

Aware that three roads led out of Château-Thierry to Soissons, La Ferté and to Rheims, I asked: 'Along which road, Sire?'

'Along the road to Soissons.'

The honour of receiving such an order from no less a person than the Emperor himself filled me with a determination to succeed. I ordered my men to advance, and in fours they rode forward over the bridge. On the other bank I allowed them to accept, without stopping, the bread, brandy, ham and sausages offered to them by the good citizens who were overjoyed to see French troops again after being made to quarter the Russians and the Prussians who had behaved very badly in this unfortified and peaceful town.

I had covered nearly three leagues when I came across a small village in flames. Its inhabitants had abandoned it to seek refuge in the woods in the middle of winter rather than submit to the brutal treatment of the enemy soldiers. I had the place searched in the hope of perhaps finding some old man who could give me information about the enemy's movements, but my men had no success. Then a sergeant whom I had ordered to dismount came to tell me that in the very last house in the village, the only one untouched by the flames, he had discovered some stragglers from the Russian army. They were stretched out by the kitchen fire, probably waiting for their meal to cook. The sergeant added that with a few other chasseurs he could capture these enemy infantrymen. This he did most skilfully. He ordered his men to aim their carbines through the window at the hearth around which the Russians were sleeping peacefully. The enemy soldiers must have been terrified to hear the bullets which whistled past their ears when the sergeant gave the word to open fire.

Immediately after the volley the sergeant and his men rushed into the room with sabres drawn and captured the Russians, none of whom was wounded. He then brought them back to the squadron which I had drawn up at the entrance to the village.

If it had not been for the fact that at that time France had been invaded by the Coalition armies, I would have found some amusement in the capture of an enormous cooking-pot in which some thirty chickens, a number of hams, potatoes and other ingredients were stewing. The bread, which had already been cut up in the room, completed a delicious meal of which the troop from my own squadron quickly took advantage.

According to the strict laws of war, and in view of the isolated position I was in, I should have had the Russian grenadiers shot immediately for I had come upon them in a village which the enemy had set on fire. But their lives were spared by the Emperor's order that I should take some prisoners for him. I even went so far as to let them have some of the food they had prepared. I thought it a little harsh to deprive them of a meal which had brought them such bad luck. From what they told me, it was their reluctance to be parted from their cherished cooking-pot that had caused them to lag behind and they had counted on making up the lost time by marching at night. I gathered from the information I extracted that I was following close behind the enemy who was withdrawing with all speed to Soissons.

I pushed forward once more, leaving my prisoners with the sergeant commanding the rearguard. At about ten o'clock in the evening when we had gone another league, my scouts came to report that the enemy was occupying the town of Oulchy-le-Château, four leagues along the road from Soissons. I quickly sent word to General Colbert, who I knew was following closely behind me with a brigade of Guard cavalry, that the enemy rearguard was in position on our side of Oulchy-le-Château, that the town was completely occupied and that, judging by the number of camp-fires, the enemy was there in force. I also informed the general that I was going to carry out the Emperor's orders and I requested the support of a few more squadrons as it was possible that the enemy would recover sufficiently to inflict considerable damage on my squadron on its way back from performing its mission. I gave my men and their horses time to rest and then I moved slowly forward with my squadron on the unpaved side of the road until I saw the enemy a hundred yards away.

At the first enemy challenge I ordered the squadron to advance at the gallop. We brushed aside the mounted sentry and took the outpost and the main post completely by surprise. Spreading alarm and confusion, we galloped through Oulchy-le-Château until we came to the Russian and Prussian bivouacs. The enemy awoke to find himself being cut down and run through by the chasseurs and the lancers and fired at by the pistols and carbines of the dragoons and the Mamelukes. My squadron had been deliberately made up of men from each of these arms of the Old Guard.

Taken by surprise in this daring night attack, the enemy thought that several cavalry regiments had come down on him. He was completely routed and lost many killed and wounded. We took a hundred prisoners, including two colonels and several officers. They were immediately sent to the Emperor who was at Fismes. From them

Napoleon learned some disastrous news; General Moreau,[1] the commander of Soissons, had opened the gates of the town to the enemy without offering any resistance.

'That name has always brought me misfortune,' said the Emperor.

The position of the enemy army would have been most critical if Soissons had not been given up. The road from Château-Thierry to La Ferté was held by Marshal Macdonald with 17,000 men. The road to Rheims was not paved and was impassable to the enemy who had consequently been forced back towards Soissons where the Emperor, Marshal Mortier and the Guard were ready to force him to submit. But now fate had shown itself to be against us!

On 5 March I was sent out by General Colbert to reconnoitre along the road to Fismes. The officer commanding his vanguard had pursued some Cossack scouts and had rashly taken his troop through a gorge full of water-mills. I had to support him with three other troops from my squadron. I then realized that I was facing vastly superior forces. I had, moreover, not been sent to engage the enemy but to reconnoitre. I gave the order to return along the gorge, but we had to do so in single file and at a walking pace. While we were thus engaged the enemy outflanked us and reached the road to Soissons before we did. We had to cut our way through almost five hundred Cossacks and our losses were heavy. I lost two officers who were wounded and captured and forty-three chasseurs who were killed, wounded or captured. I was wounded in the arm from a thrust with a lance. Nevertheless, my reconnaissance was invaluable to the army, which would have been taken from the rear as it camped in front of Soissons beyond the range of the cannon mounted on the town walls.

On my return I reported on my mission to General Colbert who commented: 'Well, you cannot always win in war'—an allusion to my highly successful attack on the night of 2 March at Oulchy-le-Château.

'That is true, sir; but at least I have the satisfaction of telling you that everyone fought well. The proof of this lies in the fact that half my squadron has been disabled. If I may make a personal request, I would like your permission to go and have the lance wound in my left arm dressed.'

In fact, my wound was not serious and it did not prevent me from continuing on active service. When France was invaded, it was the

[1] Jean-Claude Moreau (1755–1828). He was court-martialled for his surrender of Soissons, but at the Restoration he was appointed to command a department.

duty of everyone to come to her defence and I was too proud to be one of her defenders to withdraw to the rear. Some eau-de-Cologne, some lint and some water—my favourite remedy—soon had me fit again.

Two days later on 7 March the battle of Craonne took place. Generals Nansouty and Grouchy led the Guard cavalry in several highly successful charges across the plateau. In them the two generals were wounded and General Laferrière [*Lesveque de la Ferrière*], the *major* of the mounted grenadiers, had his foot carried away by a cannon-ball. The surgeons had to amputate his leg and during the operation, which he bore with great courage, the general repeatedly called out: 'Long live the Emperor!'

My friend Captain Achyntre was killed by a cannon-ball. That morning he had announced that it would be his last day alive and by two o'clock he was dead. He was an elderly officer whose service had started with the *Guides* in Egypt. He was greatly missed by the whole regiment.

I and my squadron were constantly subjected to the enemy artillery fire. Lieutenant Numance de Girardin had his scabbard shattered and his horse killed by a cannon-ball. He put down his escape to a sword-knot which a very pretty Parisienne, Mademoiselle Lavolle, had given him; he claimed it was a talisman which would save him from any danger. That evening, however, I told this young officer who was seeing action for the first time, that a cannon-ball could often cause injuries without actually hitting a man and that he should massage his thigh with some good brandy. To obtain the brandy he had to send a peasant, who was warming himself by our fire, to a village a league away. The man agreed to go and left with a napoleon. He came back at two in the morning with four bottles of brandy. There was a great shortage of brandy and it had become very expensive; the *cantinières* had none at all. Monsieur de Girardin was fast asleep on some straw and it would have been quite inhuman to rouse him. In any case, our motive in making him send for the brandy had merely been to obtain some drink with which we could celebrate his arrival in the troop for he had felt no pain in his thigh and had nothing to worry about. Monseiur de Girardin, when he awoke the next morning, took the trick we had played on him in very good part and we had, after all, emptied our glasses in honour of the lady who had given him his talisman.

I do not know what trifling incident provoked a quarrel between Captain Ibrahim Bey and Captain Lindsai, an aide-de-camp of General

Lefebvre-Desnoëttes, but the inevitable outcome was that the two parties arranged to meet behind a farm to settle their differences with sabres. I argued as well as I could with Ibrahim Bey, who had asked me to be his second. I pointed out that a duel between officers was the worst possible example to set at a time when France had been invaded and when every single one of her defenders owed his life to France alone. Captain Lindsai accepted my argument, but Ibrahim the Mameluke, with his eyes popping out of his head, merely repeated, half in French and half in Arabic:

'You must understand, my dear Parquin—when I am a friend, I am as quiet and as kind as a little dog. When I am an enemy, I am a lion and I fight.'

'Well then, be friends and shake hands. You can see that Captain Lindsai is offering his hand,' I said and finally the Mameluke agreed.

A few days later Ibrahim Bey was with some skirmishers out on the plain and there he fought like a real lion. But his turban came undone and fell over his eyes and he was struck down by Cossack lances. He was wounded and captured, though not before he had felled some half-dozen Russians.

On the 9th we were at Laon after going around Soissons which was occupied by Blücher, Sacken and Wintzingerode. That evening my squadron formed the guard and, as was my habit when in the field, I went out personally to the main post to see the mounted sentries were in position and then to the outpost. When I was coming back I met a corporal from my squadron who, in spite of my strict order to my men not to dismount before my return, was walking along with a bundle of fodder on his head.

When I reprimanded him the corporal dropped the fodder, but I was so infuriated to see my orders flouted in such serious circumstances that I struck the corporal across his back with the flat of my sabre. Immediately the poor devil pulled open his coat and in the moonlight I saw the cross he was wearing. Grasping his sabre he said:

'Captain, I have served my country and my Emperor for twenty-two years. I won this cross two years ago and now, in a matter of seconds, you have dishonoured me for ever!'

As can be imagined, I was appalled at having lost my temper with an old soldier. I hastened to say to him:

'Listen, corporal. If I were your equal in rank I should not hesitate to give you satisfaction, for I am not afraid of you. But I am your captain and I am apologizing to you. Will you shake hands?'

'Of course, sir. There is no ill-feeling on my part,' he answered, and he gripped my hand. Then he picked up his bundle of fodder and returned to the bivouac.

Half an hour later he was sharing my modest supper which was, none the less, made all the more appetizing by a bottle of brandy.

The next day, 10 March, we came under the enemy's fire and a cannon-ball hit a file of chasseurs who were in front of my squadron. Nine men were bowled over. Not since the battle of Hanau had I seen such a devastating example of the power of artillery. On the 13th we countermarched on Rheims which General Corbineau had been forced to abandon. General de Ségur, at the head of his regiment of *gardes d'honneur*, charged into the town and after a pitched battle drove out the Russians. General de Saint-Priest,[1] a French émigré who was commanding the Russians, perished in the action. A shell-burst injured the foot of the horse which I was riding; it was the same fine horse I had taken from the English officer I had unseated at Salamanca.

'Captain, we shall have to take another one for you from the enemy,' said one of my chasseurs.

'Very well,' I said, thanking him, 'but I doubt if it will be as good as the one which I have just lost and to which I was very attached.'

On the 18th the Emperor manoeuvred against the enemy at La Ferté; on the 20th we were at Arcis-sur-Aube. It was here that a shell which fell near the horse which the Emperor was riding, burst and covered him with dust. The Emperor, seeing that the incident had caused much alarm in a nearby square of Guard infantry, called out:

'Have no fear, *mes enfants*, the shell which is to kill me has not been made yet.'

On 20 March, after a halt at Saint-Dizier, we were on our way to Wassy when we heard the sound of heavy firing to our rear. It came from the army corps under Marshal Oudinot which was to relieve the headquarters at Saint-Dizier and which was being fiercely harassed by the Russian army. On hearing this news, which was brought by one of the marshal's aides-de-camp, the Emperor halted the Guard cavalry, crossed the Marne by the ford at Valcourt with it and moved against the Russian right flank.

I was riding with my men at the head of the column when the general came and ordered me to charge, regardless of cost, with my squadron against eighteen cannon which the Russians had sited in the open. I obeyed the order immediately, but when we were a hundred yards from the guns the enemy grape-shot so decimated the ranks of

[1] Saint-Priest (1776–1814) fought for the Russians against the Turks and the French. He rose to command a Russian corps.

my squadron that I gave the order to the two righthand troops and to the two lefthand troops to attack in extended order so as to be less exposed. Soon the *lanciers rouges* of the Guard arrived and after their charge we seized the guns.

A division of Russian cuirassiers, which came rushing to the help of their gunners, clashed with the lancers, who received the timely support of the 3rd and the 6th Dragoons under General Milhaud. Together they routed the enemy heavy cavalry, taking nearly 600 prisoners. In this close combat I unseated a Russian sergeant with a thrust from my sabre at his neck. A chasseur took the horse's bridle and said to me:

'You did not have long to wait for a new mount, sir.'

'Yes,' I said, 'but give the prisoner his pack. I have been a prisoner myself in Russia and I know what a soldier suffers when he loses everything.' My wishes were carried out.

This was a complete setback for the Russians. Their infantry, which was withdrawing by forced marches along the road to Bar-sur-Ornain, would have been in great trouble if night had not come and if the forest had not protected them, for the Emperor himself with sword in hand was pursuing them at the head of the Guard cavalry. As a result of this successful day, the Duc de Reggio was able to enter Saint-Dizier.

This was the last time that the Guard drew sabres against the enemy, but the action was a worthy one with which to close the splendid campaign of 1814 which, because of its manoeuvres, tacticians have compared with the Italian campaigns conducted by General Bonaparte. In the report made by General Sébastiani to the Emperor the following observation appeared:

'I have been a cavalry officer for twenty-five years and I do not ever remember seeing a more brilliant charge than the one carried out by your leading squadron.'

These words, which I learned of later, were highly complimentary to me and my squadron, but I would rather have received the cross of an officer of the *Légion d'honneur* from the Emperor. Major Kirmann, my immediate superior in this campaign, told me he had recommended me for it when I had so successfully carried out the dangerous mission which the Emperor himself had given me near the bridge at Château-Thierry on 2 March.

On the evening of the 26th I was pleasantly surprised when, back at my bivouac, I inspected the horse I had taken. In the first place it was a handsome horse in good condition; I had, moreover, acquired a bottle of champagne for my supper. My orderly found it wrapped in straw in the little canvas bag used for carrying a brush and curry-comb. I was delighted to empty the bottle with my orderly, but soon my pleasure gave way to a feeling of grief when I remembered that the Russians were encamped in Champagne. We were no longer living in the days when our bulletins were issued from Vienna, Dresden, Berlin, Moscow, Madrid or Lisbon. . . . Now the enemy was on French soil!

On 27 March from his bivouac near Saint-Dizier the Emperor, who had learned of the risings by the populations in the Vosges, Lorraine and Alsace, decided to send Captain Brice of the 1st Guard Chasseur Regiment with the perilous mission of crossing through the enemy lines and of going to the Vosges where he had been born to call for a *levée en masse*. As far as events allowed him this officer, who was one of the bravest in the army, justified the confidence the Emperor had placed in him. Disguised as a waggoner he succeeded in crossing through the enemy forces which stood between him and the province of his birth.

On the 28th the Emperor at the head of the Guard made for Troyes, passing through Brienne[1] on the way. Near this town was Brienne-le-Vieux where one of my relatives was the priest. As I wished to see him I went on ahead of the column so as to be able to spend a few hours with him. When I arrived in the village I asked a woman who was coming out of the church with a prayer-book in her hand if she could tell me where Monsieur Joffrin the priest lived.

'Alas, sir, he died yesterday. The poor man is just being buried, but he is sure to go to heaven for he did much good during his time on earth,' she said, crossing herself.

'Could you tell me the cause of the priest's death?' I asked.

'Gracious me sir, it was a surprise to everyone, for he was in excellent health for a man of seventy-six, but the Good Lord called him and he went without a word to anyone. He just dropped dead after going home from church.'

It was clear that my dear relative had had a stroke. I thanked the woman and rode slowly on. As I no longer had any reason to stay in the village I awaited the arrival of the column and rejoined my squadron.

Since I had not been able to take advantage of the leave which Major Kirmann had given me, I was again granted twenty-four hours the next day in order to ride on ahead of the regiment to Troyes which was our destination. I arrived there with my orderly on the 20th and

[1] As a boy Napoleon began his studies in France at the military school at Brienne.

on enquiry learned where Monsieur Couturier lived. He was a merchant in the town and a friend of my brother who was a lawyer. I was looking forward to seeing him and staying with him. My orderly knocked at the entrance to the house and asked if Monsieur Couturier was there.

'Yes,' replied the maidservant in tears, 'but he died this morning and has not yet been buried.'

I did not linger there but went to the inn attached to the posting-station. There I found a jolly-looking innkeeper who in return for my money gave every attention to me, my orderly and my horses.

'Could you tell me how Monsieur Couturier died?' I asked the innkeeper.

'Monsieur Couturier,' he said, 'was one of the leading merchants in this town, as well as being a member of the municipal council. As such he often went to visit the hospitals—which are now full of wounded and sick men. While performing this duty, Monsieur Couturier caught the typhus which is raging in the town at the moment and as a result he died.'

'Give me something to eat and some of your best wine so that I may drive away this spirit of death which seems to delight in going before me; yesterday, and now again today, I have learned of the deaths of people I was going to see.'

On the 30th the Emperor left Troyes with 1,000 cavalrymen whose horses were fit enough to make a hard and long journey. My horses and I had rested well at the inn and so I was a member of the expedition. We set out on the road to Fontainebleau where we arrived before nightfall on the 31st. We had ridden twenty-five leagues in twenty-seven hours!

At Fontainebleau the Emperor took a post-chaise to proceed to Paris where he was personally to take command of the army corps under Marmont and Mortier and of the National Guard, pending the arrival of the 50,000 men and the 500 guns which were coming from Troyes to Paris. However, at Villejuif he learned from General Belliard that Marshals Marmont and Mortier had capitulated. He returned to Fontainebleau where he took quarters in the château. The army continued to arrive at Fontainebleau from Troyes; the whole Guard was encamped in the forest. At the beginning of April grim news circulated among the ranks of the Guard, but such fearless soldiers were not easily dismayed.

On 3 April, after an inspection by the Emperor, the following order of the day was read aloud to each company of the Guard:

'Soldiers!

'The enemy has stolen a march on us and has taken Paris. We must drive him out. Unworthy Frenchmen, émigrés whom we had pardoned, have flaunted the white cockade and have joined with the enemy. These cowards will pay the full price for their new treachery! Let us now resolve to vanquish or to die, and to compel all to respect our tricolour cockade which for twenty years has accompanied us on the path to glory!'

Immediately everyone cried: 'Long live the Emperor! To Paris!' Hope was in everyone's heart.

The Emperor was at Fontainebleau with 50,000 men, including 25,000 of the Guard; his artillery was powerful and strong in numbers; there were the army corps of Mortier, Marmont and Souham and the light-cavalry division under General Belliard. He controlled both banks of the Seine and with these forces he would have had 100,000 men to march on Charenton.

One might justifiably have anticipated that the brave citizens of Paris would have supplied 50,000 National Guards who would have flocked to join the Emperor within two leagues of Paris. This would have resulted in an army of 150,000 men led by the Emperor, ready to strike at the rear of an enemy whose forces totalled only 130,000 men. Of these he would have had to leave at least 50,000 to guard Paris if he had wanted to oppose our march on the capital from Charenton. Moreover, the enemy army which had made the thrust on Paris had no ammunition, no artillery and no supplies. Any line of retreat back to the Rhine was completely cut. The Allied rulers were therefore in a situation where they would have to make peace at Paris or carry out their retreat to the coast and embark in the fleet which was standing by. Such were their alternatives! A defection from among our ranks was to save the Allies from their difficulties.

On 4 April the following order of the day was published, filling every soldier's heart with grief and indignation:

'The Emperor thanks the army for the loyalty it has shown to him, not least because it has recognized that he, and not the masses in the capital, embodies the true spirit of France. The soldier follows his general, his honour and his loyalties through good or bad fortune. The Duc de Raguse, however, has not inspired his companions-in-arms to act thus; he has gone over to the Allies. The Emperor cannot condone the manner in which he has acted; the Emperor cannot accept his life and liberty from the hands of one of his subjects. The Senate has seen fit to dissolve the Government; it has forgotten what it owes to the Emperor whom it now treats so disgracefully; it has forgotten that the Emperor saved half its members from the ravages of the Revolution and brought the other half from obscurity and protected it from the Nation's vengeance. The Senate has had recourse to the articles of the Constitution in order to overthrow that same Constitution. It is not ashamed to condemn the Emperor, but it fails to observe that as the foremost body in the State it has been directly involved in all that has happened. It has dared to accuse the Emperor of altering its acts before they were published. The whole world knows that there was need for the Emperor to resort to such artifices. A sign from him was an order to a Senate which was always more than ready to comply. The wellbeing of France seemed bound up in the fortunes of the Emperor; now that the die is cast only the desire of the Nation could persuade him to remain on the throne any longer. If he must be considered as the only obstacle to peace, he is quite prepared to make a last sacrifice for France.

'Consequently, he has sent the Prince de la Moskowa, the Duc de Vicence [*Caulaincourt*] and the Duc de Tarente [*Macdonald*] to Paris in order to open negotiations with the Allies. The army may be certain that the honour of the Emperor will never conflict with that of France.'

Finally on 11 April the Emperor abdicated and at noon on the 20th he bade farewell to the assembled Guard. His words, which will ever hold a place in the hearts of the soldiers of the Empire, were as follows:

'Officers, N.C.O.s and Soldiers of my Old Guard, I bid you farewell. For the twenty years we have been together I have always been proud of you. Everywhere, you have covered yourselves with glory. All the Powers of Europe have taken arms against me. Some of my generals have betrayed their duty, and France herself has chosen a course other than mine. With you and with those other brave men who have remained faithful to me I could have waged civil war. But France would have suffered! Be loyal to your new king, be obedient to your new commanders; do not abandon our beloved country. Do not pity my fate; I shall be happy if I know that you yourselves are happy. I could have chosen death;[1] if I have chosen to live, it is in order to serve your glory further. I shall write the story of the great things we have done together. I cannot embrace you all, but I can embrace your general. Come here, General Petit, so that I may

[1] Napoleon had attempted to take his own life on 12 April, but the efficacy of the poison he used had diminished.

press you to my heart. Bring me the eagle so that I may embrace that also. May the kisses that I give you, beloved eagle, resound through posterity! Farewell, *mes enfants*, my thoughts will always be with you; do not forget me.'

At these words, many were the tears that were shed by these seasoned soldiers who admired, and yet bitterly regretted, this great act of self-sacrifice. After the Emperor had left, the men as one spontaneously burned the eagles and some even swallowed the ashes so as not to be parted from them.

The officers of the Guard took their leave of the Emperor. General Krasinski who commanded the Polish Lancers was one of the last to come forward with his officers. As he took his leave of the Emperor he uttered these words, which do the greatest credit to his nation:

'Sire, if you had mounted the throne of Poland, you would have been killed upon it; but the Poles would have died at your feet to a man.'

That same day the Emperor left Fontainebleau accompanied by the Grand Marshal, Bertrand, and took the road to Lyons followed by representatives of the Allies and preceded by a battalion of the Guard which accompanied him to the island of Elba.

Thus in 1814 ended the marvellous period of the Empire which had begun in 1804.

A Russian diplomat, Monsieur de Nesselrode, has said: 'What remains of this great political drama? A Gascon in the north and a Gascon in the south.' He was referring to the throne of Sweden, occupied by Bernadotte, and the throne of Naples, occupied by Murat.

But what really does remain of this great political drama? If a serious answer to this question is required, everyone, including Monsieur de Nesselrode himself, would agree that although the extraordinary man who had presided over such great happenings had fallen, not all the changes he had sworn to bring about had vanished with him. No! The great ideals of the French Revolution—the ideals of liberty, of unity and of the future, which as everyone instinctively knows, the Emperor Napoleon personified in spite of all the theories of envious minds—these have not been finally judged. No! Defeat has not sufficed to put an end to them. Is not France, moreover, reaping even today some of their benefits? To whom does she owe her admirable administration and her powerful unity which make her still the mistress of the destinies of the world?

Appendix I

The *Chasseur à cheval* Regiment

A typical regiment of *Chasseurs à cheval* at this time consisted of the staff and four squadrons, although further squadrons were sometimes formed. The squadrons themselves comprised two troops (*compagnies*), the 1st Troop of the 1st Squadron being known as the *compagnie d'élite*. This troop was the equivalent of the grenadier company of an infantry unit, and was distinguished by wearing colpacks (busbies) instead of the shako worn by the rest of the regiment. Each troop would have four *pelotons* of about twelve to fifteen files, each under a *maréchal des logis* (sergeant) or a *brigadier* (corporal), with a *maréchal des logis-chef* (sergeant-major) as the senior N.C.O. The strength of a squadron appears to have varied between 120 and 170 men.

The officers at this period were as follows:
Colonel, *Major* (or Lieut-Colonel), two *chefs d'escadron*, quartermaster, *capitaine-adjudant-major*, *lieutenant-adjudant-major*, *chirurgien-major*, *aide-major*, *sous-aide-major*, approximately eight captains, eight lieutenants, and fifteen to twenty *sous-lieutenants*.

Within an eight-troop regiment of about 550 men, the normal N.C.O.s were: a sergeant or corporal trumpeter and eight trumpeters (one per troop), eight *maréchaux des logis-chefs*, thirty-two *maréchaux des logis*, eight *fourriers* (quartermaster sergeants), sixty-four *brigadiers*.

In the regimental line of march the C.O., the *petit état-major* consisting of the senior officers, surgeon and other specialists, and the senior trumpeter rode with the *compagnie d'élite*, while captains commanded the other troops. The two troops of each squadron rode together in pairs.

These details refer, of course, to the Line. The *Chasseurs à cheval* of the Imperial Guard were, as Parquin emphasizes, a quite different type of unit. Dressed in full 'hussar kit', their duties kept them close to the Emperor. They had five squadrons in 1811, but all at small strength, so that there were 250 men in all. They had eight squadrons in 1813, and nine squadrons later the same year. When revived in 1815 they had four squadrons.

Appendix II

La Légion d'honneur

Until the occasion when he receives his well-deserved reward, Parquin frequently expresses his burning desire to win the coveted cross of the *Légion d'honneur* and several references are made to similar ambitions on the part of his comrades. More than once Parquin portrays the Emperor bestowing the award upon his bravest soldiers. For Parquin and his contemporaries the *Légion d'honneur* was the ultimate prize which inspired them in their service and sealed the bond between Emperor and soldier. In creating the order, Napoleon had sought to achieve this result and he was completely and immediately successful in his aims.

The order was instituted by the law of 19 Floréal in the Year X (19 May 1802) at the personal instigation of the First Consul, although it was not until 22 Messidor in the Year XII (11 July 1804) that the form of the badge was decreed by Napoleon. Certain opponents protested against the creation of the order, claiming that it represented a betrayal of the revolutionary ideal of equality, but Napoleon could ask them to show him any state, ancient or modern, where distinctions had not existed. To those in the Council of State who objected to the honour and condemned it, he made his celebrated retort:

'On appelle cela des hochets. Eh bien, c'est avec des hochets qu'on mène les hommes!'

The baubles with which Napoleon was to lead men replaced the *armes d'honneur* previously given for acts of bravery. They were to be awarded to both soldiers and civilians for meritorious acts or loyal service and in this way, announced Napoleon, the illiterate soldier and the learned scientist would feel a common sense of purpose and share a common glory The order was divided into five grades:

Grands-Croix (initially, *Grands-Aigles*)
Grands Officiers
Commandeurs
Officiers
Chevaliers.

The original cross was a star with five rays with double points. The white-enamelled centre of the star was surrounded by a wreath of oak and laurel leaves and on one side showed the Emperor's head with the inscription: *Napoléon Empereur des Français.* On the reverse appeared an eagle holding a thunderbolt with the inscription: *Honneur et Patrie.* The cross, which was of silver for *chevaliers* and of gold for the other four grades, was attached to a red ribbon of watered silk. Originally, it was intended that membership should be limited to 5,500, but by 1815 some 34,000 military and 1,500 civilian awards had been made.

On 15 July 1804, shortly after being proclaimed Emperor, Napoleon appeared in great pomp at Les Invalides where for the first time the oath of the order—in effect, a promise to defend the Empire—was taken, and the first crosses were distributed. The first investiture in the field took place on 16 August of the same year at the Boulogne camp where Soult with 80,000 men of the force intended for the invasion of England were assembled.

These two ceremonies firmly established the order which was to become the supreme reward for the bravery which it itself inspired. Within a few years it had acquired such prestige that the restored king, although he altered it slightly so as to attenuate its Napoleonic associations, dared not abolish it.

Biographical Notes

The following brief biographical notes relate to a selection of the generals and marshals under whom Parquin served and who are mentioned in his memoirs. The principal source of information is the Dictionnaire Biographique des Généraux et Amiraux de la Révolution et de l'Empire, *Georges Six (2 vols, Paris, 1934).*

AUGEREAU, Charles-Pierre-François, Duc de Castiglione, Marshal of France (1757–1816). Coming from a very humble background he failed to achieve promotion in the royalist army. He served abroad in the armies of a number of nations. His courage and skill as a swordsman became legendary; Marbot devotes a chapter of his memoirs to the exploits of the future marshal. Some have questioned the accuracy of the accounts of these exploits, there being little evidence apart from Augereau's own testimony. After the Revolution his rise was rapid; by 1793 he was commanding a division. After distinguishing himself in Italy and Holland, he was made a marshal in 1804. Successful at Jena, he was less so at Eylau where his corps was almost destroyed and he himself was wounded. After fighting at Leipzig he was appointed to command the forces in the Rhône area, but was one of the first of Napoleon's generals to go over to Louis XVIII.

BERTHIER, Louis-Alexandre, Prince de Neufchâtel et de Wagram, Marshal of France (1753–1815). Under the *ancien régime* Berthier had already enjoyed a successful military career. He had served in America with Rochambeau and when the Revolution came he was made a lieutenant-colonel; as such he was appointed to command the guard at Versailles. In the uncertainty of the post-revolutionary period he fell from grace, but his appointment as chief of staff to Bonaparte in Italy marked the resumption of his rise. Honours and financial rewards came rapidly, but after the retreat from Russia and a lance wound at Brienne, he threw in his lot with the provisional government. During the Hundred Days he took refuge in Bamberg in Bavaria where he died in mysterious circumstances. He fell from the window of his room into the street, but whether this was suicide or the result of action by others has not been established.

CASTEX, Bertrand-Pierre (1771–1842). His career started auspiciously;

the same day that he joined a chasseur regiment as a volunteer he was promoted to be a sergeant. He was appointed *major* of the 20th Chasseurs on 29 October 1803. Parquin was greatly impressed by this officer and gives the outlines of his career in these memoirs. Castex was clearly a cavalryman in the traditions of the 20th, for after becoming a general he was wounded in action at least four times.

COLBERT-CHABANAIS, Pierre David (Edouard) (1774–1853). Between 1793 and 1815 Colbert served with hussars, dragoons, mamelukes, chasseurs and lancers. Present at most of the major campaigns from Egypt to Waterloo, he epitomized the dashing cavalryman and was wounded repeatedly. After being shot in the left arm at Waterloo he was imprisoned at the Second Restoration, for he had rallied to Napoleon during the Hundred Days, despite being Colonel of the royal lancers. He was not long in re-establishing himself and played a large part in the reorganization of the French cavalry.

DAVOUT, Louis-Nicolas, Duc d'Auerstadt, Prince d'Eckmühl, Marshal of France (1770–1823). His father had been an officer and he himself had been a *cadet-gentilhomme* before being commissioned into the *Royal-Champagne-cavalerie* regiment, but he was a supporter of the Revolution and was active in the defence of France in the years immediately following 1789. Possessing experience and sound strategic ability he was quick to rise under Bonaparte, and after successes in Egypt and Italy he was made a marshal in 1804. His outstanding feat as a commander was, as Parquin notes, at Auerstadt in 1806, when with his corps he routed the main body of the Prussian army. Appointed Minister of War during the Hundred Days, he was obliged to hand over Paris to the Allies and return the remnants of the French army to Louis XVIII in 1815. He never became fully reconciled to the rule of the Bourbons and retired to his country estate.

DROUET, comte d'ERLON, Jean-Baptiste, Marshal of France (1765–1844). As rapid in his rise as any of his contemporaries—from a corporal in 1792 to a brigadier-general in 1799—Drouet participated in many of the major campaigns of the period, being wounded at Friedland. In 1815 he compromised his position under the restored monarchy by being involved in an Orleanist plot and by rallying to Napoleon at Waterloo. During the reign of the Bourbons he was forced to live in exile and ran a brewery in Bayreuth; he was sentenced to death in his absence. The coming to power of Louis-Philippe in 1830 brought a resumption of his military career. He served the regime well in France and in North Africa and it was in 1843 that he became a marshal.

DUROSNEL, Antoine-Jean-Auguste-Henri (1771–1849). An *enfant de troupe* in 1783, Durosnel had by Austerlitz become a general. He was typical of the breed of cavalrymen who flourished around Napoleon and was, apart from a period after Aspern-Essling when he was wounded and captured, always to the forefront of the fighting. His personal relationship with Napoleon was a close one and he served as equerry and aide-de-camp to him, occupying the latter appointment again during the Hundred Days. After remaining in retirement between 1815 and 1830 he emerged to take an active part in politics and became an aide-de-camp to Louis-Philippe.

FOURNIER-SARLOVEZE, François (1773–1827). Parquin's unflattering portrayal of Fournier's acquisitive habits in Spain seems borne out by the fact that the general was relieved of his post or arrested on three occasions during his career. His courage and ability did not fall short of the standards expected of a Napoleonic cavalry leader, but even in 1794 when a major, he was accused of fraudulent accounting and absence without leave. In 1802 he was arrested for conspiring against the First Consul and again in 1813 he was relieved of his command for poor leadership and for expressing views which displeased the Emperor. These setbacks did not prejudice his career unduly as on each occasion he was quickly reinstated; he eventually became an inspector of cavalry under the monarchy.

LAURISTON, Jacques-Alexandre-Bernard Law, Marshal of France (1768–1828). The great-nephew of the Scottish banker Law whose *System*, which was based on the use of paper money, brought financial chaos to France at the beginning of the eighteenth century. He distinguished himself as an artillery commander, but was also entrusted with diplomatic missions. In 1801, when he was in England for the ratification of the preliminary peace proposals, members of an enthusiastic mob unharnessed his coach and pulled it themselves. He was one of the generals who accompanied the Empress Marie-Louise from Vienna and in 1811 he was appointed as ambassador to Russia. He fought successfully in Germany in 1813, but was captured at Leipzig. When he was released in 1814 he gave his loyalty to the king and was one of those who voted for the death of Ney. He became a marshal in 1823.

LEFEBVRE-DESNÖETTES, Charles (1773–1822). The son of a cloth merchant, he ran away from school to join the army and on three occasions his parents bought his release. Thanks to his enthusiasm and ability, however, he was commanding a brigade by 1806, and further honours and promotion came rapidly. After being wounded and captured by the English at Benavente in 1808 he was taken to England, but escaped to France in 1812. When Napoleon returned from Elba, Lefebvre-Desnoëttes made great efforts to win over units to the Emperor, but was unsuccessful in his attempt to seize the arsenal at La Fère. After Waterloo he went into exile in America and in his absence was condemned to death. He was drowned off the Irish coast when the ship in which he was returning to Europe sank.

MARMONT, Auguste-Frédéric-Louis Viesse de, Duc de Raguse, Marshal of France (1774–1852). A 2nd lieutenant in 1790, Marmont was by 1798 an acting brigadier-general before he had reached his twenty-fourth birthday; his conduct at the siege of Toulon, in Italy, and at the capture of Malta, had been responsible for such rapid promotion; he was created a marshal in 1809. Apart from achieving military successes he brought economic and social benefits to the area of Dalmatia where he was governor-general. His serious wound at Salamanca and painful return to France, which Parquin describes, did not prevent his participation in the later campaigns of the Empire, but with the return of Louis XVIII he associated himself fully with the fortunes of the Bourbons. He was forced to go into exile after the 1830 Revolution and never returned to France.

MASSENA, André, Duc de Rivoli, Prince d'Essling, Marshal of France (1758–1817). Massena was born in Nice, which was not French until 1792 and then only temporarily, and became naturalized at the Restoration. An orphan at an early age, he went to sea as a cabin-boy at the age of thirteen before enjoying a modest military career. When he retired as an N.C.O. in 1789 he settled in Antibes and is alleged to have lived by smuggling. The Revolution gave him the opportunity to put his experience and talent to greater effect; so successful as a commander was he in Italy that Bonaparte gave him the title of *L'Enfant chéri de la Victoire*. Even when forced to capitulate after the siege of Genoa he was allowed to evacuate his troops and was accorded the full honours of war. Successes in Germany were followed by failure in Spain and after Fuentes de Oñoro he was relieved of his command and given only minor appointments.

MONTBRUN, Louis-Pierre (1770–1812). The brother of Alexandre Montbrun, who also became a cavalry general, Louis-Pierre is described by Parquin as 'le plus bel homme de guerre que j'aie vu de ma vie'. His personal bravery had soon shown itself: at Altendorf in 1796 he covered the wounded General Richepance with his own body and prevented the general's capture. After his outstanding bravery at Austerlitz he became a brigadier-general in 1805. He was no more fortunate in the Peninsula than many of his contemporaries, but was nevertheless given the command of the 2nd Cavalry Reserve Corps in Russia. He was killed at Borodino.

MURAT, Joachim, Marshal of France and King of Naples (1767–1815). Extravagant gestures and political deviousness were essential ingredients in the make-up of this most exotic of Napoleon's leaders. Parquin, however, admires him as a cavalryman, and as such he was remarkable enough. His progress in the army had come to a halt in 1793 because of political charges. When, however, he allied himself with Bonaparte in that year it was the start of a brilliant career; by 1799 he was a major-general and it was in this rank that he won a *sabre d'honneur* for bravery at Marengo in 1800. As commander of the cavalry of the *Grande Armée* he provided an example of audacious enterprise which was copied by generals and men alike. After Leipzig political manoeuvres preoccupied him, but he was unable to retain his throne and died bravely before a firing-squad.

OUDINOT, Nicolas-Charles, Duc de Reggio, Marshal of France (1767–1847). When Oudinot died at the age of eighty he was the governor of Les Invalides. His appointment in 1842 was highly appropriate; during his career Oudinot was wounded more than twenty times. Some of his wounds were extremely serious; at Zurich in 1799 he received a bullet full in the chest; at Wagram a bullet struck him in the ear; in Russia a piece of case-shot shattered his shoulder, and at Arcis-sur-Aube his star deadened the impact of a bullet which hit him full in the chest. Despite all these wounds he served bravely in most of the major campaigns, but did not see action in Spain until 1823 when France intervened to restore the absolute monarchy.

Select Bibliography

BUCQUOY, E.-L., HOLLANDER, O. and BENIGNI, P. *Les Chasseurs à cheval de la Garde Impériale*. Strasbourg, 1926.

CHANDLER, DAVID. *The Campaigns of Napoleon*. London, 1967.

COSTELLO, EDWARD. *Adventures of a soldier*, ed. Anthony Brett-James. London, 1967.

GUEDALLA, PHILIP. *The Second Empire*. London, 1923.

HASWELL, JAMES. *Life of Napoleon III*. London, 1871.

MARBOT, General Baron de. *Mémoires*. Paris, 1891.

MARTINIEN, A. *Tableaux des Officiers tués et blessés*. Paris, *c*. 1900.

MONEGLIA, General. 'Un Héros Pyrénéen: Jean-Baptiste Guindey'. (*Vivat Hussar,* No. 2. *Revue de l'Association des Amis du Musée International des Hussards*.) Tarbes, 1967.

MORRIS, THOMAS. *Recollections*, ed. John Selby. London, 1967.

OMAN, Sir C. W. C. *History of the Peninsular War* (7 vols). Oxford, 1902–30.

SCHUERMANS, ALBERT. *Itinéraire Général de Napoléon I*. Paris, 1911.

THIEBAULT, General Baron. *Memoirs*, 1896.

Index of Persons

General Index

This Index contains the names of places and rivers mentioned by Parquin.